STEP 4

WORD
Bridge
3600

Intro

Word Bridge 3600의 수준별 학습
중학교 필수 단어에서 특목고 대비를 위한 단어까지 총 3,600 단어가 단계별로 레벨업되어 있습니다. 자신의 수준에 맞추어서 차근차근 어휘력을 다져나갈 수 있도록 하였습니다.

귀로 듣고, 입으로 따라하기
단어마다 문법과 구문법칙이 응용된 모범예문을 원어민의 정확한 발음으로 듣고 따라하다 보면 암기 효과를 두 배로 올릴 수 있도록 하였습니다.

영영정의를 통한 의미 이해
단어의 주요 의미를 영영으로 정의해 놓고 연관된 예문을 제시함으로써 그 의미를 더욱 정확하게 이해할 수 있도록 하였습니다.

반복, 반복 쏙쏙 암기
눈으로 암기하는 단어는 오래 기억되지 못합니다. 듣기, 말하기, 쓰기 등을 활용한 다양한 연습 형태를 통해 반복적으로 단어를 학습할 수 있도록 하였습니다.

교재의 구성

본 교재는 단계별로 총 5권으로 구성되어 있습니다.

각 권은 10 Part로, 각 Part는 모두 4 unit으로 구성되어 있습니다.

Listen and repeat
주요 학습 파트로 새로운 단어 18개와 단어를 활용한 모범예문이 수록되어 있으며 듣기 학습이 포함되어 있습니다.

Exercise / Review
주요 학습에서 익힌 단어와 예문을 활용하여 문제를 풀어보고 암기합니다.

▼ Step 1

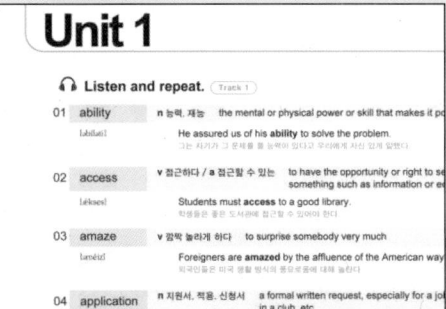

▼ Step 2

▼ Step 3

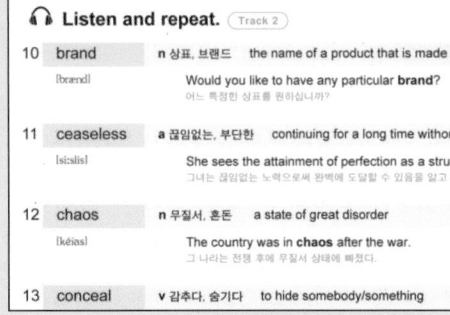

▼ Step 4

▼ Step 5

B. Fill in the word and meaning.

	Word	Meaning		Meaning	Word
01	application		01	능력, 재능	
02	bouquet		02	접근하다, 접근할 수 있는	
03	ceaseless		03	깜짝 놀라게 하다	
04	ability		04	지원서, 적용, 신청서	
05	brand		05	발생하다, 일어나다	
06	arrangement		06	준비, 배열, 정리	
07	contrary		07	평균, 평균의	
08	dare		08	의식하고, 깨달고	
09	arise		09	꽃다발, 부케	
10	contrast		10	상표, 브랜드	
11	aware		11	끊임없는, 부단한	
12	concrete		12	무질서, 혼돈	
13	amaze		13	감추다, 숨기다	
14	conceal		14	유형의, 구체적	

▼ Step 6

🎧 C. Listen, write the word and meaning. (Track 3)

	Word	Meaning		Word
01			10	
02			11	
03			12	
04			13	
05			14	
06			15	
07			16	
08			17	
09			18	

▼ Step 7

A. Read and fill in the word and meaning.

word	definition	meaning
	a state of great disorder	
	to have the opportunity or right to see or use something such as information or equipment	
	to have enough courage to do something	
	conceal to hide somebody/something	
	the mental or physical power or sill that makes it possible to do	
	unable to hear anything	
	the normal standard, amount or quality	
	a physical object rather than a quality or idea	
	a formal written request, especially for a job or a place in a club, etc	
	continuing for a long time without stopping	

교재의 학습방법

- **Step 1 - 새 단어 귀로 들으며 익히기**
  새 단어와 예문을 원어민의 발음으로 들으며 익힌다.

- **Step 2 - 단어 뜻 암기하기**
  영영 정의를 익히면서 단어의 정확한 의미를 이해하고, 예문을 해석하면서 예문 속에서 단어의 쓰임을 학습합니다.

- **Step 3 - 입으로 따라하며 암기하기**
  다시 한 번 CD를 들으면서 큰 소리로 따라합니다. 예문을 따라하면서 통째로 암기합니다.

- **Step 4 - 문장 완성하기**
  주어진 단어 힌트를 이용하여 암기한 예문을 완성합니다.

- **Step 5 - 단어와 뜻 채우기**
  제시된 영어 단어는 뜻을 우리 말로 쓰고, 단어의 뜻이 제시되어 있으면 영어 단어를 쓰면서 복습합니다.

- **Step 6 - 듣고 단어와 뜻 채우기**
  CD를 듣고 정확한 발음을 익히며 영어 단어와 뜻을 쓰면서 반복 학습합니다.

- **Step 7 - 단어 암기 확인**
  영영 정의를 읽고 암기한 영어 단어와 뜻을 쓰면서 확인 학습을 합니다.

Contents

part 1

Unit 1	6
Unit 2	10
Review 1	14
Unit 3	16
Unit 4	20
Review 2	24

part 2

Unit 5	26
Unit 6	30
Review 3	34
Unit 7	36
Unit 8	40
Review 4	44

part 3

Unit 9	46
Unit 10	50
Review 5	54

Unit 11	56
Unit 12	60
Review 6	64

part 4

Unit 13	66
Unit 14	70
Review 7	74
Unit 15	76
Unit 16	80
Review 8	84

part 5

Unit 17	86
Unit 18	90
Review 9	94
Unit 19	96
Unit 20	100
Review 10	104

WORD BRIDGE 3600

part 6

Unit 21	106
Unit 22	110
Review 11	114
Unit 23	116
Unit 24	120
Review 12	124

part 7

Unit 25	126
Unit 26	130
Review 13	134
Unit 27	136
Unit 28	140
Review 14	144

part 8

Unit 29	146
Unit 30	150
Review 15	154
Unit 31	156
Unit 32	160
Review 16	164

part 9

Unit 33	166
Unit 34	170
Review 17	174
Unit 35	176
Unit 36	180
Review 18	184

part 10

Unit 37	186
Unit 38	190
Review 19	194
Unit 39	196
Unit 40	200
Review 20	204
Total Test	207
Answer Key	229

Unit 1

🎧 Listen and repeat. (Track 1)

01 ability n 능력, 재능   the mental or physical power or skill that makes it possible to do
[əbíləti]
He assured us of his **ability** to solve the problem.
그는 자기가 그 문제를 풀 능력이 있다고 우리에게 자신 있게 말했다.

02 access v 접근하다 / a 접근할 수 있는   to have the opportunity or right to see or use something such as information or equipment
[ǽkses]
Students must **access** to a good library.
학생들은 좋은 도서관에 접근할 수 있어야 한다.

03 amaze v 깜짝 놀라게 하다   to surprise somebody very much
[əméiz]
Foreigners are **amazed** by the affluence of the American way of life.
외국인들은 미국 생활 방식의 풍요로움에 대해 놀란다.

04 application n 지원서, 적용, 신청서   a formal written request, especially for a job or a place in a club, etc
[æplikéiʃən]
When we advertised the position, we received a lot of **applications**.
우리가 그 일자리를 공고했을 때 대단히 많은 지원서가 들어왔다.

05 arise v 발생하다, 일어나다   to begin to exist; to appear
[əráiz]
Accidents **arise** from carelessness.
사고는 부주의로부터 발생한다.

06 arrangement n 준비, 배열, 정리   preparations for something that will happen in the future
[əréindʒmənt]
The mortician took care of the funeral **arrangements**.
그 장의사가 장례 준비를 맡았다.

07 average n 평균 / a 평균의   the normal standard, amount or quality
[ǽvəridʒ]
My monthly allowance is 30,000 won on **average**.
나의 한 달 용돈은 평균 3만원이다.

08 aware a 의식하고, 깨닫고   conscious of somebody/something ; realizing something
[əwέər]
I'm aware that this is a risky investment.
이것이 위험한 투자라는 것을 나는 의식하고 있다.

09 bouquet n 꽃다발, 부케   a bunch of flowers that is arranged in an attractive way
[boukéi]
I presented her with a big **bouquet** of flowers.
나는 커다란 꽃 한 다발을 그녀에게 선물했다.

key words
assure v 확신하다 / affluence n 풍요 / carelessness n 부주의함
mortician n 장의사 / allowance n 용돈, 수당

🎧 Listen and repeat. Track 2

10 brand [brænd]
n 상표, 브랜드   the name of a product that is made by a particular company
Would you like to have any particular **brand**?
어느 특정한 상표를 원하십니까?

11 ceaseless [síːslis]
a 끊임없는, 부단한   continuing for a long time without stopping
She sees the attainment of perfection as a struggle of **ceaseless** effort.
그녀는 끊임없는 노력으로써 완벽에 도달할 수 있음을 알고 있다.

12 chaos [kéias]
n 무질서, 혼돈   a state of great disorder
The country was in **chaos** after the war.
그 나라는 전쟁 후에 무질서 상태에 빠졌다.

13 conceal [kənsíːl]
v 감추다, 숨기다   to hide somebody/something
He couldn't **conceal** his envy at my success.
그는 내 성공에 대한 질투심을 감추지 못했다.

14 concrete [kánkriːt]
a 유형의, 응고한   a physical object rather than a quality or idea
The police had no **concrete** evidence.
경찰은 구체적인 증거를 갖고 있지 않았다.

15 contrary [kántreri]
a 반대의, 적합하지 않은   completely different; opposite
He took a **contrary** position to her.
그는 그녀와 반대 입장을 취했다.

16 contrast [kántraːst]
v 대조시키다 / n 대조   comparison between two people or things to show the differences
In **contrast**, your friend might have had a negative reaction.
이와는 대조적으로, 당신의 친구는 부정적인 반응을 보일 수도 있다.

17 dare [dɛər]
v 감히 ~하다   to have enough courage to do something
He will never **dare** to enter my house again.
그는 다시는 감히 내 집에 들어오지 못 할 것이다.

18 deaf [def]
a 귀머거리의, 무관심한   unable to hear anything
He had never wanted anyone to know, but he is almost **deaf**.
그는 결코 남이 아는 것을 원하지 않지만, 그는 거의 귀머거리야.

key words
attainment n 달성, 도달 / struggle n 투쟁, 분투 / disorder n 무질서, 혼란 / opposite a 정반대의

Unit 1

Exercise

A. Complete the sentence.

1. Would you like to have any particular _____?
   어느 특정한 상표를 원하십니까?

2. Students must _____ to a good library.
   학생들은 좋은 도서관에 접근할 수 있어야 한다.

3. He will never _____ to enter my house again.
   그는 다시는 감히 내 집에 들어오지 못 할 것이다.

4. When we advertised the position, we received a lot of _____.
   우리가 그 일자리를 공고했을 때 대단히 많은 지원서가 들어왔다.

5. He couldn't _____ his envy at my success.
   그는 내 성공에 대한 질투심을 감추지 못했다.

6. The mortician took care of the funeral _____.
   그 장의사가 장례 준비를 맡았다.

7. The country was in _____ after the war.
   그 나라는 전쟁 후에 무질서 상태에 빠졌다.

8. My monthly allowance is 30,000 won on _____.
   나의 한 달 용돈은 평균 3만원이다.

9. He assured us of his _____ to solve the problem.
   그는 자기가 그 문제를 풀 능력이 있다고 우리에게 자신 있게 말했다.

10. He took a _____ position to her.
    그는 그녀와 반대 입장을 취했다.

11. I'm _____ that this is a risky investment.
    이것이 위험한 투자라는 것을 나는 의식하고 있다.

12. I presented her with a big _____ of flowers.
    나는 커다란 꽃 한 다발을 그녀에게 선물했다.

13. She sees the attainment of perfection as a struggle of _____ effort.
    그녀는 끊임없는 노력으로써 완벽에 도달할 수 있음을 알고 있다.

14. Foreigners are _____ by the affluence of the American way of life.
    외국인들은 미국 생활 방식의 풍요로움에 대해 놀란다.

15. The police had no _____ evidence.
    경찰은 구체적인 증거를 갖고 있지 않았다.

16. Accidents _____ from carelessness.
    사고는 부주의로부터 발생한다.

17. In _____, your friend might have had a negative reaction.
    이와는 대조적으로, 당신의 친구는 부정적인 반응을 보일 수도 있다.

18. He had never wanted anyone to know, but he is almost _____.
    그는 결코 남이 아는 것을 원하지 않지만, 그는 거의 귀머거리야.

Hint

| application | aware | conceal | brand | arise | ability | bouquet | amaze | contrast |
| ceaseless | chaos | average | concrete | dare | contrary | arrangement | deaf | access |

Unit 1

Exercise

B. Fill in the word and meaning.

	Word	Meaning
01	application	
02	bouquet	
03	ceaseless	
04	ability	
05	brand	
06	arrangement	
07	contrary	
08	dare	
09	arise	
10	contrast	
11	aware	
12	concrete	
13	amaze	
14	conceal	
15	deaf	
16	average	
17	chaos	
18	access	

	Meaning	Word
01	능력, 재능	
02	접근하다, 접근할 수 있는	
03	깜짝 놀라게 하다	
04	지원서, 적용, 신청서	
05	발생하다, 일어나다	
06	준비, 배열, 정리	
07	평균, 평균의	
08	의식하고, 깨닫고	
09	꽃다발, 부케	
10	상표, 브랜드	
11	끊임없는, 부단한	
12	무질서, 혼돈	
13	감추다, 숨기다	
14	유형의, 응고한	
15	반대의, 적합하지 않은	
16	대조시키다, 대조	
17	감히 ~하다	
18	귀머거리의, 무관심한	

🎧 C. Listen, write the word and meaning. (Track 3)

	Word	Meaning		Word	Meaning
01			10		
02			11		
03			12		
04			13		
05			14		
06			15		
07			16		
08			17		
09			18		

Unit 2

🎧 Listen and repeat. (Track 4)

01 differ [dífər]
v 다르다, 의견이 다르다   to be different
Korean **differs** from English in many respects.
한국어는 많은 점에서 영어와 다르다.

02 digest [didʒést]
v 소화하다, 이해하다   to change food in your stomach so that it can be used by the body
I'm not going to go swimming until I've **digested** my lunch.
점심 먹은 것을 다 소화하기 전까지 수영하러 가지 않을 것이다.

03 due [djuː]
a ~할 예정인, ~에 기인하는   expected or planned to happen
When is your baby **due**?
출산예정일이 언제입니까?

04 edit [édit]
v 편집하다, 교정하다   to prepare a film or TV program by cutting and arranging in a particular order
Photo **editing** is quickly becoming popular for graphics novices.
사진 편집은 그래픽 초보자에게 빠른 속도로 인기를 얻고 있다.

05 emerge [imə́ːrdʒ]
v 나타나다, 나오다   to appear or come out from somewhere
A man **emerged** from the shadows.
한 남자가 그림자 속에서 나타났다.

06 essential [isénʃəl]
a 필수의, 본질적인   completely necessary
The possession of a passport is **essential** for foreign travel.
여권 소지는 외국 여행을 하기 위해 필수적이다.

07 export [ikspɔ́ːrt]
v 수출하다, 밖으로 전하다   to send goods, etc to another country, usually for sale
It's getting tougher and tougher to **export**.
그것은 수출하기가 점점 더 어려워지고 있다.

08 extension [iksténʃən]
n 연장, 확대   an extra period of time that you are allowed for something
She signed a contract **extension** that will keep her on staff for one additional year.
그녀는 일년 동안 더 직원으로 남게 하는 계약 연장에 서명했다.

09 folk [fouk]
n 사람들 / a 서민의, 민속의   people in general; a particular type of people
Idle **folks** only have the least leisure time.
게으른 사람들은 최소한의 여가시간만이 있을 뿐이다.

---

key words
respect n 점, 내용 / novice n 신참자 / possession n 소유 / tough a 곤란한

🎧 Listen and repeat. (Track 5)

10 foundation [faundéiʃən]
n 기초, 설립, 기반   the idea or principle on which something is based
This book aims to give students a solid **foundation** in grammar.
이 책은 학생들에게 탄탄한 문법적인 기초를 전달하는 것을 목표로 하고 있다.

11 generosity [dʒènərásəti]
n 관대, 아량   the quality of being generous
You shouldn't take advantage of his **generosity**.
너는 그의 관대함을 이용해서는 안 된다.

12 gently [dʒéntli]
ad 온화하게, 조용히, 서서히   kind and calm
If you touch the world **gently**, the world will touch you **gently** in return.
당신이 세상을 온화하게 대하면 세상도 그 보답으로 당신을 온화하게 대한다.

13 gravity [grǽvəti]
n 중력, 진지함   the natural force that makes things fall to the ground
On the Earth, **gravity** is weaker on a mountaintop than in a valley.
지구에서 중력은 계곡에서보다 산꼭대기에서 더 약하다.

14 greet [gri:t]
v 환영하다, 인사하다   to welcome somebody when you meet him/her
Native Americans **greeted** the Pilgrims who settled on the eastern shores.
북미의 원주민이 동해안에 정착했던 그 순례자들을 환영했다.

15 immigration [ìməgréiʃən]
n 이민, 이주   the process of coming to live permanently in a country that is not your own
Immigration in the United States has been increasing rapidly.
미국 내의 이민은 급격히 증가해왔다.

16 importance [impɔ́:rtəns]
n 중요성, 중대성   the quality of being important
He emphasized the **importance** of careful driving.
그는 조심스런 운전의 중요성을 강조했다.

17 irregular [irégjələr]
a 불규칙한, 고르지 못한   not allowed according to the rules
I have to stop my **irregular** life style now.
나는 이제 불규칙적인 생활을 끝내야겠다.

18 isolated [áisəlèitid]
a 고립된, 멀리 떨어진   alone or apart from other people or things
They found an **isolated** house and shouted with joy.
그들은 고립된 집 한 채를 발견하고 기쁨으로 소리를 질렀다.

---

key words
aim n 목표 / Pilgrim n 순례자 / settle v 정착하다 / permanently ad 영구적으로 / emphasize v 강조하다

Unit 2 11

Exercise

A. Complete the sentence.

1. The possession of a passport is _____ for foreign travel.
   어권 소지는 외국 여행을 하기 위해 필수적이다.

2. I'm not going to go swimming until I've _____ my lunch.
   점심 먹은 것을 다 소화하기 전까지 수영하러 가지 않을 것이다.

3. I have to stop my _____ life style now.
   나는 이제 불규칙적인 생활을 끝내야겠다.

4. When is your baby _____?
   출산예정일이 언제입니까?

5. A man _____ from the shadows.
   한 남자가 그림자 속에서 나타났다.

6. She signed a contract _____ that will keep her on staff for one additional year.
   그녀는 일년 동안 더 직원으로 남게 하는 계약 연장에 서명했다.

7. If you touch the world _____, the world will touch you _____ in return.
   당신이 세상을 온화하게 대하면 세상도 그 보답으로 당신을 온화하게 대한다.

8. Korean _____ from English in many respects.
   한국어는 많은 점에서 영어와 다르다.

9. You shouldn't take advantage of his _____.
   너는 그의 관대함을 이용해서는 안 된다.

10. Idle _____ only have the least leisure time.
    게으른 사람들은 최소한의 여가시간만이 있을 뿐이다.

11. This book aims to give students a solid _____ in grammar.
    이 책은 학생들에게 탄탄한 문법적인 기초를 전달하는 것을 목표로 하고 있다.

12. _____ in the United States has been increasing rapidly.
    미국 내의 이민은 급격히 증가해왔다.

13. On the Earth, _____ is weaker on a mountaintop than in a valley.
    지구에서 중력은 계곡에서보다 산꼭대기에서 더 약하다.

14. It's getting tougher and tougher to _____.
    그것은 수출하기가 점점 더 어려워지고 있다.

15. Native Americans _____ the Pilgrims who settled on the eastern shores.
    북미의 원주민들이 동해안에 정착했던 그 순례자들을 환영했다.

16. Photo _____ is quickly becoming popular for graphics novices.
    사진 편집은 그래픽 초보자에게 빠른 속도로 인기를 얻고 있다.

17. He emphasized the _____ of careful driving.
    그는 조심스런 운전의 중요성을 강조했다.

18. They found an _____ house and shouted with joy.
    그들은 고립된 집 한 채를 발견하고 기쁨으로 소리를 질렀다.

Hint

generosity   edit   digest   immigration   export   gently   isolated   folk   irregular
foundation   differ   greet   extension   importance   essential   emerge   due   gravity

Exercise

B. Fill in the word and meaning.

	Word	Meaning
01	gently	
02	differ	
03	immigration	
04	due	
05	emerge	
06	foundation	
07	isolated	
08	digest	
09	greet	
10	extension	
11	irregular	
12	edit	
13	gravity	
14	export	
15	folk	
16	importance	
17	essential	
18	generosity	

	Meaning	Word
01	다르다, 의견이 다르다	
02	소화하다, 이해하다	
03	~할 예정인, ~에 기인하는	
04	편집하다, 교정하다	
05	나타나다, 나오다	
06	필수의, 본질적인	
07	수출하다, 밖으로 전하다	
08	연장, 확대	
09	사람들, 서민의, 민속의	
10	기초, 설립, 기반	
11	관대, 아량	
12	온화하게, 조용히, 서서히	
13	중력, 진지함	
14	환영하다, 인사하다	
15	이민, 이주	
16	중요성, 중대성	
17	불규칙한, 고르지 못한	
18	고립된, 멀리 떨어진	

C. Listen, write the word and meaning. Track 6

	Word	Meaning		Word	Meaning
01			10		
02			11		
03			12		
04			13		
05			14		
06			15		
07			16		
08			17		
09			18		

Review 1

A. Read and fill in the word and meaning.

word	definition	meaning
chaos	a state of great disorder	
access	to have the opportunity or right to see or use something such as information or equipment	
dare	to have enough courage to do something	
conceal	conceal to hide somebody/something	
ability	the mental or physical power or sill that makes it possible to do	
deaf	unable to hear anything	
average	the normal standard, amount or quality	
concrete	a physical object rather than a quality or idea	
application	a formal written request, especially for a job or a place in a club, etc	
ceaseless	continuing for a long time without stopping	
contrary	completely different; opposite	
amaze	to surprise somebody very much	
contrast	comparison between two people or things to show the differences	
aware	realizing something; conscious of somebody/something	
bouquet	a bunch of flowers that is arranged in an attractive way	
arise	to begin to exist; to appear	
brand	the name of a product that is made by a particular company	
arrangement	preparations for something that will happen in the future	

Hint

application aware conceal brand arise ability bouquet amaze contrast
ceaseless chaos average concrete dare contrary arrangement deaf access

Review 1

B. Read and fill in the word and meaning.

word	definition	meaning
	to be different	
	to change food in your stomach so that it can be used by the body	
	the natural force that makes things fall to the ground	
	the idea or principle on which something is based	
	the quality of being generous	
	to welcome somebody when you meet him/her	
	to prepare a film or TV program by cutting and arranging in a particular order	
	kind and calm	
	completely necessary	
	the quality of being important	
	people in general, a particular type of people	
	expected or planned to happen	
	the process of coming to live permanently in a country that is not your own	
	an extra period of time that you are allowed for something	
	alone or apart from other people or things	
	to appear or come out from somewhere	
	not allowed according to the rules	
	to send goods, etc to another country, usually for sale	

Hint

generosity edit digest immigration export gently isolated folk irregular
foundation differ greet extension importance essential emerge due gravity

Unit 3

🎧 Listen and repeat. (Track 7)

01 location [loukéiʃən]
n 위치, 장소   a place or position
That pharmacy moved to another **location**.
그 약국은 다른 장소로 옮겼습니다.

02 logic [ládʒik]
n 논리, 사고, 논리학   sound and clear thinking or reasoning
She uses **logic** to make decisions.
그녀는 결정을 할 때에 논리를 사용한다.

03 majestic [mədʒéstik]
a 장엄한, 위엄 있는   impressive because of its size or beauty
He was very impressed when he saw a **majestic** mountain landscape.
그는 장엄한 산의 풍경을 보고 매우 감명 받았다.

04 metropolitan [mètrəpálitən]
a 대도시의, 주요 도시의   belonging to or typical of a large busy city
Cleveland, the greatest **metropolitan** area in Ohio, lies on the southern shore of Lake Erie.
오하이오 주에서 가장 큰 대도시인 클리브랜드는 에리 호수의 남쪽 연안에 놓여있다.

05 mode [moud]
n 방식, 방법   a type of something or way of doing something
Many factors influenced new **modes** of production.
많은 요소들이 새로운 생산방식에 영향을 주었다.

06 moderation [màdəréiʃən]
n 절제, 중용   the quality of being reasonable and not being extreme
I have to show great **moderation** in eating.
나는 음식을 먹는 일에 있어서 엄청난 절제를 보여주어야 한다.

07 numerous [njú:mərəs]
a 다수의, 수많은   existing in large numbers
The latest research shows that laughter may have **numerous** benefits.
최근의 조사는 웃음이 많은 이점을 가지고 있을 것이라는 것을 보여준다.

08 oar [ɔ:r]
n 노   a long pole that you use for moving a small boat
Father handed him the **oars**, knowing the water was shallow.
아버지는 물 수심이 낮다는 것을 알기 때문에 그에게 노를 건네주었다.

09 object [ábdʒikt]
n 물체, 목적, 대상   a thing that can be seen and touched, but is not alive
A squid will follow any moving **object** during the first few days of its existence.
오징어는 그것이 태어난 지 처음 며칠 동안 움직이는 어떤 물체든지 쫓아가려고 한다.

---

key words
pharmacy n 약국 / landscape n 풍경 / shore n 연안 / influence v 영향을 끼치다 / shallow a 얕은

🎧 Listen and repeat. (Track 8)

10 paste [peist]
n 풀 / **v** 풀로 붙이다   a soft, wet mixture used for sticking things
Paste is used to make one surface adhere to another.
풀은 한 면을 다른 표면에 붙일 때 쓰인다.

11 peninsula [pinínsələ]
n 반도   an area of land that is almost surrounded by water
Korea **peninsula** borders the land of Russia on the northeast and China on the northwest.
한반도는 북동쪽으로는 러시아, 북서쪽으로는 중국과 국경을 이루고 있다.

12 performance [pərfɔ́ːrməns]
n 상연, 공연, 실행   the act of performing something in front of an audience
His passionate **performance** was so impressive.
그의 열정적인 공연이 매우 인상적이었다.

13 precious [préʃəs]
a 귀중한, 소중한   of great value, loved very much
Don't waste your **precious** time on trivial matters.
사소한 문제들로 귀중한 시간을 낭비하지 마라.

14 probably [prábəbli]
ad 아마, 필시   almost certainly
They will **probably** arrive on Friday evening.
그들은 필시 금요일 저녁에 도착할 것입니다.

15 process [práses]
n 진행, 과정 / **v** (가공)처리하다   a series of actions that you do for a particular purpose
I'm in the **process** of faxing you some documents.
나는 서류를 팩스로 보내는 일을 진행 중이다.

16 receipt [risíːt]
n 영수증, 수령   a piece of paper that is given to show that you have paid for something
As I asked for a refund, they asked me to show the **receipt**.
내가 환불을 요구하자, 그들은 영수증을 보여 달라고 했다.

17 recognize [rékəgnàiz]
v 알아보다, 인정하다   to know again somebody that you have seen
He had changed so much that I couldn't **recognize** him.
그가 너무 많이 변해서 알아 볼 수가 없었다.

18 reflection [riflékʃən]
n 반영, 반사, 반성   a particular person's attitude or situation that reveals something about it
Your clothes are a **reflection** of your personality.
당신의 옷은 당신 인격의 반영이다.

---

key words
adhere **v** 접착하다 / passionate **a** 열정적인 / trivial **a** 하찮은, 사소한 / refund **n** 환불
reveal **v** 드러내다

Exercise

A. Complete the sentence.

1. She uses _____ to make decisions.
   그녀는 결정을 할 때에 논리를 사용한다.
2. _____ is used to make one surface adhere to another.
   풀은 한 면을 다른 표면에 붙일 때 쓰인다.
3. He was very impressed when he saw a _____ mountain landscape.
   그는 장엄한 산의 풍경을 보고 매우 감명 받았다.
4. Many factors influenced new _____ of production.
   많은 요소들이 새로운 생산방식에 영향을 주었다.
5. As I asked for a refund, they asked me to show the _____.
   내가 환불을 요구하자, 그들은 영수증을 보여 달라고 했다.
6. That pharmacy moved to another _____.
   그 약국은 다른 장소로 옮겼습니다.
7. The latest research shows that laughter may have _____ benefits.
   최근의 조사는 웃음이 많은 이점을 가지고 있을 것이라는 것을 보여준다.
8. Father handed him the _____, knowing the water was shallow.
   아버지는 물 수심이 낮다는 것을 알기 때문에 그에게 노를 건네주었다.
9. Cleveland, the greatest _____ area in Ohio, lies on the southern shore of Lake Erie.
   오하이오 주에서 가장 큰 대도시인 클리브랜드는 에리 호수의 남쪽 연안에 놓여있다.
10. Korea _____ borders the land of Russia on the northeast and China on the northwest.
    한반도는 북동쪽으로는 러시아, 북서쪽으로는 중국과 국경을 이루고 있다.
11. A squid will follow any moving _____ during the first few days of its existence.
    오징어는 그것이 태어난 지 처음 며칠 동안 움직이는 어떤 물체든지 쫓아가려고 한다.
12. They will _____ arrive on Friday evening.
    그들은 필시 금요일 저녁에 도착할 것입니다.
13. I have to show great _____ in eating.
    나는 음식을 먹는 일에 있어서 엄청난 절제를 보여주어야 한다.
14. His passionate _____ was so impressive.
    그의 열정적인 공연이 매우 인상적이었다.
15. He had changed so much that I couldn't _____ him.
    그가 너무 많이 변해서 알아 볼 수가 없었다.
16. I'm in the _____ of faxing you some documents.
    나는 서류를 팩스로 보내는 일을 진행 중이다.
17. Your clothes are a _____ of your personality.
    당신의 옷은 당신 인격의 반영이다.
18. Don't waste your _____ time on trivial matters.
    사소한 문제들로 귀중한 시간을 낭비하지 마라.

Hint

performance   receipt   precious   numerous   moderation   process   logic   majestic   oar
metropolitan   location   reflection   peninsula   probably   recognize   paste   object   mode

Exercise

B. Fill in the word and meaning.

	Word	Meaning
01	metropolitan	
02	probably	
03	oar	
04	majestic	
05	recognize	
06	peninsula	
07	location	
08	reflection	
09	precious	
10	numerous	
11	performance	
12	receipt	
13	moderation	
14	process	
15	object	
16	paste	
17	logic	
18	mode	

	Meaning	Word
01	위치, 장소	
02	논리, 사고, 논리학	
03	장엄한, 위엄 있는	
04	대도시의, 주요 도시의	
05	방식, 방법	
06	절제, 중용	
07	다수의, 수많은	
08	노	
09	물체, 목적, 대상	
10	풀, 풀로 붙이다	
11	반도	
12	상연, 공연, 실행	
13	귀중한, 소중한	
14	아마, 필시	
15	진행, 과정, (가공)처리하다	
16	영수증, 수령	
17	알아보다, 인정하다	
18	반영, 반사, 반성	

🎧 C. Listen, write the word and meaning. (Track 9)

	Word	Meaning		Word	Meaning
01			10		
02			11		
03			12		
04			13		
05			14		
06			15		
07			16		
08			17		
09			18		

Unit 4

🎧 Listen and repeat. Track 10

01 rob [rab]
v 빼앗다, 훔치다   to take money, property, etc from a person or place illegally
They knocked him down and **robbed** his watch.
그들은 그를 때려눕히고 시계를 빼앗았다.

02 robbery [rábəri]
n 강도(짓), 약탈   the crime of stealing, especially using violence or threats
The **robbery** occurred in broad daylight in a crowded street.
그 강도 사건은 대낮에 사람들이 붐비는 거리에서 일어났다.

03 rod [rad]
n 막대, 낚싯대   a thin straight piece of wood, metal, etc
While holding a fishing **rod** on the river bank, a little girl suddenly felt something moving.
강둑에서 낚싯대를 잡고 있는 동안, 한 어린 소녀가 갑자기 무언가 움직이는 것을 느꼈다.

04 shepherd [ʃépərd]
n 양치는 사람 / v 이끌다   a person whose job is to look after sheep
He urges his master to get better so that they may be **shepherds** together.
그는 주인에게 빨리 병이 나아서 함께 목동이 되자고 재촉한다.

05 shore [ʃɔːr]
n 해안, 호숫가   the land at the edge of a sea or lake
The land inclines toward the **shore**.
그 땅은 해안 쪽으로 기울어져 있다.

06 shortage [ʃɔ́ːrtidʒ]
n 부족, 결핍   a situation where there is not enough of something
They suffered from the **shortage** of food, water and medicine.
그들은 음식, 물, 의약품 등의 부족으로 고통을 받았다.

07 spare [spɛər]
v 나누어주다, 절약하다 / a 여분의   to be able to give something to somebody
We would be honored if you could **spare** the time to have lunch with us.
저희들과 함께 점심식사를 할 시간을 나눠주신다면 영광이겠는데요.

08 spread [spred]
v 펴다, 늘이다   to open something that has been folded so that it covers a larger area
I **spread** the napkin over my lap.
나는 냅킨을 무릎 위에 폈다.

09 starve [staːrv]
v 굶주리다, 굶어 죽다   to suffer or die because you do not have enough food to eat
They got lost in the desert and **starved** to death.
그들은 사막에서 길을 잃고 굶어 죽었다.

---

key words
illegally ad 불법으로 / urge v 재촉하다 / incline v 기울다 / suffer v 고통을 겪다 / honor a 명예로운

🎧 Listen and repeat. Track 11

10 summary [sʌ́məri]
n 요약, 개요   a short description of the main ideas but without any details
Write me a one-page **summary** of this report.
이 보고서를 한 페이지로 요약해서 써주세요.

11 supply [səplái]
v 공급하다, 보충하다   to give or provide something
The company **supplies** its goods only to the trade.
그 회사는 무역업자들에게만 상품을 공급한다.

12 support [səpɔ́:rt]
v 지지하다, 후원하다   to help somebody saying that you agree with him/her
I cannot **support** your opinion.
당신의 의견을 지지할 수 없습니다.

13 tiny [táini]
a 매우 작은 / n 작은 것   very small
Tiny blossoms have come out all over the river bank.
작은 꽃들이 강둑 전체에 가득 피었다.

14 tissue [tíʃu:]
n 조직, 티슈   the mass of cells that form the bodies
Muscle **tissue** consists of a lot of cells.
근육 조직은 많은 세포로 이루어져 있다.

15 torch [tɔ:rtʃ]
n 횃불 / v 태우다   a light made by burning wood, flax, etc. and carried by hand
We used a **torch** to light our way.
우리는 길을 밝히기 위해 횃불을 이용했다.

16 victim [víktim]
n 희생자, 피해자   a person or animal that is injured, killed or hurt
I paid my respects to a lot of war **victims**.
나는 많은 전쟁 희생자들에게 경의를 표했다.

17 violent [váiələnt]
a 격렬한, 맹렬한   very strong and impossible to control
This **violent** weather destroyed nine homes near the downtown area.
이 격렬한 날씨 때문에 도심 인근의 가옥 9채가 파괴되었다.

18 virus [váiərəs]
n 바이러스, 병균   a living thing, too small to be seen, that causes disease
That scientist will study the **virus**.
저 과학자가 그 바이러스를 연구할 것입니다.

key words
bank n 둑, 제방 / flax n 아마 섬유 / injure v 상처를 입히다 / pay v (존경, 경의를) 표하다

Unit 4 21

Exercise

A. Complete the sentence.

1. While holding a fishing _____ on the river bank, a little girl suddenly felt something moving.
   강둑에서 낚싯대를 잡고 있는 동안, 한 어린 소녀가 갑자기 무언가 움직이는 것을 느꼈다.

2. He urges his master to get better so that they may be _____ together.
   그는 주인에게 빨리 병이 나아서 함께 목동이 되자고 재촉한다.

3. _____ blossoms have come out all over the river bank.
   작은 꽃들이 강둑 전체에 가득 피었다.

4. They suffered from the _____ of food, water and medicine.
   그들은 음식, 물, 의약품 등의 부족으로 고통을 받았다.

5. They knocked him down and _____ his watch.
   그들은 그를 때려눕히고 시계를 빼앗았다.

6. We would be honored if you could _____ the time to have lunch with us.
   저희들과 함께 점심식사를 할 시간을 나눠주신다면 영광이겠는데..

7. That scientist will study the _____.
   저 과학자가 그 바이러스를 연구할 것입니다.

8. I _____ the napkin over my lap.
   나는 냅킨을 무릎 위에 폈다.

9. The _____ occurred in broad daylight in a crowded street.
   그 강도 사건은 대낮에 사람들이 붐비는 거리에서 일어났다.

10. They got lost in the desert and _____ to death.
    그들은 사막에서 길을 잃고 굶어 죽었다.

11. The company _____ its goods only to the trade.
    그 회사는 무역업자들에게만 상품을 공급한다.

12. This _____ weather destroyed nine homes near the downtown area.
    이 격렬한 날씨 때문에 도심 인근의 가옥 9채가 파괴되었다.

13. I cannot _____ your opinion.
    당신의 의견을 지지할 수 없습니다.

14. Muscle _____ consists of a lot of cells.
    근육 조직은 많은 세포로 이루어져 있다.

15. The land inclines toward the _____.
    그 땅은 해안 쪽으로 기울어져 있다.

16. We used a _____ to light our way.
    우리는 길을 밝히기 위해 햇불을 이용했다.

17. I paid my respects to a lot of war _____.
    나는 많은 전쟁 희생자들에게 경의를 표했다.

18. Write me a one-page _____ of this report.
    이 보고서를 한 페이지로 요약해서 써주세요.

Hint

| victim | robbery | shore | torch | spread | rod | tiny | summary | virus |
| supply | shortage | rob | shepherd | violent | starve | support | tissue | spare |

Exercise

B. Fill in the word and meaning.

	Word	Meaning
01	rod	
02	shore	
03	victim	
04	summary	
05	rob	
06	spread	
07	virus	
08	tissue	
09	spare	
10	robbery	
11	supply	
12	starve	
13	violent	
14	torch	
15	shortage	
16	tiny	
17	support	
18	shepherd	

	Meaning	Word
01	빼앗다, 훔치다	
02	강도(짓), 약탈	
03	막대, 낚싯대	
04	양치는 사람, 이끌다	
05	해안, 호숫가	
06	부족, 결핍	
07	나누어주다, 절약하다, 여분의	
08	펴다, 늘이다	
09	굶주리다, 굶어 죽다	
10	요약, 개요	
11	공급하다, 보충하다	
12	지지하다, 후원하다	
13	매우 작은, 작은 것	
14	조직, 티슈	
15	횃불, 태우다	
16	희생자, 피해자	
17	격렬한, 맹렬한	
18	바이러스, 병균	

🎧 C. Listen, write the word and meaning. (Track 12)

	Word	Meaning		Word	Meaning
01			10		
02			11		
03			12		
04			13		
05			14		
06			15		
07			16		
08			17		
09			18		

Review 2

A. Read and fill in the word and meaning.

word	definition	meaning
	a long pole that you use for moving a small boat	
	sound and clear thinking or reasoning	
	almost certainly	
	a piece of paper that is given to show that you have paid for something	
	a place or position	
	a particular person's attitude or situation that reveals something about it	
	existing in large numbers	
	a type of something or way of doing something	
	a soft, wet mixture used for sticking things	
	a thing that can be seen and touched, but is not alive	
	impressive because of its size or beauty	
	of great value, loved very much	
	belonging to or typical of a large busy city	
	a series of actions that you do for a particular purpose	
	the act of performing something in front of an audience	
	the quality of being reasonable and not being extreme	
	an area of land that is almost surrounded by water	
	to know again somebody that you have seen	

Hint

performance   receipt   precious   numerous   moderation   process   logic   majestic   oar
metropolitan   location   reflection   peninsula   probably   recognize   paste   object   mode

B. Read and fill in the word and meaning.

word	definition	meaning
rob	to take money, property, etc from a person or place illegally	
shortage	a situation where there is not enough of something	
virus	a living thing, too small to be seen, that causes disease	
spare	to be able to give something to somebody	
robbery	the crime of stealing , especially using violence or threats	
shore	the land at the edge of a sea or lake	
support	to help somebody saying that you agree with him/her	
rod	a thin straight piece of wood, metal, etc	
tiny	very small	
shepherd	a person whose job is to look after sheep	
torch	a light made by burning wood, flax, etc. and carried by hand	
summary	a short description of the main ideas but without any details	
tissue	the mass of cells that form the bodies	
starve	to suffer or die because you do not have enough food to eat	
supply	to give or provide something	
victim	a person or animal that is injured, killed or hurt	
spread	to open something that has been folded so that it covers a larger area	
violent	very strong and impossible to control	

Hint

victim   robbery   shore   torch   spread   rod   tiny   summary   virus
supply   shortage   rob   shepherd   violent   starve   support   tissue   spare

Unit 5

🎧 Listen and repeat. Track 13

01 accomplish
[əkámpliʃ]
v 이룩하다, 성취하다, 완성하다   to succeed in doing something difficult that you planned to do
It will be a long time before he **accomplishes** his plan.
그가 자기의 계획을 성취하기까지는 긴 시간이 걸릴 것이다.

02 account
[əkáunt]
n 설명, 이유, 은행구좌   somebody's report or description of something that has happened
There is no **accounting** for tastes.
취향을 말로 설명할 수 없다.

03 ancient
[éinʃənt]
a 고대의, 옛날의, 구식의   belonging to a period of history that is thousands of years in the past
Her specialty is **ancient** Greek poetry.
그녀의 전공은 고대 그리스 시이다.

04 animated
[ǽnəmèitid]
a 만화영화의   connected with a film using a process which makes pictures appear to move
He worked on **animated** movies, like the famous Puss in Boots.
그는 유명한 Puss in Boots와 같은 만화영화를 제작하였다.

05 arrest
[ərést]
v 체포하다, 저지하다 / n 체포   to take prisoner in order to question him/her about a crime
He was **arrested** on charges of armed robbery.
그는 무장 강도 혐의로 체포되었다.

06 aside
[əsáid]
ad 옆에(으로), 떨어져서   to one side; apart from
Stir the mixture until it foams, then set it **aside**.
그 혼합물을 거품이 날 때까지 저은 다음 옆에 놓습니다.

07 awful
[ɔ́:fəl]
a 무서운, 대단한   terrible; very great
You must think that we are **awful** people.
당신은 우리 모두가 무서운 사람들이라고 생각하실 거에요.

08 bald
[bɔ:ld]
a 벗어진, 대머리의   having little or no hair on your head
I hope I don't go **bald** like my father did.
아버지처럼 머리가 벗어지는 일은 없었으면 좋겠어요.

09 beam
[bi:m]
n 광선, 기둥 / v 빛나다   a line of light
The distance from the earth to the moon can easily be measured today by laser **beams**.
오늘 지구에서 달까지의 거리는 레이저 광선으로 쉽게 측정할 수 있다.

---

key words
taste n 취향, 취미 / specialty n 전공, 전문 / armed a 무장한 / stir v 젓다 / foam n 거품 / laser n 레이저

🎧 Listen and repeat. Track 14

10 bump
[bʌmp]
v 충돌하다, 부딪치다   to hit somebody/something by accident when you are moving
I saw stars when I **bumped** into the door.
문에 부딪히니 별이 보였다.

11 bunch
[bʌntʃ]
n 다발, 묶음   a number of things fastened or growing together
He bought her a **bunch** of flowers for her birthday.
그는 그녀의 생일날 꽃 한 다발을 가져 왔다.

12 civilize
[sívəlàiz]
v 문명화하다, 세련되게 하다   to make people or a society develop from a low level to a more advanced
Throughout much of **civilized** history, people have made distinctions between the arts.
많은 문명화된 역사를 통해서 사람들은 예술 사이에도 차이를 두게 되었다.

13 colonial
[kəlóuniəl]
a 식민(지)의, 식민지풍의   connected with a country that controls another country
She collects **colonial** antiques.
그녀는 식민지의 골동품을 수집한다.

14 confess
[kənfés]
v 자백하다, 인정하다, 고백하다   to admit that you have done something bad or wrong
Did the kidnapper **confess** his crime?
납치범이 범죄를 자백했나요?

15 convenience
[kənvíːnjəns]
n 편리, 편의   something that makes things easier, quicker or more comfortable
The house has all the latest **conveniences**.
그 집은 모든 최신 편의 시설들을 갖추고 있다.

16 courteous
[kə́ːrtiəs]
a 예의 바른, 친절한   polite and pleasant, showing respect for other people
The bishop of the town offers him lodging and **courteous** treatment.
마을의 주교는 그에게 숙소를 제공하고 예의 바른 접대를 베풀었다.

17 decade
[dékeid]
n 10년간   a period of ten years
It's been one of the worst years I've seen in a **decade**.
올해는 10년 만에 겪는 최악의 한 해랍니다.

18 deck
[dek]
n 갑판   one of the floors of a ship or bus
Rain splashed on the ship's **deck**.
배의 갑판 위로 빗방울이 튀겼다.

---

key words
distinction n 차이, 구별 / kidnapper n 유괴범 / bishop n 주교
lodging n 숙소, 하숙집 / splash v 튀기다

Unit 5 27

Exercise

A. Complete the sentence.

1. Did the kidnapper _____ his crime?
   납치범이 범죄를 자백했나요?
2. It will be a long time before he _____ his plan.
   그가 자기의 계획을 성취하기까지는 긴 시간이 걸릴 것이다.
3. Rain splashed on the ship's _____.
   배의 갑판 위로 빗방울이 튀겼다.
4. There is no _____ for tastes.
   취향을 말로 설명할 수 없다.
5. She collects _____ antiques.
   그녀는 식민지의 골동품을 수집한다.
6. He worked on _____ movies, like the famous Puss in Boots.
   그는 유명한 Puss in Boots와 같은 만화영화를 제작하였다.
7. I hope I don't go _____ like my father did.
   아버지처럼 머리가 벗어지는 일은 없었으면 좋겠어요.
8. The distance from the earth to the moon can easily be measured today by laser _____.
   오늘날 지구에서 달까지의 거리는 레이저 광선으로 쉽게 측정할 수 있다.
9. You must think that we are _____ people.
   당신은 우리 모두가 무서운 사람들이라고 생각하실 거예요.
10. I saw stars when I _____ into the door.
    문에 부딪히니 별이 보였다.
11. The house has all the latest _____.
    그 집은 모든 최신 편의 시설들을 갖추고 있다.
12. Her specialty is _____ Greek poetry.
    그녀의 전공은 고대 그리스 시이다.
13. He bought her a _____ of flowers for her birthday.
    그는 그녀의 생일날 꽃 한 다발을 가져 왔다.
14. He was _____ on charges of armed robbery.
    그는 무장 강도 혐의로 체포되었다.
15. Throughout much of _____ history, people have made distinctions between the arts.
    많은 문명화된 역사를 통해서 사람들은 예술 사이에도 차이를 두게 되었다.
16. Stir the mixture until it foams, then set it _____.
    그 혼합물을 거품이 날 때까지 저은 다음 옆에 놓습니다.
17. The bishop of the town offers him lodging and _____ treatment.
    마을의 주교는 그에게 숙소를 제공하고 예의 바른 접대를 베풀었다.
18. It's been one of the worst years I've seen in a _____.
    올해는 10년 만에 겪는 최악의 한 해랍니다.

Hint

| bald | account | bump | civilize | confess | courteous | animated | beam | accomplish |
| awful | bunch | deck | arrest | ancient | aside | | colonial | decade | convenience |

Exercise

B. Fill in the word and meaning.

	Word	Meaning
01	awful	
02	bald	
03	accomplish	
04	civilize	
05	account	
06	bump	
07	convenience	
08	arrest	
09	colonial	
10	decade	
11	aside	
12	courteous	
13	bunch	
14	ancient	
15	deck	
16	beam	
17	confess	
18	animated	

	Meaning	Word
01	이룩하다, 성취하다, 완성하다	
02	설명, 이유, 은행구좌	
03	고대의, 옛날의, 구식의	
04	만화영화의	
05	체포하다, 저지하다, 체포	
06	옆에(으로), 떨어져서	
07	무서운, 대단한	
08	벗어진, 대머리의	
09	광선, 기둥, 빛나다	
10	충돌하다, 부딪치다	
11	다발, 묶음	
12	문명화하다, 세련되게 하다	
13	식민(지)의, 식민지풍의	
14	자백하다, 인정하다, 고백하다	
15	편리, 편의	
16	예의 바른, 친절한	
17	10년간	
18	갑판	

C. Listen, write the word and meaning. Track 15

	Word	Meaning		Word	Meaning
01			10		
02			11		
03			12		
04			13		
05			14		
06			15		
07			16		
08			17		
09			18		

Unit 6

🎧 Listen and repeat. (Track 16)

01 declare [diklέər]
v 선언하다, 단언하다 to state something publicly or to make something known in a firm way
The meat was **declared** unfit for human consumption.
그 고기는 인간이 소비하기에는 부적합하다고 선언되었다.

02 disappointment [dìsəpɔ́intmənt]
n 실망, 실망거리 to make somebody sad because what is less good then he/she had hoped
To my **disappointment**, he went away without a word.
실망스럽게도 그는 한마디 말없이 가 버렸다.

03 efficiency [ifíʃənsi]
n 능률, 효율 an ability to work well without wasting time and energy
An **efficiency** of the work depends on their conversation.
그 직업의 능률은 그들의 의사소통에 달려있다.

04 elect [ilékt]
v 뽑다, 선거하다 to choose somebody by voting
If he withdraws his support, I don't see how I can be **elected**.
그가 지지를 철회하면 내가 어떻게 뽑힐 수 있을지 알 수가 없다.

05 establish [istǽbliʃ]
v 설립하다, 확립하다 to start or create an organization, a system, etc
The United States struggled to **establish** its own economic and financial system.
미국은 자신들만의 경제적, 금융적 시스템을 설립하려고 노력했다.

06 estate [istéit]
n 광대한 토지, 재산 a large area of land in the countryside that is owned by one person or family
His **estates** were sold, and the family moved into hired lodgings.
그의 토지는 팔렸고 가족은 임대 주택으로 이사를 갔다.

07 facility [fəsíləti]
n 시설, 특징, 장소 a service, building, etc that makes it possible to do something
They took full advantage of the hotel's **facilities**.
그들은 호텔 시설들을 최대한 활용했다.

08 fancy [fǽnsi]
n 공상, 상상 / v 공상하다 an imagination or vision
When I was five I started to pour out my **fancies** onto my note.
다섯 살이었을 때 나는 나의 상상들을 노트에 쏟아 붓기 시작했다.

09 financial [finǽnʃəl]
a 재정(상)의, 재무의 of finance or the management of money
Financial markets reacted cautiously to the increase in interest rates.
금융시장은 이율 인상에 조심스런 반응을 보였다.

---

key words
publicly ad 공개적으로 / consumption n 소비 / withdraw v 철회하다
struggle v 애쓰다, 노력하다 / hired a 임대의

🎧 Listen and repeat. Track 17

10 fossil [fásl]
n 화석 / a 화석의, 구식의   an animal or plant that lived thousands of years ago which has turned into rock
The vast continent is abundant in **fossil** fuels.
그 광대한 대륙은 화석 연료가 풍부하다.

11 geography [dʒiːágrəfi]
n 지리학, 지리   the study of the world's surface, physical qualities, climate, etc
The **geography** class has gone on a trip to Wales.
지리학과는 웨일즈로 여행을 갔다 왔다.

12 gesture [dʒéstʃər]
n 몸짓, 제스처   a movement of the hand, head, etc that expresses something
In pantomime actors use **gestures** in place of words to convey ideas.
판토마임에서 배우들은 의사를 전달하기 위해서 말 대신에 제스처를 사용한다.

13 growth [grouθ]
n 성장, 발육   the process of growing and developing
Light is a stimulus to **growth** in plants.
빛은 식물의 성장에 자극제가 된다.

14 homesick [hóumsik]
a 향수병에 걸린   sad because you are away from home and you miss it
What do you do when you get **homesick**?
여러분은 향수병을 어떻게 달래십니까?

15 industrious [indʌ́striəs]
a 근면한, 부지런한   always working hard
I always try to be an **industrious** worker.
나는 항상 근면한 노동자가 되려고 노력한다.

16 influence [ínfluːəns]
n 영향, 세력 / v 영향을 미치다   to have an effect on or power over somebody /something
The book had the most **influence** on me.
그 책이 나에게 가장 많은 영향을 끼쳤다.

17 issue [íʃuː]
n 문제, 논쟁, 발행   a problem or subject for discussion
We want to know your idea about the price **issue** before we make a final decision.
최종 결정을 하기 전에 가격 문제에 대한 당신의 의견을 듣고 싶습니다.

18 jail [dʒeil]
n 감옥, 교도소   a prison
You should have gone to **jail** for that.
당신은 그 일로 감옥에 갔어야 했어요.

key words
vast a 광대한, 거대한 / abundant a 풍부한 / convey v 전달하다 / stimulus n 자극제, 자극

Unit 6 31

Exercise

A. Complete the sentence.

1. In pantomime actors use _____ in place of words to convey ideas.
   판토마임에서 배우들은 의사를 전달하기 위해서 말 대신에 제스처를 사용한다.

2. To my _____, he went away without a word.
   실망스럽게도 그는 한마디 말없이 가 버렸다.

3. I always try to be an _____ worker.
   나는 항상 근면한 노동자가 되려고 노력한다.

4. An _____ of the work depends on their conversation.
   그 직업의 능률은 그들의 의사소통에 달려있다.

5. If he withdraws his support, I don't see how I can be _____.
   그가 지지를 철회하면 내가 어떻게 뽑힐 수 있을지 알 수가 없다.

6. The United States struggled to _____ its own economic and financial system.
   미국은 자신들만의 경제적, 금융적 시스템을 설립하려고 노력했다.

7. They took full advantage of the hotel's _____.
   그들은 호텔 시설들을 최대한 활용했다.

8. The meat was _____ unfit for human consumption.
   그 고기는 인간이 소비하기에는 부적합하다고 선언되었다.

9. When I was five I started to pour out my _____ onto my note.
   다섯 살이었을 때 나는 나의 상상들을 노트에 쏟아 붓기 시작했다.

10. _____ markets reacted cautiously to the increase in interest rates.
    금융시장은 이율 인상에 조심스런 반응을 보였다.

11. His _____ were sold, and the family moved into hired lodgings.
    그의 토지는 팔렸고 가족은 임대 주택으로 이사를 갔다.

12. The _____ class has gone on a trip to Wales.
    지리학과는 웨일즈로 여행을 갔다 왔다.

13. Light is a stimulus to _____ in plants.
    빛은 식물의 성장에 자극제가 된다.

14. The vast continent is abundant in _____ fuels.
    그 광대한 대륙은 화석 연료가 풍부하다.

15. You should have gone to _____ for that.
    당신은 그 일로 감옥에 갔어야 했어요.

16. What do you do when you get _____?
    여러분은 향수병을 어떻게 달래십니까?

17. The book had the most _____ on me.
    그 책이 나에게 가장 많은 영향을 끼쳤다.

18. We want to know your idea about the price _____ before we make a final decision.
    최종 결정을 하기 전에 가격 문제에 대한 당신의 의견을 듣고 싶습니다.

Hint

| fancy | elect | financial | growth | disappointment | gesture | industrious | establish | fossil |
| issue | facility | efficiency | declare | geography | | estate | homesick | influence | jail |

Exercise

B. Fill in the word and meaning.

	Word	Meaning
01	disappointment	
02	fossil	
03	estate	
04	growth	
05	declare	
06	financial	
07	gesture	
08	influence	
09	elect	
10	issue	
11	industrious	
12	establish	
13	jail	
14	fancy	
15	homesick	
16	geography	
17	facility	
18	efficiency	

	Meaning	Word
01	선언하다, 단언하다	
02	실망, 실망거리	
03	능률, 효율	
04	뽑다, 선거하다	
05	설립하다, 확립하다	
06	광대한 토지, 재산	
07	시설, 특징, 장소	
08	공상, 상상, 공상하다	
09	재정(상)의, 재무의	
10	화석, 화석의, 구식의	
11	지리학, 지리	
12	몸짓, 제스처	
13	성장, 발육	
14	향수병에 걸린	
15	근면한, 부지런한	
16	영향, 세력, 영향을 미치다	
17	문제, 논쟁, 발행	
18	감옥, 교도소	

C. Listen, write the word and meaning. Track 18

	Word	Meaning		Word	Meaning
01			10		
02			11		
03			12		
04			13		
05			14		
06			15		
07			16		
08			17		
09			18		

Review 3

A. Read and fill in the word and meaning.

word	definition	meaning
	to admit that you have done something bad or wrong	
	having little or no hair on your head	
	to succeed in doing something difficult that you planned to do	
	something that makes things easier, quicker or more comfortable	
	terrible; very great	
	one of the floors of a ship or bus	
	somebody's report or description of something that has happened	
	polite and pleasant, showing respect for other people	
	a line of light	
	belonging to a period of history that is thousands of years in the past	
	a period of ten years	
	connected with a film using a process which makes pictures appear to move	
	connected with a country that controls another country	
	to one side; apart from	
	a number of things fastened or growing together	
	to take prisoner in order to question him/her about a crime	
	to make people or a society develop from a low level to a more advanced	
	to hit somebody/something by accident when you are moving	

Hint

bald   account   bump   civilize   confess   courteous   animated   beam   accomplish
awful   bunch   deck   arrest   ancient   aside   colonial   decade   convenience

B. Read and fill in the word and meaning.

word	definition	meaning
gesture	a movement of the hand, head, etc that expresses something	
disappointment	to make somebody sad because what is less good then he/she had hoped	
elect	to choose somebody by voting	
geography	the study of the world's surface, physical qualities, climate, etc	
declare	to state something publicly or to make something known in a firm way	
growth	the process of growing and developing	
efficiency	an ability to work well without wasting time and energy	
industrious	always working hard	
fossil	an animal or plant that lived thousands of years ago which has turned into rock	
estate	a large area of land in the countryside that is owned by one person or family	
homesick	sad because you are away from home and you miss it	
financial	of finance or the management of money	
influence	to have an effect on or power over somebody/something	
establish	to start or create an organization, a system, etc	
facility	a service, building, etc that makes it possible to do something	
issue	a problem or subject for discussion	
fancy	an imagination or vision	
jail	a prison	

Hint
fancy   elect   financial   growth   disappointment   gesture   industrious   establish   fossil
issue   facility   efficiency   declare   geography   estate   homesick   influence   jail

Unit 7

🎧 Listen and repeat. Track 19

01 maintenance
[méintinəns]
n 유지, 정비, 주장   the process of keeping something in good condition checking and repairing
We bought an old house that needs **maintenance**.
우리는 보수가 필요한 오래된 집을 구입했다.

02 manner
[mǽnəːr]
n 태도, 방법   the way that somebody behaves towards other people
You will be satisfied with their **manner** of doing business.
그늘의 영업태도에 만족하실 수 있으리라 생각합니다.

03 mine
[main]
n 광산 / v 채광하다   a deep hole, or a system of passages under the ground
He got a serious problem in his health because he had worked for a coal **mine**.
그는 탄광에서 일해 왔기 때문에 건강에 심각한 문제가 생겼다.

04 minimum
[mínəmən]
a 최소의 / n 최소   the smallest amount of level that is possible
Some countries have a **minimum** wage set by law.
몇몇 나라에서는 법으로 정해진 최소 임금이 있다.

05 mostly
[móustli]
ad 주로, 대개   in almost every case; almost all the time
My patients are **mostly** professional athletes.
나의 환자들은 대게 프로 운동선수들이다.

06 murder
[mə́ːrdəːr]
n 살인사건 / v 살해하다   the crime of killing person
There is no evidence to connect him with the **murder**.
그를 그 살인 사건과 관련시킬 증거가 없다.

07 occupy
[ákjəpài]
v 차지하다, 점령하다   to take control of building, country, etc by force
The piano seemed to **occupy** the whole room.
그 피아노가 방 전체를 차지하고 있는 것 같았다.

08 occur
[əkə́ːr]
v 일어나다, 생기다   to happen in a way that has not been planed
Without trees, the soil is washed away by storms, making it much easier for floods to **occur**.
나무가 없으면 흙은 비바람에 씻겨 내려가게 되어, 홍수가 훨씬 더 쉽게 일어나게 된다.

09 offend
[əfénd]
v 성나게하다, 위반하다   to hurt somebody's feelings
I won't be **offended** with what others say from now on.
나는 지금부터 남이 하는 말에 성내지 않을 것이다.

key words
satisfied a 만족한 / coal n 석탄 / evidence n 증거 / flood n 홍수

🎧 Listen and repeat. Track 20

10 permit [pə:rmít]
v 허락하다, 용인하다   to allow somebody to do something
Permit me to give you a word or two.
제가 당신에게 한 두 마디 할 수 있도록 허락해주십시오.

11 perplex [pərpléks]
v 당혹케하다, 복잡케하다   to make somebody/something confused
His strange silence **perplexes** me.
그의 이상한 침묵이 나를 당황하게 만든다.

12 plentiful [pléntifəl]
a 풍부한, 넉넉한   more than enough; abundant
Tomatoes are now cheap because they are **plentiful**.
토마토가 풍작이라 지금 값이 싸다.

13 product [prádəkt]
n 산물, 생산품   something that is made in a factory
We sell only real leather **products**.
우리는 가죽으로 된 생산품만 팔아요.

14 progress [prágrəs]
n 전진, 진보   movement forwards or towards achieving something
Without struggle, there is no **progress**.
투쟁 없이는 어떤 진전도 없다.

15 properly [prápərli]
ad 적당히, 정확히   in a proper manner; correctly
Your seat and mirrors need to be **properly** adjusted.
좌석과 거울을 적당히 조절해야만 합니다.

16 reaction [ri:ǽkʃən]
n 반작용, 반동, 반응   an opposing action; a response to some force
Action is inevitably followed by **reaction**.
작용이 있으면 반드시 반작용이 있다.

17 relative [rélətiv]
n 친척 / a 상대적인   a member of your family
Several of our **relatives** will come and stay for a few days.
친척 몇 분이 오셔서 며칠 묵으실 것이다.

18 religion [rilídʒən]
n 종교, 신앙   the belief in a god or gods
The subject of today's discussion was about **religion**.
오늘의 토론 주제는 종교에 관한 것이었다.

---

key words
confused a 혼란스러운, 당황한 / abundant a 풍부한, 많은 / leather n 가죽 / adjust v 조절하다
inevitably ad 불가피하게

Unit 7   37

Exercise

A. Complete the sentence.

1. _____ me to give you a word or two.
   제가 당신에게 한 두 마디 할 수 있도록 허락해주십시오.

2. Some countries have a _____ wage set by law.
   몇몇 나라에서는 법으로 정해진 최소 임금이 있다.

3. My patients are _____ professional athletes.
   나의 환자들은 대게 프로 운동선수들이다.

4. The subject of today's discussion was about _____.
   오늘의 토론 주제는 종교에 관한 것이었다.

5. There is no evidence to connect him with the _____.
   그를 그 살인 사건과 관련시킬 증거가 없다.

6. His strange silence _____ me.
   그의 이상한 침묵이 나를 당황하게 만든다.

7. We bought an old house that needs _____.
   우리는 보수가 필요한 오래된 집을 구입했다.

8. The piano seemed to _____ the whole room.
   그 피아노가 방 전체를 차지하고 있는 것 같았다.

9. Without trees, the soil is washed away by storms, making it much easier for floods to _____.
   나무가 없으면 흙은 비바람에 씻겨 내려가게 되어, 홍수가 훨씬 더 쉽게 일어나게 된다.

10. I won't be _____ with what others say from now on.
    나는 지금부터 남이 하는 말에 성내지 않을 것이다.

11. Tomatoes are now cheap because they are _____.
    토마토가 풍작이라 지금 값이 싸다.

12. He got a serious problem in his health because he had worked for a coal _____.
    그는 탄광에서 일해 왔기 때문에 건강에 심각한 문제가 생겼다.

13. Without struggle, there is no _____.
    투쟁 없이는 어떤 진전도 없다.

14. You will be satisfied with their _____ of doing business.
    그들의 영업태도에 만족하실 수 있으리라 생각합니다.

15. Your seat and mirrors need to be _____ adjusted.
    좌석과 거울을 적당히 조절해야만 합니다.

16. Action is inevitably followed by _____.
    작용이 있으면 반드시 반작용이 있다.

17. We sell only real leather _____.
    우리는 가죽으로 된 생산품만 팔아요.

18. Several of our _____ will come and stay for a few days.
    친척 몇 분이 오셔서 며칠 묵으실 것이다.

Hint

| product | minimum | perplex | occur | reaction | manner | occupy | murder | properly |
| offend | progress | relative | mine | plentiful | religion | mostly | permit | maintenance |

Unit 7

Exercise

B. Fill in the word and meaning.

	Word	Meaning
01	minimum	
02	occupy	
03	plentiful	
04	maintenance	
05	product	
06	offend	
07	murder	
08	perplex	
09	reaction	
10	manner	
11	religion	
12	permit	
13	properly	
14	mine	
15	relative	
16	progress	
17	occur	
18	mostly	

	Meaning	Word
01	유지, 정비, 주장	
02	태도, 방법	
03	광산, 채광하다	
04	최소의, 최소	
05	주로, 대개	
06	살인사건, 살해하다	
07	차지하다, 점령하다	
08	일어나다, 생기다	
09	성나게하다, 위반하다	
10	허락하다, 용인하다	
11	당혹케하다, 복잡케하다	
12	풍부한, 넉넉한	
13	산물, 생산품	
14	전진, 진보	
15	적당히, 정확히	
16	반작용, 반동, 반응	
17	친척, 상대적인	
18	종교, 신앙	

🎧 C. Listen, write the word and meaning. (Track 21)

	Word	Meaning		Word	Meaning
01			10		
02			11		
03			12		
04			13		
05			14		
06			15		
07			16		
08			17		
09			18		

Unit 8

🎧 Listen and repeat. Track 22

01 rotate [róuteit]
v 회전하다, 교대하다   to turn in circles round a central point
The owl can **rotate** its head in an almost complete circle.
올빼미는 그 머리를 거의 완전한 원의 모양으로 회전할 수 있다.

02 rub [rʌb]
v 문지르다, 비비다   to move your hand, etc backwards and forwards on the surface
Rubbing the body stimulates the circulation of blood.
몸을 문지르면 혈액 순환이 활발해진다.

03 rumor [rú:mər]
n 소문, 풍문   news that many people are talking about but that is possibly not true
He often comments on the **rumor** of other's private life.
그는 남의 사생활에 대한 소문에 관해 말을 종종 한다.

04 shuttle [ʃʌtl]
n 왕복 운행 / v (정기적으로)왕복하다   a plane, bus or train that travels regularly between two places
There won't be a space **shuttle** flight for at least two more months.
최소한 두 달 동안은 우주를 왕복 운행하는 비행은 없을 것입니다.

05 silly [síli]
a 어리석은, 시시한   not showing understanding; foolish
Do you know how **silly** you're sounding?
당신 말이 얼마나 어리석게 들리는지 알아요?

06 similar [símələ:r]
a 유사한, 닮은   like somebody/something but not exactly the same
I bought new shoes which are very **similar** to a pair I had before.
나는 전에 가지고 있던 신발과 유사한 것을 새로 샀다.

07 statistics [stətístiks]
n 통계, 통계학   numbers that have been collected in order to provide information
The calculations are based on the latest **statistics**.
그 계산은 최신의 통계에 근거를 둔 것이다.

08 status [stéitəs]
n 지위, 신분   your social or professional position
Obviously, they are jealous of his wealth and **status**.
확실히 그들은 그의 부와 지위를 시샘하고 있다.

09 stock [stak]
n 주식, 재고   the amount of money which the company has through selling shares
The **stock** market crashed, so I regret buying **stocks**.
주식 시장이 폭락해서 나는 주식을 산 일이 후회된다.

---

key words
stimulate v 자극하다 / circulation n 순환 / obviously ad 확실히, 눈에 띄게 / jealous a 시샘하는
share n 주식, 지분 / crash v 무너지다

🎧 Listen and repeat. Track 23

10 swallow [swálou]
v 삼키다, 들이켜다   to make food, drink, etc go down your throat to your stomach
Doctors suggest that you read the directions carefully before **swallowing** any medicine.
의사들은 어떤 약이든 삼키기 전에 사용설명서를 유심히 읽으라고 제안한다.

11 symbolize [símbəlàiz]
v 상징하다, 부호로 나타내다   to represent something
A wedding ring **symbolizes** the union of husband and wife.
결혼반지는 부부 결합의 상징이다.

12 sympathy [símpəθi]
n 동정, 공감   an understanding of other people's feelings
These people need our help and **sympathy**.
이 사람들은 우리의 도움과 동정을 필요로 한다.

13 toward [tɔːrd]
prep ~쪽으로, ~편으로   in the direction of somebody/something
Everybody in the resort area was running **toward** the party.
그 리조트에 있는 모든 사람들이 파티장 쪽으로 달려가고 있었다.

14 track [træk]
n 통로, 흔적   marks that are left in the ground
The muddy **track** descends to a valley.
그 진흙의 흔적은 계곡까지 내려가 있다.

15 traditional [trədíʃənəl]
a 전통적인, 전통의   having a custom, belief or way of doing from the past to the present
Where can I see the **traditional** Korean dresses?
한국의 전통 의상을 어디서 볼 수 있지요?

16 visible [vízəbəl]
a 눈에 보이는, 명백한   that can be seen or noticed
Make yourself more **visible** to traffic at night by wearing reflective clothing.
빛이 반사되는 옷을 입음으로써 밤에 자동차가 너 자신을 더 잘 볼 수 있도록 해라.

17 vogue [voug]
n 유행, 인기 / a 유행하는   a fashion of something
I bought a sweater in **vogue**.
나는 유행하는 스웨터를 한 벌 샀다.

18 vomit [vámit]
v 토하다, 게우다   to bring food up from the stomach and out of the mouth
It can cause excessive sweating and **vomiting**.
그것은 과도하게 땀을 흘리게 하거나 구토를 일으킬 수 있다.

key words
descend v 내려가다, 경사지다 / reflective a 반사하는 / excessive a 과도의, 지나친

Exercise

A. Complete the sentence.

1. I bought new shoes which are very _____ to a pair I had before.
   나는 전에 가지고 있던 신발과 유사한 것을 새로 샀다.

2. _____ the body stimulates the circulation of blood.
   몸을 문지르면 혈액 순환이 활발해진다.

3. There won't be a space _____ flight for at least two more months.
   최소한 두 달 동안은 우주를 왕복 운행하는 비행은 없을 것입니다.

4. I bought a sweater in _____.
   나는 유행하는 스웨터를 한 벌 샀다.

5. Do you know how _____ you're sounding?
   당신 말이 얼마나 어리석게 들리는지 알아요?

6. The owl can _____ its head in an almost complete circle.
   올빼미는 그 머리를 거의 완전한 원의 모양으로 회전할 수 있다.

7. The calculations are based on the latest _____.
   그 계산은 최신의 통계에 근거를 둔 것이다.

8. The _____ market crashed, so I regret buying _____.
   주식 시장이 폭락해서 나는 주식을 산 일이 후회된다.

9. The muddy _____ descends to a valley.
   그 진흙의 흔적은 계곡까지 내려가 있다.

10. Doctors suggest that you read the directions carefully before _____ any medicine.
    의사들은 어떤 약이든 삼키기 전에 사용설명서를 유심히 읽으라고 제안한다.

11. He often comments on the _____ of other's private life.
    그는 남의 사생활에 대한 소문에 관해 말을 종종 한다.

12. A wedding ring _____ the union of husband and wife.
    결혼반지는 부부 결합의 상징이다.

13. Everybody in the resort area was running _____ the party.
    그 리조트에 있는 모든 사람들이 파티장 쪽으로 달려가고 있었다.

14. Obviously, they are jealous of his wealth and _____.
    확실히 그들은 그의 부와 지위를 시샘하고 있다.

15. Where can I see the _____ Korean dresses?
    한국의 전통 의상을 어디서 볼 수 있지요?

16. Make yourself more _____ to traffic at night by wearing reflective clothing.
    빛이 반사되는 옷을 입음으로써 밤에 자동차가 너 자신을 더 잘 볼 수 있도록 해라.

17. These people need our help and _____.
    이 사람들은 우리의 도움과 동정을 필요로 한다.

18. It can cause excessive sweating and _____.
    그것은 과도하게 땀을 흘리게 하거나 구토를 일으킬 수 있다.

Hint

statistics	visible	symbolize	shuttle	track	rub	stock	rotate	silly
traditional	swallow	sympathy	rumor	vogue	similar	vomit	status	toward

Exercise

B. Fill in the word and meaning.

	Word	Meaning
01	shuttle	
02	toward	
03	sympathy	
04	rotate	
05	silly	
06	traditional	
07	swallow	
08	rub	
09	similar	
10	vogue	
11	status	
12	vomit	
13	statistics	
14	visible	
15	stock	
16	track	
17	symbolize	
18	rumor	

	Meaning	Word
01	회전하다, 교대하다	
02	문지르다, 비비다	
03	소문, 풍문	
04	왕복운행, 왕복하다	
05	어리석은, 시시한	
06	유사한, 닮은	
07	통계, 통계학	
08	지위, 신분	
09	주식, 재고	
10	삼키다, 들이켜다	
11	상징하다, 부호로 나타내다	
12	동정, 공감	
13	~쪽으로, ~편으로	
14	통로, 흔적	
15	전통적인, 전통의	
16	눈에 보이는, 명백한	
17	유행, 인기, 유행하는	
18	토하다, 게우다	

C. Listen, write the word and meaning. Track 24

	Word	Meaning		Word	Meaning
01			10		
02			11		
03			12		
04			13		
05			14		
06			15		
07			16		
08			17		
09			18		

Review 4

A. Read and fill in the word and meaning.

word	definition	meaning
	to take control of building, country, etc by force	
	an opposing action; a response to some force	
	the smallest amount of level that is possible	
	a member of your family	
	in a proper manner; correctly	
	the process of keeping something in good condition checking and repairing	
	movement forwards or towards achieving something	
	a deep hole, or a system of passages under the ground	
	the belief in a god or gods	
	something that is made in a factory	
	the way that somebody behaves towards other people	
	more than enough; abundant	
	in almost every case; almost all the time	
	to make somebody/something confused	
	to hurt somebody's feelings	
	to allow somebody to do something	
	the crime of killing person	
	to happen in a way that has not been planed	

Hint

product   minimum   perplex   occur   reaction   manner   occupy   murder   properly
offend   progress   relative   mine   plentiful   religion   mostly   permit   maintenance

B. Read and fill in the word and meaning.

word	definition	meaning
	to make food, drink, etc go down your throat to your stomach	
	to turn in circles round a central point	
	to bring food up from the stomach and out of the mouth	
	the amount of money which the company has through selling shares	
	to move your hand, etc backwards and forwards on the surface	
	to represent something	
	a plane, bus or train that travels regularly between two places	
	in the direction of somebody/something	
	an understanding of other people's feelings	
	news that many people are talking about but that is possibly not true	
	your social or professional position	
	marks that are left in the ground	
	not showing understanding; foolish	
	having a custom, belief or way of doing from the past to the present	
	numbers that have been collected in order to provide information	
	that can be seen or noticed	
	like somebody/something but not exactly the same	
	a fashion of something	

Hint
statistics   visible   symbolize   shuttle   track   rub   stock   rotate   silly
traditional   swallow   sympathy   rumor   vogue   similar   vomit   status   toward

Review 4

Unit 9

🎧 Listen and repeat. Track 25

01 actually [ǽktʃuəli] — **ad** 현실로, 실제로   really; in fact
The clock is simply for ornament, it doesn't **actually** work.
그 시계는 장식용일 뿐이지 실제로 작동은 하지 않는다.

02 admire [ædmáiər] — **v** 감탄하다, 칭찬하다   to look at somebody/something with pleasure
I **admired** her dedication to her family.
나는 가족에 대한 그녀의 헌신에 감탄했다.

03 announcer [ənáunsər] — **n** 아나운서, 발표자   a person who introduces or gives information on television
What does the **announcer** suggest?
아나운서가 제안하고 있는 것은 무엇인가?

04 annoy [ənɔ́i] — **v** 괴롭히다, 귀찮다   trouble; to make somebody angry
He always is **annoying** his sister by pulling her hair.
그는 누나의 머리카락을 잡아당겨 그녀를 항상 괴롭히고 있다.

05 associate [əsóuʃièit] — **v** 연상하다, 연합하다, 교제하다   to make a connection between people or things in your mind
Most people **associate** haze with pollution, but it's not just pollution.
대부분의 사람들은 연무를 공해라고 연상하지만 그것은 공해가 아니다.

06 astronomical [æstrənámikəl] — **a** 천문학(상)의   connected with astronomy
I want to have an **astronomical** instrument to observe the heavenly bodies.
나는 천체를 관찰하기 위한 천문학용 기계가 갖고 싶다.

07 bankrupt [bǽŋkrʌpt] — **a** 파산한 / **n** 파산자   not having enough money to pay your debts
Beggars can never be **bankrupt**.
거지는 파산할 염려가 없다.

08 blend [blend] — **v** 섞다, 섞이다   to mix
I **blended** milk and butter into the flour.
나는 밀가루에 우유와 버터를 섞었다.

09 bush [buʃ] — **n** 관목, 덤불, 수풀   a plant like a small, thick tree with many low branches
If he does something bad, he always hides in the **bushes**.
그는 나쁜 일을 저지르면 항상 그 덤불 속으로 숨는다.

key words
ornament **n** 장식 / dedication **n** 헌신 / haze **n** 연무

🎧 Listen and repeat. (Track 26)

10 cancer [kǽnsər] **n** 암 — a very serious disease in which lumps grow in the body
Research has established a link between smoking and lung **cancer**.
흡연과 폐암 사이의 관련성은 연구로 입증되었다.

11 classify [klǽsəfài] **v** 분류하다, 등급으로 나누다 — to put somebody/something into a group of a similar type
The books in the library are **classified** according to the subject.
그 도서관의 책들은 주제별로 분류되어 있다.

12 clockwise [klákwàiz] **a** 시계 방향의 — in the same direction as the hands of a clock
We'll walk to the **clockwise** direction.
우리는 시계 방향으로 걸을 거예요.

13 confidence [kánfidəns] **n** 신뢰, 신용, 자신감 — firm belief; trust
It gives your parents **confidence** in you.
그것은 부모님에게 당신에 대한 신뢰를 줄 것이다.

14 congress [káŋgris] **n** 의회, 국회 — the group of people who are elected to make the laws
The function of **Congress** is to make laws.
의회의 기능은 법을 만드는 것이다.

15 coward [káuərd] **n** 겁쟁이, 소심한 사람 — a person who has no courage
They called me a **coward** because I would not fight.
그들은 내가 싸우려 하지 않았기 때문에 나를 겁쟁이라고 불렀다.

16 deduct [didʌ́kt] **v** 빼다, 공제하다 — to take something such as money or points
A monthly service charge will be **deducted**.
서비스 요금은 매월 공제될 겁니다.

17 defeat [difíːt] **v** 쳐부수다, 패배시키다 — to win a game, a fight, a vote, etc against somebody
The army **defeated** the rebels after three days of fighting.
3일간의 싸움 끝에 군대가 그 반역자들을 쳐부수었다.

18 defect [difékt] **n** 결함, 장애 — something that is missing from somebody/something
Generally speaking, it was okay, but some of them had serious **defects**.
대체적으로는 괜찮습니다만 몇 개는 심한 결함이 있었다.

---

key words
lump **n** 덩어리 / establish **v** 입증하다 / rebel **n** 반역자

Exercise

A. Complete the sentence.

1. We'll walk to the _____ direction.
   우리는 시계 방향으로 걸을 거예요.
2. I _____ her dedication to her family.
   나는 가족에 대한 그녀의 헌신에 감탄했다.
3. He always is _____ his sister by pulling her hair.
   그는 누나의 머리카락을 잡아당겨 그녀를 항상 괴롭히고 있다.
4. Research has established a link between smoking and lung _____.
   흡연과 폐암 사이의 관련성은 연구로 입증되었다.
5. The army _____ the rebels after three days of fighting.
   3일간의 싸움 끝에 군대가 그 반역자들을 쳐부수었다.
6. Beggars can never be _____.
   거지는 파산할 염려가 없다.
7. They called me a _____ because I would not fight.
   그들은 내가 싸우려 하지 않기 때문에 나를 겁쟁이라고 불렀다.
8. What does the _____ suggest?
   아나운서가 제안하고 있는 것은 무엇인가?
9. A monthly service charge will be _____.
   서비스 요금은 매월 공제될 겁니다.
10. Most people _____ haze with pollution, but it's not just pollution.
    대부분의 사람들은 연무를 공해라고 연상하지만 그것은 공해가 아니다.
11. The books in the library are _____ according to the subject.
    그 도서관의 책들은 주제별로 분류되어 있다.
12. Generally speaking, it was okay, but some of them had serious _____.
    대체적으로는 괜찮습니다만 몇 개는 심한 결함이 있었다.
13. I want to have an _____ instrument to observe the heavenly bodies.
    나는 천체를 관찰하기 위한 천문학용 기계를 갖고 싶다.
14. I _____ milk and butter into the flour.
    나는 밀가루에 우유와 버터를 섞었다.
15. It gives your parents _____ in you.
    그것은 부모님에게 당신에 대한 신뢰를 줄 것이다.
16. The function of _____ is to make laws.
    의회의 기능은 법을 만드는 것이다.
17. The clock is simply for ornament, it doesn't _____ work.
    그 시계는 장식용일 뿐이지 실제로 작동은 하지 않는다.
18. If he does something bad, he always hides in the _____.
    그는 나쁜 일을 저지르면 항상 그 덤불 속으로 숨는다.

Hint

classify   bankrupt   bush   blend   deduct   announcer   cancer   annoy   astronomical
associate   clockwise   defeat   admire   coward   congress   actually   defect   confidence

Exercise

B. Fill in the word and meaning.

	Word	Meaning
01	blend	
02	actually	
03	deduct	
04	cancer	
05	admire	
06	congress	
07	astronomical	
08	defect	
09	annoy	
10	classify	
11	defeat	
12	associate	
13	confidence	
14	bankrupt	
15	coward	
16	bush	
17	announcer	
18	clockwise	

	Meaning	Word
01	현실로, 실제로	
02	감탄하다, 칭찬하다	
03	아나운서, 발표자	
04	괴롭히다, 귀찮다	
05	연상하다, 연합하다, 교제하다	
06	천문학(상)의	
07	파산한, 파산자	
08	섞다, 섞이다	
09	관목, 덤불, 수풀	
10	암	
11	분류하다, 등급으로 나누다	
12	시계 방향의	
13	신뢰, 신용, 자신감	
14	의회, 국회	
15	겁쟁이, 소심한 사람	
16	빼다, 공제하다	
17	쳐부수다, 패배시키다	
18	결함, 장애	

C. Listen, write the word and meaning. Track 27

	Word	Meaning		Word	Meaning
01			10		
02			11		
03			12		
04			13		
05			14		
06			15		
07			16		
08			17		
09			18		

Unit 10

🎧 Listen and repeat. Track 28

01 definite [défənit]
a 명확한, 확실한   having a clear, exact meaning
We have to commit him to make a **definite** decision.
명확한 결정을 위해 그를 병원으로 보내야 한다.

02 discomfort [diskʌ́mfərt]
n 불편, 불쾌   a slight feeling of pain
Today's **discomfort** index is very high.
오늘은 불쾌지수가 높은 날이다.

03 dispute [dispjúːt]
n 논쟁 / v 논쟁하다   a disagreement or argument between two people or groups
There was some **dispute** between Julie and her boss about whose fault it was.
줄리와 그녀의 상사 사이에 누구의 잘못인지에 관한 약간의 논쟁이 있었다.

04 embarrass [imbǽrəs]
v 곤란케 하다, 당황케 하다   to make somebody feel uncomfortable or shy
He seemed to be **embarrassed** when we asked where the money was.
그는 돈이 어디에 있는가라고 우리가 물었을 때 당황한 듯 보였다.

05 eternal [itə́ːrnəl]
a 영원한, 불후의   existing or continuing for ever
Keep in mind that youth is not **eternal**.
젊음은 영원하지 않다는 것을 항상 잊지 마라.

06 evaluation [ivæ̀ljuèiʃən]
n 평가, 값을 구함   forming an opinion about something
Evaluation records will be used to calculate employee bonuses.
직원들의 보너스 산출에 업무평가 기록이 이용될 것이다.

07 fantastic [fæntǽstik]
a 환상적인, 멋진   very good; excellent
He has **fantastic** passing and tackling ability.
그는 환상적인 패스 능력과 태클 능력을 지니고 있다.

08 fertile [fə́ːrtl]
a 비옥한, 풍부한   that plants grow well
They had no choice but to make the journey north to more **fertile** ground.
그들은 더 비옥한 땅이 있는 북쪽으로 장기간의 여행을 떠나지 않을 수 없었다.

09 frail [freil]
a 약한, 덧없는   weak or not healthy
My aunt is still very **frail** after her accident.
숙모님은 사고 후 계속해서 매우 약하시다.

---

key words
commit v 넘기다, 위임하다 / index n 지수 / tackle v 달려들다 / no choice but ~하지 않을 수 없다

🎧 Listen and repeat. Track 29

10 genuine [dʒénjuin]
a 진짜의, 순수한   real; true
He thought that he had bought a **genuine** Rolex watch but it was a cheap fake.
그는 진짜 Rolex 시계를 샀다고 생각했지만 그것은 싸구려 모조품이었다.

11 glide [glaid]
v 미끄러지다, 미끄러지듯 나가다   to move smoothly without noise or effort
I watched the skiers **gliding** down the slope.
나는 스키 타는 사람들이 비탈 아래로 활주하는 것을 보았다.

12 global [glóubəl]
a 지구의, 전 세계의   affecting the whole world
Truly the Internet is making the world a **global** society.
참으로 인터넷은 세계를 지구촌으로 만들고 있는 것이다.

13 horizon [həráizən]
n 수평선, 지평선   the line where the earth and sky appear to meet
We could see another ship coming over the **horizon**.
우리들은 수평선 너머로 다가오는 또 다른 배 한 척을 볼 수 있었다.

14 hunchback [hÁntʃbæk]
n 곱사등(이)   a person with a back that has a round lump on it
The **hunchback** is touched to the point of tears by this unexpected act.
예기치 못한 이 행동에 곱사등이는 감동이 되어 눈물을 흘린다.

15 insult [insÁlt]
v 모욕하다, 무례한 짓을 하다   to speak or act rudely to somebody
I felt very **insulted** when I didn't even get an answer to my letter.
나는 편지에 대한 답장을 받지 못해 무척 모욕감을 느꼈다.

16 insure [inʃúər]
v 보험 계약하다, 보증하다   to buy or to provide insurance
They **insured** the painting for $100,000 against theft.
그들은 절도에 대비하여 그림에 대한 10만 달러의 보험을 들었다.

17 journey [dʒə́ːrni]
n 여행, 여정   the act of travelling from one place to another
A long **journey** begins with the first step.
긴 여행도 첫 걸음부터 시작 된다.

18 justify [dʒÁstəfài]
v 정당화하다, 옳다고 하다   to give or be a good reason for something
Nothing **justifies** cheating on an exam.
그 무엇도 시험에서의 부정행위를 정당화 하지 못한다.

---

key words
fake **n** 모조품, 위조품 / slope **n** 비탈, 사면 / rudely **ad** 무례하게

Unit 10 **51**

Exercise

A. Complete the sentence.

1. He seemed to be _____ when we asked where the money was.
   그는 돈이 어디에 있는가라고 우리가 물었을 때 당황한 듯 보였다.

2. They had no choice but to make the journey north to more _____ ground.
   그들은 더 비옥한 땅이 있는 북쪽으로 장기간의 여행을 떠나지 않을 수 없었다.

3. Today's _____ index is very high.
   오늘은 불쾌지수가 높은 날이다.

4. I felt very _____ when I didn't even get an answer to my letter.
   나는 편지에 대한 답장을 받지 못해 무척 모욕감을 느꼈다.

5. I watched the skiers _____ down the slope.
   나는 스키 타는 사람들이 비탈 아래로 활주하는 것을 보았다.

6. _____ records will be used to calculate employee bonuses.
   직원들의 보너스 산출에 업무평가 기록이 이용될 것이다.

7. A long _____ begins with the first step.
   긴 여행도 첫 걸음부터 시작 된다.

8. We could see another ship coming over the _____.
   우리들은 수평선 너머로 다가오는 또 다른 배 한 척을 볼 수 있었다.

9. There was some _____ between Julie and her boss about whose fault it was.
   줄리와 그녀의 상사 사이에 누구의 잘못인지에 관한 약간의 논쟁이 있었다.

10. Keep in mind that youth is not _____.
    젊음은 영원하지 않다는 것을 항상 잊지 마라.

11. He has _____ passing and tackling ability.
    그는 환상적인 패스 능력과 태클 능력을 지니고 있다.

12. He thought that he had bought a _____ Rolex watch but it was a cheap fake.
    그는 진짜 Rolex 시계를 샀다고 생각했지만 그것은 싸구려 모조품이었다.

13. We have to commit him to make a _____ decision.
    명확한 결정을 위해 그를 병원으로 보내야 한다.

14. Truly the Internet is making the world a _____ society.
    참으로 인터넷이 세계를 지구촌으로 만들고 있는 것이다.

15. The _____ is touched to the point of tears by this unexpected act.
    예기치 못한 이 행동에 곱사등이는 감동이 되어 눈물을 흘린다.

16. They _____ the painting for $100,000 against theft.
    그들은 절도에 대비하여 그림에 대한 10만 달러의 보험을 들었다.

17. My aunt is still very _____ after her accident.
    숙모님은 사고 후 계속해서 매우 약하시다.

18. Nothing _____ cheating on an exam.
    그 무엇도 시험에서의 부정행위를 정당화 하지 못한다.

Hint

evaluation hunchback eternal frail   dispute insult   justify genuine fantastic
discomfort embarrass global   definite insure fertile glide   journey horizon

Exercise

B. Fill in the word and meaning.

	Word	Meaning
01	fertile	
02	genuine	
03	definite	
04	hunchback	
05	embarrass	
06	glide	
07	insult	
08	dispute	
09	global	
10	eternal	
11	journey	
12	evaluation	
13	insure	
14	horizon	
15	discomfort	
16	frail	
17	justify	
18	fantastic	

	Meaning	Word
01	명확한, 확실한	
02	불편, 불쾌	
03	논쟁, 논쟁하다	
04	곤란케 하다, 당황케 하다	
05	영원한, 불후의	
06	평가, 값을 구함	
07	환상적인, 멋진	
08	비옥한, 풍부한	
09	약한, 덧없는	
10	진짜의, 순수한	
11	미끄러지다, 미끄러지듯 나가다	
12	지구의, 전 세계의	
13	수평선, 지평선	
14	곱사등(이)	
15	모욕하다, 무례한 짓을 하다	
16	보험 계약하다, 보증하다	
17	여행, 여정	
18	정당화하다, 옳다고 하다	

C. Listen, write the word and meaning. Track 30

	Word	Meaning		Word	Meaning
01			10		
02			11		
03			12		
04			13		
05			14		
06			15		
07			16		
08			17		
09			18		

Review 5

A. Read and fill in the word and meaning.

word	definition	meaning
	connected with astronomy	
	not having enough money to pay your debts	
	to put somebody/something into a group of a similar type	
	really; in fact	
	to make a connection between people or things in your mind	
	firm belief; trust	
	in the same direction as the hands of a clock	
	to mix	
	a person who introduces or gives information on television	
	a person who has no courage	
	to look at somebody/something with pleasure	
	a very serious disease in which lumps grow in the body	
	trouble; to make somebody angry	
	the group of people who are elected to make the laws	
	to take something such as money or points	
	a plant like a small, thick tree with many low branches	
	something that is missing from somebody/something	
	to win a game, a fight, a vote, etc against somebody	

Hint

classify　bankrupt　bush　blend　deduct　announcer　cancer　annoy　astronomical
associate　clockwise　defeat　admire　coward　congress　actually　defect　confidence

B. Read and fill in the word and meaning.

word	definition	meaning
	that plants grow well	
	forming an opinion about something	
	the act of travelling from one place to another	
	very good; excellent	
	to move smoothly without noise or effort	
	to make somebody feel uncomfortable or shy	
	real; true	
	to buy or to provide insurance	
	weak or not healthy	
	a disagreement or argument between two people or groups	
	existing or continuing for ever	
	a person with a back that has a round lump on it	
	affecting the whole world	
	a slight feeling of pain	
	to speak or act rudely to somebody	
	the line where the earth and sky appear to meet	
	to give or be a good reason for something	
	having a clear, exact meaning	

Hint
evaluation hunchback eternal frail dispute insult justify genuine fantastic
discomfort embarrass global definite insure fertile glide journey horizon

Unit 11

🎧 Listen and repeat. Track 31

01 manufacture v 제조하다 / n 제조   to make something in large quantities using machines
[mǽnjəfæktʃəːr]   Our local factory **manufactures** furniture.
우리 지역 공장은 가구를 제조한다.

02 marble n 대리석 / a 대리석의, 단단한   a hard attractive stone that is used to make statues and parts of buildings
[máːrbəl]   Write injury in the sand and benefit in **marble**.
손해는 모래에 써놓고 은혜는 대리석에 써 놓아라.

03 minor a 주요하지 않은 / n 미성년자   not very big, serious or important
[máinər]   A couple of flights were delayed on account of a **minor** accident.
경미한 사고 때문에 비행기 두 세편의 출발이 지연되었다.

04 minstrel n 음유시인   a singer and musician who travelled around and entertained noble families
[mínstrəl]   You should never listen to **minstrels'** fancies.
너는 음유 시인들의 공상을 들어서는 안 된다.

05 mystery n 신비, 불가사의   a thing that you cannot understand or explain
[místəri]   Something went wrong somewhere, but just where and when is complete **mystery**.
무엇인가 어딘가에서 잘못 되었는데, 언제 어디서 그렇게 되었는지는 정말 불가사의다.

06 narrator n 해설자, 내레이터   the person who tells a story or explains what is happening
[næréitər]   The **narrator** made a big mistake at the first time of his work.
그 해설자는 일하는 중에 처음으로 큰 실수를 했다.

07 odd a 기묘한, 홀수의   strange; unusual
[ad]   The anthropologist says **odd** customs to persist in the region.
그 인류학자는 그 지역에 기묘한 풍습들이 지금도 계속되고 있다고 말한다.

08 offence n 위반, 화냄   a crime; an illegal action
[əféns]   I believe you not to do an **offence** against rules.
나는 당신이 규칙을 위반하지 않았다고 믿어요.

09 opponent n 상대, 반대자   a person who plays against somebody
[əpóunənt]   The communist gave in to his tough **opponent** at last.
그 공산주의자는 힘든 상대에게 결국 굴복했다.

key words
anthropologist n 인류학자 / persist v 지속하다 / communist n 공산주의자

🎧 Listen and repeat. Track 32

10 organize
[ɔ́ːrɡənàiz]
v 조직하다, 계획하다 to put or arrange things into a system
Teenagers can plan and **organize** their lives.
10대들은 자신의 삶을 계획하고 조직할 수 있다.

11 plow
[plau]
n 쟁기 / v 쟁기로 갈다 a large farm tool which is pulled by a vehicle or an animal
In the 1800's store owners sold everything from a needle to a **plow**.
1800년대에 가게 주인들은 바늘에서 쟁기까지 무엇이든지 팔았다.

12 political
[pəlítikəl]
a 정치상의, 정치적인 connected with politics and government
His decision seems to show a lack of **political** judgment.
그의 결정은 정치적 판단력이 부족함을 보여 주는 것 같다.

13 property
[prápərti]
n 재산, 소유물 a thing or things that belong to somebody
The stolen **property** must be restored to its owner.
도난 당한 재산은 마땅히 그 주인에게 돌려주어야 한다.

14 protect
[prətékt]
v 보호하다, 막다 to keep somebody/something safe
The seat belt can **protect** me, so I decide to fasten my seat belt from now on.
안전벨트가 나를 보호해 줄 수 있으므로, 이제부터는 꼭 매기로 했다.

15 punch
[pʌntʃ]
v 주먹으로 치다 to hit somebody/something hard with your closed hand
I **punched** the seat a couple times in anger.
화가 나서 의자를 주먹으로 몇 번 쳤어요.

16 remedy
[rémədi]
n 치료, 치료약 / v 고치다 something that makes you better when you are ill
This **remedy** will do you good overnight.
이 치료법을 쓰면 하룻밤 사이에 좋아질 것입니다.

17 remodel
[riːmádl]
v 개조하다, 개작하다 to make a building or a room into a different form
Building a new house is cheaper than **remodeling** an old house.
새집을 짓는 것이 오래된 집을 개조하는 것보다 저렴하다.

18 remote
[rimóut]
a 먼, 외딴 far away from where other people live
The power plant supplies the **remote** county with electricity.
발전소는 멀리 떨어진 마을에 전기를 공급하고 있다.

key words
restore v 되돌려주다 / fasten v 매다, 묶다 / overnight ad 하룻밤 사이에

Unit 11 57

Exercise

A. Complete the sentence.

1. Teenagers can plan and _____ their lives.
   10대들은 자신의 삶을 계획하고 조직할 수 있다.

2. Write injury in the sand and benefit in _____.
   손해는 모래에 써놓고 은혜는 대라석에 써 놓아라.

3. Building a new house is cheaper than _____ an old house.
   새집을 짓는 것이 오래된 집을 개조하는 것보다 저렴하다.

4. You should never listen to _____' fancies.
   너는 음유 시인들의 공상을 들어서는 안 된다.

5. The _____ made a big mistake at the first time of his work.
   그 해설자는 일하는 중에 처음으로 큰 실수를 했다.

6. The anthropologist says _____ customs to persist in the region.
   그 인류학자는 그 지역에 기묘한 풍습들이 지금도 계속되고 있다고 말한다.

7. Our local factory _____ furniture.
   우리 지역 공장은 가구를 제조한다.

8. The communist gave in to his tough _____ at last.
   그 공산주의자는 힘든 상대에게 결국 굴복했다.

9. In the 1800's store owners sold everything from a needle to a _____.
   1800년대에 가게 주인들은 바늘에서 쟁기까지 무엇이든지 팔았다.

10. I believe you not to do an _____ against rules.
    나는 당신이 규칙을 위반하지 않았다고 믿어요.

11. His decision seems to show a lack of _____ judgment.
    그의 결정은 정치적 판단력이 부족함을 보여 주는 것 같다.

12. The stolen _____ must be restored to its owner.
    도난 당한 재산은 마땅히 그 주인에게 돌려주어야 한다.

13. A couple of flights were delayed on account of a _____ accident.
    경미한 사고 때문에 비행기 두 세편의 출발이 지연되었다.

14. I _____ the seat a couple times in anger.
    화가 나서 의자를 주먹으로 몇 번 쳤어요.

15. This _____ will do you good overnight.
    이 치료법을 쓰면 하룻밤 사이에 좋아질 것입니다.

16. Something went wrong somewhere, but just where and when is complete _____.
    무엇인가 어딘가에서 잘못 되었는데, 언제 어디서 그렇게 되었는지는 정말 불가사의다.

17. The seat belt can _____ me, so I decide to fasten my seat belt from now on.
    안전벨트가 나를 보호해 줄 수 있으므로, 이제부터는 꼭 매기로 했다.

18. The power plant supplies the _____ county with electricity.
    발전소는 멀리 떨어진 마을에 전기를 공급하고 있다.

Hint

| odd | remote | offence | punch | protect | minstrel | property | manufacture | organize |
| plow | mystery | remodel | opponent | narrator | remedy | marble | political | minor |

Exercise

B. Fill in the word and meaning.

	Word	Meaning
01	odd	
02	plow	
03	manufacture	
04	opponent	
05	property	
06	marble	
07	punch	
08	offence	
09	remedy	
10	minor	
11	organize	
12	remodel	
13	protect	
14	mystery	
15	remote	
16	narrator	
17	political	
18	minstrel	

	Meaning	Word
01	제조하다, 제조	
02	대리석, 대리석의, 단단한	
03	주요하지 않은, 미성년자	
04	음유시인	
05	신비, 불가사의	
06	해설자, 내레이터	
07	기묘한, 홀수의	
08	위반, 화냄	
09	상대, 반대자	
10	조직하다, 계획하다	
11	쟁기, 쟁기로 갈다	
12	정치상의, 정치적인	
13	재산, 소유물	
14	보호하다, 막다	
15	주먹으로 치다	
16	치료, 치료약, 고치다	
17	개조하다, 개작하다	
18	먼, 외딴	

C. Listen, write the word and meaning. (Track 33)

	Word	Meaning		Word	Meaning
01			10		
02			11		
03			12		
04			13		
05			14		
06			15		
07			16		
08			17		
09			18		

Unit 12

🎧 Listen and repeat. (Track 34)

01 satisfy
[sǽtisfài]
v 만족시키다, 충족시키다   to make somebody pleased by doing or giving what he/she wants
I felt **satisfied** because I thought I had a good vacation.
방학을 알차게 보낸 것 같아 만족스럽다.

02 scan
[skæn]
v 훑어보다, 자세히 조사하다   to look at every part of something quickly
Bill **scanned** the list until he found his own name.
Bill은 그의 이름을 찾을 때끼지 명단을 훑어보았다.

03 scary
[skɛ́əri]
a 무서운, 두려운   frightening
The film was so **scary** that it had people running out of the theater.
그 영화는 너무 무서워 관객들이 도중에 밖으로 뛰쳐나왔다.

04 skill
[skil]
n 기술, 실력   an ability that you need in order to do a job, an activity, etc well
The course will help you to develop your reading and listening **skills**.
그 과정은 당신의 독해와 듣기 기술을 향상시키는데 도움이 될 것이다.

05 skyscraper
[skáiskrèipəːr]
n 고층건물   an extremely tall building
All of a sudden the thirty-story **skyscraper** went up in flames.
갑자기 30층짜리 고층 빌딩이 불길에 휩싸이며 폭발했다.

06 slippery
[slípəri]
a 미끄러운, 잘 빠져나가는   difficult to walk on or hold because it is smooth
I descended the mountain slowly because the path was **slippery**.
길이 미끄러워서 나는 산을 천천히 내려왔다.

07 stomachache
[stʌ́məkèik]
n 복통, 위통   a pain in your stomach
This medicine works well for your **stomachache**.
복통에는 이 약이 잘 듣는다.

08 straighten
[stréitn]
v 똑바르게 하다, 정리하다   to make something straight
Let's try to **straighten** out this confusion.
이 혼란을 바로잡도록 노력합시다.

09 strict
[strikt]
a 엄격한, 엄밀한   not allowing people to break rules or behave badly
The **strict** teacher broke me of a bad habit of being late.
엄격한 선생님께서 나의 지각하는 나쁜 버릇을 고쳐 주셨다.

key words
story n (건물의) 층 / descend v 내려가다 / confusion n 혼란

🎧 Listen and repeat. Track 35

10 symptom [símptəm]
n 징후, 증상 — a sign of illness in your body
It is said that the first **symptom** of the disease is a very high temperature.
그 질병의 첫 징후는 고열이라고 한다.

11 tame [teim]
a 길든, 유순한 — not wild or afraid of people
A girl was puzzled when **tame** pigeons took flight out of town.
그 소녀는 길들인 비둘기가 마을에서 날아가 버려 어쩔 줄 몰라했다.

12 tap [tæp]
v 가볍게 두드리다 — to touch or hit quickly and lightly
He **tapped** me on the shoulder.
그는 내 어깨를 가볍게 쳤다.

13 translate [trænsléit]
v 번역하다, 통역하다, 바꾸다 — to change something written or spoken from one language to another
Most poetry doesn't **translate** well.
대부분의 시들은 제대로 번역이 되지 않는다.

14 transport [trænspɔ́ːrt]
v 수송하다 / **n** 수송, 운송 — to carry or take people or goods
Trains **transport** the coal to the ports.
기차가 항구로 그 석탄을 수송한다.

15 unify [júːnəfài]
v 통합하다, 통일하다 — to join separate parts together to make one unit
The martial arts were **unified** into one national art called taegwondo.
그 무술은 태권도라 불리는 국기로 통합되었다.

16 vote [vout]
v 투표하다 / **n** 투표 — to show formally a choice by marking a piece of paper
He **voted** from Spain by absentee ballot.
그는 부재자 투표로 스페인에서 투표했다.

17 weed [wiːd]
n 잡초, 쓸모없는 것 — a wild plant that is not wanted in a garden
I can't tell the **weeds** from the grass.
나는 잡초와 풀을 구별 할 수가 없다.

18 western [wéstəːrn]
a 서쪽의, 서부 지방의 — in or of the west
The vehicles are produced at the factory, located in **western** China.
이 차량들은 중국 서부에 있는 공장에서 생산되는 것들이다.

key words
puzzle **v** 어쩔 줄 모르다 / absentee **n** 부재자 / ballot **n** 투표

Unit 12

Exercise

A. Complete the sentence.

1. Bill _____ the list until he found his own name.
   Bill은 그의 이름을 찾을 때까지 명단을 훑어보았다.
2. The martial arts were _____ into one national art called taegwondo.
   그 무술은 태권도라 불리는 국기로 통합되었다.
3. The _____ teacher broke me of a bad habit of being late.
   엄격한 선생님께서 나의 지각하는 나쁜 버릇을 고쳐 주셨다.
4. A girl was puzzled when _____ pigeons took flight out of town.
   그 소녀는 길들인 비둘기가 마을에서 날아가 버려 어쩔 줄 몰라했다.
5. I felt _____ because I thought I had a good vacation.
   방학을 알차게 보낸 것 같아 만족스럽다.
6. He _____ me on the shoulder.
   그는 내 어깨를 가볍게 쳤다.
7. This medicine works well for your _____.
   복통에는 이 약이 잘 듣는다.
8. Most poetry doesn't _____ well.
   대부분의 시들은 제대로 번역이 되지 않는다.
9. All of a sudden the thirty-story _____ went up in flames.
   갑자기 30층짜리 고층 빌딩이 불길에 휩싸이며 폭발했다.
10. Trains _____ the coal to the ports.
    기차가 항구로 그 석탄을 수송한다.
11. Let's try to _____ out this confusion.
    이 혼란을 바로잡도록 노력합시다.
12. He _____ from Spain by absentee ballot.
    그는 부재자 투표로 스페인에서 투표했다.
13. I descended the mountain slowly because the path was _____.
    길이 미끄러워서 나는 산을 천천히 내려왔다.
14. I can't tell the _____ from the grass.
    나는 잡초와 풀을 구별 할 수가 없다.
15. The film was so _____ that it had people running out of the theater.
    그 영화는 너무 무서워 관객들이 도중에 밖으로 뛰쳐나왔다.
16. It is said that the first _____ of the disease is a very high temperature.
    그 질병의 첫 징후는 고열이라고 한다.
17. The vehicles are produced at the factory, located in _____ China.
    이 차량들은 중국 서부에 있는 공장에서 생산되는 것들이다.
18. The course will help you to develop your reading and listening _____.
    그 과정은 당신의 독해와 듣기 기술을 향상시키는데 도움이 될 것이다.

Hint

| transport | western | symptom | tap | skill | vote | scary | scan | stomachache |
| straighten | slippery | translate | strict | tame | satisfy | weed | unify | skyscraper |

Unit 12

Exercise

B. Fill in the word and meaning.

	Word	Meaning
01	straighten	
02	translate	
03	satisfy	
04	symptom	
05	tame	
06	scan	
07	strict	
08	unify	
09	scary	
10	weed	
11	stomachache	
12	western	
13	skill	
14	transport	
15	skyscraper	
16	vote	
17	tap	
18	slippery	

	Meaning	Word
01	만족시키다, 충족시키다	
02	훑어보다, 자세히 조사하다	
03	무서운, 두려운	
04	기술, 실력	
05	고층건물	
06	미끄러운, 잘 빠져나가는	
07	복통, 위통	
08	똑바르게 하다, 정리하다	
09	엄격한, 엄밀한	
10	징후, 증상	
11	길든, 유순한	
12	가볍게 두드리다	
13	번역하다, 통역하다, 바꾸다	
14	수송하다, 수송, 운송	
15	통합하다, 통일하다	
16	투표하다, 투표	
17	잡초, 쓸모없는 것	
18	서쪽의, 서부 지방의	

C. Listen, write the word and meaning. Track 36

	Word	Meaning		Word	Meaning
01			10		
02			11		
03			12		
04			13		
05			14		
06			15		
07			16		
08			17		
09			18		

Unit 12

Review 6

A. Read and fill in the word and meaning.

word	definition	meaning
remedy	something that makes you better when you are ill	
protect	to keep somebody/something safe	
minor	not very big, serious or important	
odd	strange; unusual	
remodel	to make a building or a room into a different form	
offence	a crime; an illegal action	
punch	to hit somebody/something hard with your closed hand	
remote	far away from where other people live	
opponent	a person who plays against somebody	
political	connected with politics and government	
mystery	a thing that you cannot understand or explain	
organize	to put or arrange things into a system	
narrator	the person who tells a story or explains what is happening	
property	a thing or things that belong to somebody	
minstrel	a singer and musician who travelled around and entertained noble families	
manufacture	to make something in large quantities using machines	
plow	a large farm tool which is pulled by a vehicle or an animal	
marble	a hard attractive stone that is used to make statues and parts of buildings	

Hint

odd   remote   offence   punch   protect   minstrel   property   manufacture   organize
plow   mystery   remodel   opponent   narrator   remedy   marble   political   minor

B. Read and fill in the word and meaning.

word	definition	meaning
	not allowing people to break rules or behave badly	
	not wild or afraid of people	
	in or of the west	
	to make somebody pleased by doing or giving what he/she wants	
	to touch or hit quickly and lightly	
	to make something straight	
	a wild plant that is not wanted in a garden	
	a sign of illness in your body	
	to look at every part of something quickly	
	to change something written or spoken from one language to another	
	difficult to walk on or hold because it is smooth	
	to carry or take people or goods	
	a pain in your stomach	
	frightening	
	to join separate parts together to make one unit	
	to show formally a choice by marking a piece of paper	
	an ability that you need in order to do a job, an activity, etc well	
	an extremely tall building	

Hint

transport   western   symptom   tap   skill   vote   scary   scan   stomachache
straighten   slippery   translate   strict   tame   satisfy   weed   unify   skyscraper

Review 6

Unit 13

🎧 Listen and repeat. (Track 37)

01 admit v 인정하다, 허가하다   accept as true or sure; allow to enter
[ædmít]
When she asked for details he **admitted** that he was not doing too well.
그녀가 자세한 내역을 묻자 그는 별로 성과가 좋지 않다는 것을 인정했다.

02 adolescence n 사춘기, 청년기   the period of a person's life between a child and an adult
[ædəlésəns]
That very tune remained me of my **adolescence**.
바로 지 곡이 나의 사춘기 시절을 떠오르게 했다.

03 apologize v 사과하다, 변명하다   to say that you are sorry for something that you have done
[əpάlədʒàiz]
I **apologized** for stepping on her foot.
나는 그녀의 발을 밟은 것에 대해 사과했다.

04 appetite n 식욕, 욕구   a strong desire for something, especially food
[ǽpitàit]
A clear soup has very little nutritious value but stimulates the **appetite**.
맑은 스프는 영양가는 거의 없지만 식욕을 자극한다.

05 athlete n 운동선수   a person who takes part in sports competitions, etc
[ǽθli:t]
Many **athletes** try to retire before they get old.
많은 운동선수들은 그들이 늙기 전에 은퇴하려고 한다.

06 attractive a 매력적인, 흥미를 돋우는   beautiful or nice to look at
[ətrǽktiv]
The tamarind is an **attractive** tropical tree that may grow as tall as seventy-five feet.
타마린드는 75 피트의 높이까지 자라는 매력적인 열대나무이다.

07 bet v 걸다, 내기를 하다   to risk money on a race by trying to predict the result
[bet]
I **bet** you can't eat all that food that you've got on your plate.
나는 네가 접시에 있는 음식을 다 먹지 못한다는데 걸겠어.

08 bless v 은총을 내리다, 축복하다   to ask for God's help and protection
[bles]
She told us, "God **bless** you," and headed for the subway.
그녀는 우리에게 "신이 당신을 축복하시길." 이라고 말하고는 지하철역으로 향했다.

09 capacity n 수용력, 능력   the ability to do something
[kəpǽsəti]
I'll let you know as soon as I check the production **capacity**.
생산능력을 확인해 보고 곧 알려드리겠습니다.

---

key words
tune n 곡 / nutritious a 영양이 되는 / predict v 예언하다

🎧 Listen and repeat. Track 38

10 capture
[kǽptʃər]
v 붙잡다, 생포하다   to take a person or animal prisoner
The rebel was finally **captured** and confined to jail.
그 반역자는 결국 붙잡혀 감옥에 수감되었다.

11 clone
[kloun]
v 복제하다   to copy of a plant or animal that is produced from one of its cells
The firm claimed that it succeeded in **cloning** the first human.
그 회사는 최근 첫 인간 복제에 성공하였다고 주장하였다.

12 compare
[kəmpέər]
v 비교하다, 비유하다   to consider people or things to see how similar or different they are
Their product can't **compare** with ours when it comes to quality.
품질을 놓고 볼 때, 그들의 생산품은 우리들 것과 비교 할 수 없다.

13 conscious
[kánʃəs]
a 의식이 있는, 의식적인   noticing or realizing that something exists
She didn't seem **conscious** of the danger.
그녀는 위험을 의식하지 못한 것 같았다.

14 constantly
[kánstəntli]
ad 항상, 끊임없이, 자주   always; without stopping
The situation situation is **constantly** changing.
상황은 항상 변한다.

15 crisis
[kráisis]
n 위기, 어려운 상황   a time of great danger or difficulty
Many people think of **crisis** as being connected only with unhappy events.
많은 사람들이 위기를 오직 불행한 사건들과 관련된 것으로만 생각한다.

16 crowded
[kráudid]
a 붐비는, 혼잡한   full of people
The bank was **crowded**, so I had to stand in line.
은행에 사람이 붐벼서 나는 줄을 서야만 했다.

17 defend
[difénd]
v 막다, 지키다   to protect somebody/something from harm or danger
Taegwondo is a method of **defending** yourself with your hands and feet.
태권도란 손과 발로 자신을 지키는 방법을 말한다.

18 deposit
[dipázit]
v 예금하다, 두다, 쌓이다   to put money into an account at a bank
He **deposited** $20 a week into his savings account.
그는 매주 저축계좌에 20달러를 예금했다.

key words
confine v 가두다 / save v 저축하다

Unit 13 67

Exercise

A. Complete the sentence.

1. She told us, "God _____ you," and headed for the subway.
   그녀는 우리에게 "신이 당신을 축복하시길." 이라고 말하고는 지하철역으로 향했다.

2. When she asked for details he _____ that he was not doing too well.
   그녀가 자세한 내역을 묻자 그는 별로 성과가 좋지 않다는 것을 인정했다.

3. The situation is _____ changing.
   상황은 항상 변한다.

4. That very tune remained me of my _____.
   바로 저 곡이 나의 사춘기 시절을 떠오르게 했다.

5. The firm claimed that it succeeded in _____ the first human.
   그 회사는 최근 첫 인간 복제에 성공하였다고 주장하였다.

6. A clear soup has very little nutritious value but stimulates the _____.
   맑은 스프는 영양가는 거의 없지만 식욕을 자극한다.

7. He _____ $20 a week into his savings account.
   그는 매주 저축계좌에 20달러를 예금했다.

8. The tamarind is an _____ tropical tree that may grow as tall as seventy-five feet.
   타마린드는 75 피트의 높이까지 자라는 매력적인 열대나무이다.

9. I _____ you can't eat all that food that you've got on your plate.
   나는 네가 접시에 있는 음식을 다 먹지 못한다는데 걸겠어.

10. I'll let you know as soon as I check the production _____.
    생산능력을 확인해 보고 곧 알려드리겠습니다.

11. The rebel was finally _____ and confined to jail.
    그 반역자는 결국 붙잡혀 감옥에 수감되었다.

12. Many _____ try to retire before they get old.
    많은 운동선수들은 그들이 늙기 전에 은퇴 하려고 한다.

13. Their product can't _____ with ours when it comes to quality.
    품질을 놓고 볼 때, 그들의 생산품은 우리들 것과 비교 할 수 없다.

14. She didn't seem _____ of the danger.
    그녀는 위험을 의식하지 못한 것 같았다.

15. Taegwondo is a method of _____ yourself with your hands and feet.
    태권도란 손과 발로 자신을 지키는 방법을 말한다.

16. Many people think of _____ as being connected only with unhappy events.
    많은 사람들이 위기를 오직 불행한 사건들과 관련된 것으로만 생각한다.

17. I _____ for stepping on her foot.
    나는 그녀의 발을 밟은 것에 대해 사과했다.

18. The bank was _____, so I had to stand in line.
    은행에 사람이 붐벼서 나는 줄을 서야만 했다.

Hint

athlete   defend   bless   attractive   capacity   admit   compare   bet   adolescence
capture   crowded   deposit   conscious   apologize   crisis   appetite   clone   constantly

Exercise

B. Fill in the word and meaning.

	Word	Meaning
01	bless	
02	capture	
03	admit	
04	conscious	
05	attractive	
06	clone	
07	crowded	
08	adolescence	
09	crisis	
10	bet	
11	constantly	
12	appetite	
13	compare	
14	deposit	
15	apologize	
16	capacity	
17	defend	
18	athlete	

	Meaning	Word
01	인정하다, 허가하다	
02	사춘기, 청년기	
03	사과하다, 변명하다	
04	식욕, 욕구	
05	운동선수	
06	매력적인, 흥미를 돋우는	
07	걸다, 내기를 하다	
08	은총을 내리다, 축복하다	
09	수용력, 능력	
10	붙잡다, 생포하다	
11	복제하다	
12	비교하다, 비유하다	
13	의식이 있는, 의식적인	
14	항상, 끊임없이, 자주	
15	위기, 어려운 상황	
16	붐비는, 혼잡한	
17	막다, 지키다	
18	예금하다, 두다, 쌓이다	

C. Listen, write the word and meaning. (Track 39)

	Word	Meaning		Word	Meaning
01			10		
02			11		
03			12		
04			13		
05			14		
06			15		
07			16		
08			17		
09			18		

Unit 14

🎧 Listen and repeat. (Track 40)

01 disease [diziːz]
n 병, 질병   an illness of the body in humans or animals
These children suffer from a rare **disease**.
이 아이들은 희귀한 병을 앓고 있다.

02 dispose [dispóuz]
v 배치하다, 배열하다   to place something in a particular position
He **disposed** soldiers for the battle to prepare for the great war.
그는 대전을 준비하기 위해 병사를 전장에 배치했다.

03 emotion [imóuʃən]
n 감정, 감동, 감격   a strong feeling such as love, anger, etc
He showed no **emotion** as the police took him away.
경찰들이 그를 붙잡아 갔을 때 그는 어떤 감정도 보이지 않았다.

04 employ [emplói]
v 고용하다, 사용하다   to pay somebody to work for you
Three people are **employed** on the task of designing a new computer system.
새로운 컴퓨터 체계를 설계하는 일에 세 명의 사람들이 고용되었다.

05 eventual [ivéntʃuəl]
a 최종적인, 최후의   happening as a result at the end of a process
It is impossible to say what the **eventual** cost will be.
최종적인 가격이 어떻게 될지는 말하기 어렵다.

06 evidence [évidəns]
n 증거, 흔적   the facts, signs, etc that make you believe something
The witnesses to the accident will be asked to give **evidence** in court.
그 사건의 목격자들은 법정에서 증거를 제출하라는 요청을 받을 것이다.

07 finance [fináens]
n 재정, 자금 / v 융자하다   the management of large amounts of money
He is in charge of the company **finance**.
그는 회사의 재정을 관리하고 있다.

08 firm [fəːrm]
a 단단한, 굳은   strong and steady or not likely to change
Love is a relationship built on a **firm** foundation.
사랑이란 단단한 토대 위에 세워진 관계이다.

09 frighten [fráitn]
v 두려워하게 하다, 놀라게 하다   to make somebody/something afraid
The little girl was **frightened** that her mother wouldn't come back.
그 어린 소녀는 엄마가 돌아오지 않을까 봐 두려웠다.

---

key words
rare a 희한한 / court n 법정 / in charge of ~을 맡고 있는 / foundation n 토대, 기초

🎧 Listen and repeat. Track 41

10 frustrate
[frʌ́streit]
v 실패하게 하다, 헛되게 하다 — to prevent somebody from doing something
The rescue work has been **frustrated** by bad weather conditions.
그 구조 작업은 좋지 않은 날씨 상태로 실패하게 되었다.

11 glorious
[glɔ́:riəs]
a 영광스러운, 찬려한, 유쾌한 — having or deserving fame or success
The city has a **glorious** history.
그 도시는 영광스러운 역사를 가지고 있다.

12 governor
[gʌ́vərnər]
n 주지사, 총독 — a person who rules or controls a region or state
The **governor** granted liberty to many prisoners.
그 총독은 많은 죄수들에게 자유를 부여했다.

13 immoral
[imɔ́:rəl]
a 부도덕한, 품행이 나쁜 — considered wrong or not honest by most people
Did you play a part in this **immoral** act?
당신은 이 부도덕한 일에 동참을 했습니까?

14 independent
[indipéndənt]
a 독립한, 독립심이 강한 — not controlled by another person, country, etc
The Vatican is an **independent** enclave in Italy.
바티칸은 이탈리아 안에 있는 독립된 영토다.

15 intend
[inténd]
v 의도하다, 작정이다 — to plan or mean to do something
I **intend** to study abroad next year.
나는 내년에 유학 갈 작정이다.

16 invade
[invéid]
v 침입하다, 침해하다 — to enter a country with an army to take control of it
The border of China was **invaded** frequently by foreigners.
중국의 변방은 외적의 침입을 자주 받았다.

17 lack
[læk]
n 부족, 결핍 — the state of not having something
The reason for the change is **lack** of money, pure and simple.
그렇게 변경한 이유는 순전히 돈이 부족해서다.

18 landscape
[lǽndskèip]
n 풍경, 경치 — everything you can see when you look across a large area of land
Elephants may seem out of place in this **landscape**.
코끼리들은 이 풍경에 어울리지 않는 존재인 것 같아요.

key words
fame n 명성 / grant v 주다, 인정하다 / enclave n 타국의 영토 / border n 국경

Exercise

A. Complete the sentence.

1. He _____ soldiers for the battle to prepare for the great war.
   그는 대전을 준비하기 위해 병사를 전장에 배치했다.
2. The _____ granted liberty to many prisoners.
   그 총독은 많은 죄수들에게 자유를 부여했다.
3. He showed no _____ as the police took him away.
   경찰들이 그를 붙잡아 갔을 때 그는 어떤 감정도 보이지 않았다.
4. Love is a relationship built on a _____ foundation.
   사랑이란 단단한 토대 위에 세워진 관계이다.
5. The witnesses to the accident will be asked to give _____ in court.
   그 사건의 목격자들은 법정에서 증거를 제출하라는 요청을 받을 것이다.
6. Elephants may seem out of place in this _____.
   코끼리들은 이 풍경에 어울리지 않는 존재인 것 같아요.
7. These children suffer from a rare _____.
   이 아이들은 희귀한 병을 앓고 있다.
8. The Vatican is an _____ enclave in Italy.
   바티칸은 이탈리아 안에 있는 독립된 영토다.
9. It is impossible to say what the _____ cost will be.
   최종적인 가격이 어떻게 될지는 말하기 어렵다.
10. He is in charge of the company _____.
    그는 회사의 재정을 관리하고 있다.
11. Three people are _____ on the task of designing a new computer system.
    새로운 컴퓨터 체계를 설계하는 일에 세 명의 사람들이 고용되었다.
12. The rescue work has been _____ by bad weather conditions.
    그 구조 작업은 좋지 않은 날씨 상태로 실패하게 되었다.
13. The border of China was _____ frequently by foreigners.
    중국의 변방은 외적의 침입을 자주 받았다.
14. The city has a _____ history.
    그 도시는 영광스러운 역사를 가지고 있다.
15. The little girl was _____ that her mother wouldn't come back.
    그 어린 소녀는 엄마가 돌아오지 않을까 봐 두려웠다.
16. Did you play a part in this _____ act?
    당신은 이 부도덕한 일에 동참을 했습니까?
17. I _____ to study abroad next year.
    나는 내년에 유학 갈 작정이다.
18. The reason for the change is _____ of money, pure and simple.
    그렇게 변경한 이유는 순전히 돈이 부족해서다.

Hint

employ   frustrate   intend   eventual   lack   dispose   governor   emotion   landscape
immoral   disease   frighten   glorious   firm   finance   evidence   invade   independent

Exercise

B. Fill in the word and meaning.

	Word	Meaning
01	eventual	
02	disease	
03	governor	
04	finance	
05	intend	
06	dispose	
07	invade	
08	firm	
09	glorious	
10	landscape	
11	emotion	
12	independent	
13	frighten	
14	lack	
15	employ	
16	immoral	
17	frustrate	
18	evidence	

	Meaning	Word
01	병, 질병	
02	배치하다, 배열하다	
03	감정, 감동, 감격	
04	고용하다, 사용하다	
05	최종적인, 최후의	
06	증거, 흔적	
07	재정, 자금, 융자하다	
08	단단한, 굳은	
09	두려워하게 하다, 놀라게 하다	
10	실패하게 하다, 헛되게 하다	
11	영광스러운, 장려한, 유쾌한	
12	주지사, 총독	
13	부도덕한, 품행이 나쁜	
14	독립한, 독립심이 강한	
15	의도하다, 작정이다	
16	침입하다, 침해하다	
17	부족, 결핍	
18	풍경, 경치	

C. Listen, write the word and meaning. Track 42

	Word	Meaning		Word	Meaning
01			10		
02			11		
03			12		
04			13		
05			14		
06			15		
07			16		
08			17		
09			18		

Review 7

A. Read and fill in the word and meaning.

word	definition	meaning
	to take a person or animal prisoner	
	full of people	
	accept as true or sure; allow to enter	
	to copy of a plant or animal that is produced from one of its cells	
	the ability to do something	
	to put money into an account at a bank	
	the period of a person's life between a child and an adult	
	to ask for God's help and protection	
	to protect somebody/something from harm or danger	
	to consider people or things to see how similar or different they are	
	to say that you are sorry for something that you have done	
	to risk money on a race by trying to predict the result	
	beautiful or nice to look at	
	a time of great danger or difficulty	
	a strong desire for something, especially food	
	noticing or realizing that something exists	
	always; without stopping	
	a person who takes part in sports competitions, etc	

Hint

athlete   defend   bless   attractive   capacity   admit   compare   bet   adolescence
capture   crowded   deposit   conscious   apologize   crisis   appetite   clone   constantly

B. Read and fill in the word and meaning.

word	definition	meaning
	having or deserving fame or success	
	considered wrong or not honest by most people	
	the state of not having something	
	to pay somebody to work for you	
	a person who rules or controls a region or state	
	to place something in a particular position	
	to prevent somebody from doing something	
	not controlled by another person, country, etc	
	a strong feeling such as love, anger, etc	
	to make somebody/something afraid	
	to plan or mean to do something	
	strong and steady or not likely to change	
	an illness of the body in humans or animals	
	everything you can see when you look across a large area of land	
	to enter a country with an army to take control of it	
	happening as a result at the end of a process	
	the management of large amounts of money	
	the facts, signs, etc that make you believe something	

Hint

employ frustrate intend eventual lack dispose governor emotion landscape
immoral disease frighten glorious firm finance evidence invade independent

Unit 15

🎧 Listen and repeat. Track 43

01 marine [məríːn]
a 바다의, 해양의   connected with the sea
A fund was set up to preserve endangered **marine** life.
멸종위기의 해양 생물을 보호하기 위해 기금이 마련되었다.

02 match [mætʃ]
v 어울리다 / **n** 시합   to look good with something else
Your shirt and jacket don't **match**.
당신의 셔츠와 재킷은 서로 어울리지 않는다.

03 miserable [mízərəbəl]
a 불쌍한, 비참한, 궁핍한   very unhappy
She led a **miserable** life and died alone last night.
그녀는 비참한 인생을 살다가 어젯밤 홀로 죽었다.

04 misleading [mislíːdiŋ]
a 오해하게 하는, 현혹시키는   making somebody have the wrong idea or opinion
It is against the law to put out advertisement **misleading** the public.
대중을 현혹시키는 광고를 내는 것은 위법이다.

05 necessary [nésəsèri]
a 필요한, 필연적인   that is needed for a purpose
It's not **necessary** for you all to come.
여러분 모두가 올 필요는 없습니다.

06 neglect [niglékt]
v 무시하다, 방치하다   to give too little or no attention
The old house had stood **neglected** for years.
그 오래된 집은 여러 해 동안 방치된 채 있었다.

07 opportunity [àpərtjúːnəti]
n 기회, 호기   a chance to do something
I'll take the **opportunity** to ask him a few personal questions.
그에게 몇 가지 개인적인 질문을 할 기회를 잡을 것이다.

08 oriental [ɔ̀ːriéntl]
a 동양의, 동양적인   coming from or belonging to the East
He specializes in **Oriental** history.
그는 동양역사를 전공한다.

09 original [ərídʒənəl]
a 독창적인 / **n** 원본   different from others of its type
There are no **original** ideas in his report.
그의 보고서에는 독창적인 아이디어가 전혀 없어요.

key words
preserve **v** 보호하다, 지키다 / endangered **a** 멸종위기에 처한 / specialize **v** 전공하다

🎧 Listen and repeat. Track 44

10 polite [pəláit]
a 공손한, 예의 바른   having good manners and showing respect for others
My offer met with a **polite** refusal.
나의 제안은 공손히 거절 당했다.

11 politician [pàlətíʃən]
n 정치가, 출세주의자   a person whose job is in politics
Politicians of all parties supported the war.
모든 정당의 정치가들이 그 전쟁을 지지했다.

12 pollute [pəlúːt]
v 오염시키다, 불결하게 하다   to make air, rivers, etc dirty and dangerous
It is not possible to burn garbage, because that **pollutes** the air.
쓰레기 소각은 공기를 오염시키기 때문에 태우는 것이 불가능하다.

13 purpose [pə́ːrpəs]
n 목적, 의도, 요점   the aim or intention of something
The **purpose** of a tour is to see more of the world.
여행의 목적은 더 많은 세상을 보는 것이다.

14 quarrel [kwɔ́ːrəl]
v 싸우다 / n 싸움   to have an angry argument or disagreement
They were good neighbors, never **quarreling** over unimportant matters.
그들은 좋은 이웃들이어서 사소한 문제로 싸우지 않았다.

15 quote [kwout]
v 인용하다, 예시하다 / n 인용구   to repeat exactly something that somebody else has said before
He's always **quoting** verses from the Bible.
그는 항상 성경에 나오는 구절들을 인용한다.

16 resemble [rizémbəl]
v 닮다, 공통점이 있다   to be or look like somebody/something else
She **resembles** her mother in appearance but not in character.
그녀의 외모는 어머니를 닮았지만 성격은 닮지 않았다.

17 reservation [rèzərvéiʃən]
n 예약, 보류   a seat, table, room, etc that you have booked
I've been busy, so I had to cancel the **reservation**.
나는 바빠서 예약을 취소해야만 했다.

18 result [rizʌ́lt]
n 결과, 성과   something that happens because of something else
The child's bad behavior is the **result** of emotional problems.
그 아이의 나쁜 행동은 정서적인 문제가 낳은 결과이다.

---

key words
refusal n 거절, 거부 / verse n 구절, 시구 / emotional a 감정적인

Unit 15

Exercise

A. Complete the sentence.

1. He specializes in _____ history.
   그는 동양역사를 전공한다.

2. Your shirt and jacket don't _____.
   당신의 셔츠와 재킷은 서로 어울리지 않는다.

3. _____ of all parties supported the war.
   모든 정당의 정치가들이 그 전쟁을 지지했다.

4. I've been busy, so I had to cancel the _____.
   나는 바빠서 예약을 취소해야만 했다.

5. They were good neighbors, never _____ over unimportant matters.
   그들은 좋은 이웃들이어서 사소한 문제로 싸우지 않았다.

6. She led a _____ life and died alone last night.
   그녀는 비참한 인생을 살다가 어젯밤 홀로 죽었다.

7. The old house had stood _____ for years.
   그 오래된 집은 여러 해 동안 방치된 채 있었다.

8. I'll take the _____ to ask him a few personal questions.
   그에게 몇 가지 개인적인 질문을 할 기회를 잡을 것이다.

9. My offer met with a _____ refusal.
   나의 제안은 공손히 거절 당했다.

10. A fund was set up to preserve endangered _____ life.
    멸종위기의 해양 생물을 보호하기 위해 기금이 마련되었다.

11. It is not possible to burn garbage, because that _____ the air.
    쓰레기 소각은 공기를 오염시키기 때문에 태우는 것이 불가능하다.

12. The _____ of a tour is to see more of the world.
    여행의 목적은 더 많은 세상을 보는 것이다.

13. He's always _____ verses from the Bible.
    그는 항상 성경에 나오는 구절들을 인용한다.

14. She _____ her mother in appearance but not in character.
    그녀의 외모는 어머니를 닮았지만 성격은 닮지 않았다.

15. There are no _____ ideas in his report.
    그의 보고서에는 독창적인 아이디어가 전혀 없어요.

16. It's not _____ for you all to come.
    여러분 모두가 올 필요는 없습니다.

17. It is against the law to put out advertisement _____ the public.
    대중을 현혹시키는 광고를 내는 것은 위법이다.

18. The child's bad behavior is the _____ of emotional problems.
    그 아이의 나쁜 행동은 정서적인 문제가 낳은 결과이다.

Hint

misleading   quote   original   politician   result   miserable   oriental   polite   opportunity
reservation   match   quarrel   resemble   pollute   necessary   marine   neglect   purpose

Exercise

B. Fill in the word and meaning.

	Word	Meaning
01	necessary	
02	original	
03	polite	
04	marine	
05	purpose	
06	neglect	
07	pollute	
08	match	
09	quote	
10	opportunity	
11	reservation	
12	quarrel	
13	miserable	
14	result	
15	politician	
16	misleading	
17	resemble	
18	oriental	

	Meaning	Word
01	바다의, 해양의	
02	어울리다, 시합	
03	불쌍한, 비참한, 궁핍한	
04	오해하게 하는, 현혹시키는	
05	필요한, 필연적인	
06	무시하다, 방치하다	
07	기회, 호기	
08	동양의, 동양적인	
09	독창적인, 원본	
10	공손한, 예의 바른	
11	정치가, 출세주의자	
12	오염시키다, 불결하게 하다	
13	목적, 의도, 요점	
14	싸우다, 싸움	
15	인용하다, 예시하다, 인용구	
16	닮다, 공통점이 있다	
17	예약, 보류	
18	결과, 성과	

C. Listen, write the word and meaning. Track 45

	Word	Meaning		Word	Meaning
01			10		
02			11		
03			12		
04			13		
05			14		
06			15		
07			16		
08			17		
09			18		

Unit 16

🎧 Listen and repeat. Track 46

01 scatter
[skǽtəːr]
v 흩뿌리다, 흩어지다   to drop or throw things in different directions
The wind **scattered** the papers all over the room.
그 바람이 종이들을 방 안에 온통 흩뿌렸다.

02 semester
[siméstər]
n 한 학기, 반 년간   one of the two main periods into which the year is divided in colleges and universities
There's only one **semester** left before graduation.
졸업이 한 학기 밖에 남지 않았다.

03 separate
[sépərit]
a 분리된, 분산된   apart; not together
You should always keep your cash and credit cards **separate**.
항상 현금과 신용 카드는 분리해서 보관해야 한다.

04 snatch
[snætʃ]
v 와락 붙잡다, 잡아채다   to take something with a quick rough movement
A boy **snatched** her handbag and ran off.
한 소년이 그녀의 핸드백을 잡아채고는 도망갔다.

05 soak
[souk]
v 젖다, 적시다   to become or make something completely wet
The dog came out of the river and shook itself, **soaking** everyone.
개가 강에서 나와 몸을 털어서 모두를 젖게 했다.

06 solid
[sálid]
a 고체의, 단결된   hard and firm
Solid waste has been dumped in the oceans, buried underground, and burned.
고체 쓰레기는 바다에 던져지고, 땅에 묻히고 또는 태워진다.

07 stumble
[stʌ́mbəl]
v 주춤하다, 비틀거리다   to put your foot down awkwardly while you are walking or running
A good horse never **strumbles**, a good wife never grumbles.
좋은 말은 비틀거리지 않고 좋은 부인은 불평하지 않는다.

08 submit
[səbmít]
v 복종하다, 제출하다   to accept the power or control
I would rather die than **submit**.
나는 복종하느니 차라리 죽겠다.

09 suddenly
[sʌ́dnli]
ad 갑자기, 별안간   quickly and unexpectedly
Suddenly, she looked ten years older.
갑자기 그녀가 십 년쯤 나이 들게 보였다.

key words
apart a 떨어져, 분리된 / shake v 흔들다 / dump v (쓰레기를) 내버리다
awkwardly ad 서투르게 / grumble v 투덜거리다

🎧 Listen and repeat. (Track 47)

10 tender [téndər]
a 부드러운, 다정한, 예민한   soft and easy to cut or bite
Boil the beans until they are **tender**.
콩이 부드러워질 때까지 끓어라.

11 term [tə:rm]
n 기간, 임기   a period of time for which something lasts
The **term** shall be extended for two years upon agreement between both sides.
쌍방의 동의 하에 그 기한을 2년 더 연장할 것이다.

12 terrific [tərífik]
a 아주 좋은, 멋진   extremely nice or good
He came up with a **terrific** solution to the complex problem.
그는 복잡한 그 문제를 푸는 멋진 해결책을 생각해냈다.

13 unconscious [ʌnkánʃəs]
a ~을 모르는, 무의식의   in a state that is like sleep, because of injury or illness
He is brought home to his grandfather, **unconscious** and almost dead.
할아버지가 있는 집으로 옮겨졌을 때 그는 의식을 잃고 거의 죽은 상태이다.

14 urban [á:rbən]
a 도시의, 도회풍의   connected with a town or city
The explosion broke out at one **urban** gas supply station.
폭발은 도시의 가스 공급기지에서 일어났다.

15 utility [ju:tíləti]
n 실용성, 공공사업   the quality of being useful
The **utility** of the rescue equipment has to be tested in a real emergency.
구조 장비의 실용성은 진짜 위급상황 속에서 시험 받아야 한다.

16 wetland [wétlænd]
n 습지대   an area of very wet, muddy land
Wetlands are important to many kinds of animals and plants that live there.
습지는 그 곳에 사는 많은 종류의 동물과 식물에게 중요하다.

17 while [hwail]
n 잠시 / **conj** ~하는 동안   during the time that
He always phones **while** we're having lunch.
그는 점심 식사를 하는 동안 늘 전화를 한다.

18 witty [wíti]
a 재치 있는, 기지 있는   clever and amusing
She entertained them with a **witty** monologue.
그녀는 재치 있는 독백으로 그들을 즐겁게 했다.

---

key words
extend **v** 연장하다 / complex **a** 복잡한 / explosion **v** 폭발 / monologue **n** 독백극

Exercise

A. Complete the sentence.

1. _____, she looked ten years older.
   갑자기 그녀가 십 년쯤 나이 들게 보였다.
2. She entertained them with a _____ monologue.
   그녀는 재치 있는 독백으로 그들을 즐겁게 했다.
3. The wind _____ the papers all over the room.
   그 바람이 종이들을 방 안에 온통 흩뿌렸다.
4. _____ are important to many kinds of animals and plants that live there.
   습지는 그 곳에 사는 많은 종류의 동물과 식물에게 중요하다.
5. The _____ of the rescue equipment has to be tested in a real emergency.
   구조 장비의 실용성은 진짜 위급상황 속에서 시험 받아야 한다.
6. There's only one _____ left before graduation.
   졸업이 한 학기 밖에 남지 않았다.
7. The explosion broke out at one _____ gas supply station.
   폭발은 도시의 가스 공급기지에서 일어났다.
8. A boy _____ her handbag and ran off.
   한 소년이 그녀의 핸드백을 잡아채고는 도망갔다.
9. _____ waste has been dumped in the oceans, buried underground, and burned.
   고체 쓰레기는 바다에 던져지고, 땅에 묻히고 또는 태워진다.
10. A good horse never _____, a good wife never grumbles.
    좋은 말은 비틀거리지 않고 좋은 부인은 불평하지 않는다.
11. Boil the beans until they are _____.
    콩이 부드러워질 때까지 끓여라.
12. You should always keep your cash and credit cards _____.
    항상 현금과 신용 카드는 분리해서 보관해야 한다.
13. The _____ shall be extended for two years upon agreement between both sides.
    쌍방의 동의 하에 그 기한을 2년 더 연장할 것이다.
14. The dog came out of the river and shook itself, _____ everyone.
    개가 강에서 나와 몸을 털어서 모두를 젖게 했다.
15. He came up with a _____ solution to the complex problem.
    그는 복잡한 그 문제를 푸는 멋진 해결책을 생각해냈다.
16. He is brought home to his grandfather, _____ and almost dead.
    할아버지가 있는 집으로 옮겨졌을 때 그는 의식을 잃고 거의 죽은 상태이다.
17. He always phones _____ we're having lunch.
    그는 점심 식사를 하는 동안 늘 전화를 한다.
18. I would rather die than _____.
    나는 복종하느니 차라리 죽겠다.

Hint

| snatch | urban | suddenly | term | scatter | submit | soak | stumble | unconscious |
| tender | while | wetland | solid | terrific | utility | witty | separate | semester |

Exercise

B. Fill in the word and meaning.

	Word	Meaning
01	snatch	
02	suddenly	
03	tender	
04	scatter	
05	utility	
06	solid	
07	term	
08	semester	
09	urban	
10	stumble	
11	while	
12	terrific	
13	separate	
14	witty	
15	submit	
16	wetland	
17	soak	
18	unconscious	

	Meaning	Word
01	흩뿌리다, 흩어지다	
02	한 학기, 반 년간	
03	분리된, 분산된	
04	와락 붙잡다, 잡아채다	
05	젖다, 적시다	
06	고체의, 단결된	
07	주춤하다, 비틀거리다	
08	복종하다, 제출하다	
09	갑자기, 별안간	
10	부드러운, 다정한, 예민한	
11	기간, 임기	
12	아주 좋은, 멋진	
13	~을 모르는, 무의식의	
14	도시의, 도회풍의	
15	실용성, 공공사업	
16	습지대	
17	잠시, ~하는 동안	
18	재치 있는, 기지 있는	

🎧 **C. Listen, write the word and meaning.** (Track 48)

	Word	Meaning		Word	Meaning
01			10		
02			11		
03			12		
04			13		
05			14		
06			15		
07			16		
08			17		
09			18		

Review 8

A. Read and fill in the word and meaning.

word	definition	meaning
	having good manners and showing respect for others	
	something that happens because of something else	
	different from others of its type	
	to make air, rivers, etc dirty and dangerous	
	connected with the sea	
	a person whose job is in politics	
	coming from or belonging to the East	
	the aim or intention of something	
	to have an angry argument or disagreement	
	to look good with something else	
	to give too little or no attention	
	to be or look like somebody/something else	
	a chance to do something	
	very unhappy	
	to repeat exactly something that somebody else has said before	
	that is needed for a purpose	
	a seat, table, room, etc that you have booked	
	making somebody have the wrong idea or opinion	

Hint

misleading   quote   original   politician   result   miserable   oriental   polite   opportunity
reservation   match   quarrel   resemble   pollute   necessary   marine   neglect   purpose

B. Read and fill in the word and meaning.

word	definition	meaning
	to become or make something completely wet	
	clever and amusing	
	to take something with a quick rough movement	
	an area of very wet, muddy land	
	hard and firm	
	during the time that	
	apart; not together	
	in a state that is like sleep, because of injury or illness	
	to put your foot down awkwardly while you are walking or running	
	to drop or throw things in different directions	
	extremely nice or good	
	one of the two main periods into which the year is divided in colleges and universities	
	the quality of being useful	
	quickly and unexpectedly	
	soft and easy to cut or bite	
	connected with a town or city	
	to accept the power or control	
	a period of time for which something lasts	

Hint

snatch   urban   suddenly   term   scatter   submit   soak   stumble   unconscious
tender   while   wetland   solid   terrific   utility   witty   separate   semester

Review 8

Unit 17

🎧 Listen and repeat. (Track 49)

01 abolish [əbáliʃ]
v 폐지하다, 없애다   to end a law or system officially
Should the death penalty be **abolished**?
사형 제도는 폐지되어야 합니까?

02 advertise [ǽdvərtàiz]
v 광고하다, 알리다   to put information in order to persuade people
We need to cut our **advertising** costs.
우리는 광고비를 줄일 필요가 있다.

03 appreciate [əprí:ʃièit]
v 인정하다, 감상하다, 인식하다   to understand the value of somebody/something
Two things are only **appreciated** when we no longer have them, health and youth.
두 가지, 즉 건강과 젊음은 그것을 잃고 난 뒤에야 그 가치가 인정된다.

04 approach [əpróutʃ]
v ~에 접근하다, 가까이 가다   to come near to somebody/something
When you **approach** the village you will see a garage on your left.
마을에 가까이 가면 왼편으로 차고가 보일 것이다.

05 approve [əprú:v]
v 찬성하다, 승인하다   to agree formally to something
My father did not **approve** my sister's marriage.
나의 아버지께서는 언니의 결혼에 찬성하지 않으셨다.

06 available [əvéiləbəl]
a 이용할 수 있는, 입수 가능한   that you can get, buy, use, etc
This information is easily **available** to everyone at the local library.
이 정보는 모든 사람들이 지역 도서관에서 쉽게 이용할 수 있다.

07 blossom [blásəm]
n 꽃 / v 꽃이 피다   a flower
The apple trees began to put forth their **blossoms**.
사과나무에서 꽃이 피어나기 시작했다.

08 bold [bould]
a 대담한, 뻔뻔스러운   confident and not afraid
Not many people are **bold** enough to say exactly what they think.
많은 사람들이 자신들의 생각을 정확히 말 할 수 있을 만큼 충분히 대담하지 못하다.

09 bond [band]
n 유대, 결속, 끈   something that joins more people together such as a feeling of friendship
Group rubbing to otters not only refreshes their coats, but strengthens social **bonds**.
수달에게 서로 비비대는 것은 외피를 고르는 것뿐 아니라 사회적인 유대를 강화 시킨다.

key words
penalty n 처벌, 형벌 / put forth (싹 등이) 나오다 / rub v 비비다 / strengthen v 강하게 하다

🎧 Listen and repeat. Track 50

10 boundary [báundəri]
n 경계, 경계선 — a line that marks the limits and divides it from other things
He stood on the **boundary** of the country and looked back his hometown.
그는 조국의 경계선에 서서 고향 땅을 돌아보았다.

11 competitive [kəmpétətiv]
a 경쟁력 있는, 경쟁에 의한 — involving people or organizations competing against each other
The travel industry is a highly **competitive** business.
여행 산업은 매우 경쟁력 있는 사업이다.

12 complex [kəmpléks]
a 복잡한 / n 복합시설, 열등감 — made up of several connected parts
This protein's structure is particularly **complex**.
이 단백질 구조는 특히 복잡하다.

13 continent [kántənənt]
n 대륙, 육지 — one of the seven main areas of land on the Earth
These, the highest mountains of the world, were created by the collision of **continents**.
세계에서 가장 높은 이 산들은 대륙 간의 충돌로 생성 되었다.

14 contract [kántrækt]
n 계약, 계약서 — a written legal agreement
Would you like to renew our **contract**?
우리의 계약을 갱신하고 싶습니까?

15 cultural [kʌ́ltʃərəl]
a 문화의, 교양의 — connected with the customs, ideas, etc of a society or country
The country's **cultural** diversity is a result of taking in immigrants from all over the world.
그 나라 문화의 다양성은 세계 도처에서 온 이민자들이 건너온 까닭이다.

16 curious [kjúəriəs]
a 호기심 있는, 기묘한 — wanting to know or learn something
They were very **curious** about the people who lived upstairs.
그들은 위층에 사는 사람들에 대한 호기심이 많았다.

17 despite [dispáit]
prep ~에도 불구하고 — without being affected by the thing mentioned
Despite all my efforts to persuade him, he wouldn't agree.
그를 설득하려는 나의 모든 노력에도 불구하고 그는 동의하려 하지 않았다.

18 diameter [daiǽmitər]
n 지름, 직경 — a straight line that goes from one side to the other
The tree measures almost 2 feet in **diameter**.
그 나무는 지름이 거의 2피트이다.

key words
protein n 단백질 / collision n 충돌, 격돌 / renew v 갱신하다, 새롭게 하다 / diversity n 다양성

Exercise

A. Complete the sentence.

1. My father did not _____ my sister's marriage.
   나의 아버지께서는 언니의 결혼에 찬성하지 않으셨다.
2. _____ all my efforts to persuade him, he wouldn't agree.
   그를 설득하려는 나의 모든 노력에도 불구하고 그는 동의하려 하지 않았다.
3. The apple trees began to put forth their _____.
   사과나무에서 꽃이 피어나기 시작했다.
4. They were very _____ about the people who lived upstairs.
   그들은 위층에 사는 사람들에 대한 호기심이 많았다.
5. We need to cut our _____ costs.
   우리는 광고비를 줄일 필요가 있다.
6. Would you like to renew our _____?
   우리의 계약을 갱신하고 싶습니까?
7. Two things are only _____ when we no longer have them, health and youth.
   두 가지, 즉 건강과 젊음은 그것을 잃고 난 뒤에야 그 가치가 인정된다.
8. These, the highest mountains of the world, were created by the collision of _____.
   세계에서 가장 높은 이 산들은 대륙 간의 충돌로 생성 되었다.
9. Not many people are _____ enough to say exactly what they think.
   많은 사람들이 자신들의 생각을 정확히 말 할 수 있을 만큼 충분히 대담하지 못하다.
10. This information is easily _____ to everyone at the local library.
    이 정보는 모든 사람들이 지역 도서관에서 쉽게 이용할 수 있다.
11. Group rubbing to otters not only refreshes their coats, but strengthens social _____.
    수달에게 서로 비벼대는 것은 외피를 고르는 것뿐 아니라 사회적인 유대를 강화 시킨다.
12. Should the death penalty be _____?
    사형 제도는 폐지되어야 합니까?
13. He stood on the _____ of the country and looked back his hometown.
    그는 조국의 경계선에 서서 고향 땅을 돌아보았다.
14. The country's _____ diversity is a result of taking in immigrants from all over the world.
    그 나라 문화의 다양성은 세계 도처에서 온 이민자들이 건너온 까닭이다.
15. When you _____ the village you will see a garage on your left.
    마을에 가까이 가면 왼편으로 차고가 보일 것이다.
16. This protein's structure is particularly _____.
    이 단백질 구조는 특히 복잡하다.
17. The tree measures almost 2 feet in _____.
    그 나무는 지름이 거의 2피트이다.
18. The travel industry is a highly _____ business.
    여행 산업은 매우 경쟁력 있는 사업이다.

Hint

available bold curious appreciate approve diameter blossom complex boundary
approach bond despite competitive contract cultural advertise abolish continent

Exercise

B. Fill in the word and meaning.

	Word	Meaning
01	approve	
02	boundary	
03	abolish	
04	continent	
05	blossom	
06	cultural	
07	advertise	
08	despite	
09	bold	
10	appreciate	
11	curious	
12	competitive	
13	approach	
14	diameter	
15	bond	
16	contract	
17	available	
18	complex	

	Meaning	Word
01	폐지하다, 없애다	
02	광고하다, 알리다	
03	인정하다, 감상하다, 인식하다	
04	~에 접근하다, 가까이 가다	
05	찬성하다, 승인하다	
06	이용할 수 있는, 입수 가능한	
07	꽃, 꽃이 피다	
08	대담한, 뻔뻔스러운	
09	유대, 결속, 끈	
10	경계, 경계선	
11	경쟁력 있는, 경쟁에 의한	
12	복잡한, 복합시설, 열등감	
13	대륙, 육지	
14	계약, 계약서	
15	문화의, 교양의	
16	호기심 있는, 기묘한	
17	~에도 불구하고	
18	지름, 직경	

🎧 **C. Listen, write the word and meaning.** Track 51

	Word	Meaning		Word	Meaning
01			10		
02			11		
03			12		
04			13		
05			14		
06			15		
07			16		
08			17		
09			18		

Unit 18

🎧 Listen and repeat. Track 52

01 dictation [diktéiʃən]
n 구술, 받아쓰기   spoken words that somebody else must write
The teacher gave us two English **dictations** today.
선생님이 오늘 우리들에게 영어 받아쓰기 시험을 두 번 실시하셨다.

02 diminish [dəmíniʃ]
v 줄어들다, 감소하다   to become or to make something smaller
The bad news did nothing to **diminish** her enthusiasm for the plan.
나쁜 소식은 그 계획에 대한 그녀의 열정을 줄어들게 하지 못했다.

03 employee [implóii:]
n 피고용자, 종업원   a person who works for somebody
The employer dismissed three **employees**.
그 고용주는 세 명의 종업원을 해고했다.

04 equality [i(ː)kwáləti]
n 평등, 같음   the situation in which everyone has the same rights
For them, **equality** means that everyone should have equal chance to run the race.
그들에게 있어, 평등이란 모든 이가 경주 할 수 있는 동등한 기회를 가져야 한다는 것을 뜻한다.

05 existence [igzístəns]
n 존재, 생존   the state of existing
This is the oldest Hebrew manuscript in **existence**.
이것은 현존하는 히브리어 필사본 중에서 가장 오래된 것이다.

06 explorer [iksplɔ́ːrər]
n 탐험가, 조사자   a person who travels round a place
Through the centuries **explorers** have shown enthusiasm in writing about their travels.
수세기에 걸쳐서 탐험가들은 그들의 여행에 관하여 글 쓰는 일에 열의를 보여 왔다.

07 flexible [fléksəbəl]
a 구부리기 쉬운, 유연성이 있는   able to bend or move easily without breaking
The most **flexible** group in a society tends to be its youth.
한 사회에서 가장 유연성이 있는 그룹은 그 사회의 젊은 층인 경향이 있다.

08 flush [flʌʃ]
v 얼굴이 붉어지다, 분출하다   to go red
She **flushed** and could not hide her embarrassment.
그녀는 얼굴이 붉어져서 당혹스러움을 감추지 못했다.

09 gallon [gǽlən]
n 갤런, 대량   a measure of liquid; 4.5 liters
The oil tanker spilled millions of **gallons** of oil into the sea.
유조선이 바다에다 수백만 갤런의 기름을 유출시켰습니다.

---

key words
enthusiasm n 열정, 열의 / dismiss v 해고하다 / manuscript n 손으로 쓴 것, 사본
embarrassment n 당황, 난처 / spill v 엎지르다, 흩뜨리다

🎧 Listen and repeat. Track 53

10 generally [dʒénərəli]
ad 대개, 일반적으로   by most people, usually
The building of the pyramids was **generally** started during the dry season of May and June.
피라미드의 건설은 일반적으로 5월과 6월의 건기에 시작되었다.

11 grab [græb]
v 붙잡다, 가로채다   to take something with a sudden movement
Someone had arrived before us and **grabbed** all the seats.
누군가 우리보다 먼저 와서 모든 좌석을 가로챘다.

12 graduate [grǽdʒuèit]
v 졸업하다, 학위를 수여하다   to complete a course at a school, college, etc
I am **graduating** from school with mixed emotions.
학교를 졸업하자니 여러 가지 감정이 뒤섞인다.

13 illustrate [íləstrèit]
v 설명하다, 삽화를 넣다   to explain or make something clear by using pictures, etc
This graph **illustrates** the fact clearly.
이 도표가 그 사실을 분명하게 설명해주고 있다.

14 immediate [imíːdiit]
a 즉석의, 가장 가까운   happening or done without delay
Without **immediate** treatment, the illness will be fatal.
즉석으로 치료를 하지 않으면 그 병은 치명적인 것이 될 것이다.

15 invasion [invéiʒən]
n 침입, 침략   the action of entering another country with your army
Much of this temple was destroyed by fire during the Japanese **invasion**.
이 사찰의 상당 부분이 일제 침략 시에 화재로 손실되었다.

16 invest [invést]
v 투자하다, 돈을 쓰다   to put money into a bank, business to make a profit
I'll have to start thinking of ways to **invest** it if I want to see it grow.
나는 그것을 불리기 위해 투자할 방법을 생각해야 할 것이다.

17 leak [liːk]
v 새다 / n 새는 곳   to allow liquid or gas to get through a hole or crack
Apparently a gas pipe **leaked**, and a spark caused their home to explode.
분명히 가스관이 샜고 그 바람에 불꽃이 일어 그들의 집이 폭발하게 되었다.

18 loaf [louf]
n 덩어리   bread baked in one piece
Half a **loaf** is better than no bread.
반 덩어리 빵이라도 없는 것보다 낫다.

key words
fatal **a** 치명적인 / crack **n** 갈라진 틈 / apparently **ad** 분명히

Unit 18

Exercise

A. Complete the sentence.

1. The most _____ group in a society tends to be its youth.
   한 사회에서 가장 유연성이 있는 그룹은 그 사회의 젊은 층인 경향이 있다.
2. The bad news did nothing to _____ her enthusiasm for the plan.
   나쁜 소식은 그 계획에 대한 그녀의 열정을 줄어들게 하지 못했다.
3. Much of this temple was destroyed by fire during the Japanese _____.
   이 사찰의 상당 부분이 일제 침략 시에 화재로 손실되었다.
4. Someone had arrived before us and _____ all the seats.
   누군가 우리보다 먼저 와서 모든 좌석을 가로챘다.
5. The employer dismissed three _____.
   그 고용주는 세 명의 종업원을 해고했다.
6. The oil tanker spilled millions of _____ of oil into the sea.
   유조선이 바다에다 수백만 갤런의 기름을 유출시켰습니다.
7. For them, _____ means that everyone should have equal chance to run the race.
   그들에게 있어, 평등이란 모든 이가 경주 할 수 있는 동등한 기회를 가져야 한다는 것을 뜻한다.
8. This is the oldest Hebrew manuscript in _____.
   이것은 현존하는 히브리어 필사본 중에서 가장 오래된 것이다.
9. Without _____ treatment, the illness will be fatal.
   즉석으로 치료를 하지 않으면 그 병은 치명적인 것이 될 것이다.
10. Through the centuries _____ have shown enthusiasm in writing about their travels.
    수세기에 걸쳐서 탐험가들은 그들의 여행에 관하여 글 쓰는 일에 열의를 보여 왔다.
11. The teacher gave us two English _____ today.
    선생님이 오늘 우리들에게 영어 받아쓰기 시험을 두 번 실시하셨다.
12. The building of the pyramids was _____ started during the dry season of May and June.
    피라미드의 건설은 일반적으로 5월과 6월의 건기에 시작되었다.
13. I am _____ from school with mixed emotions.
    학교를 졸업하자니 여러 가지 감정이 뒤섞인다.
14. I'll have to start thinking of ways to _____ it if I want to see it grow.
    나는 그것을 불리기 위해 투자할 방법을 생각해야 할 것이다.
15. Apparently a gas pipe _____, and a spark caused their home to explode.
    분명히 가스관이 샜고 그 바람에 불꽃이 일어 그들의 집이 폭발하게 되었다.
16. She _____ and could not hide her embarrassment.
    그녀는 얼굴이 붉어져서 당혹스러움을 감추지 못했다.
17. This graph _____ the fact clearly.
    이 도표가 그 사실을 분명하게 설명해주고 있다.
18. Half a _____ is better than no bread.
    반 덩어리 빵이라도 없는 것보다 낫다.

Hint

explorer   dictation   employee   leak   invasion   flush   generally   illustrate   graduate
diminish   equality   immediate   grab   flexible   loaf   existence   gallon   invest

Exercise

B. Fill in the word and meaning.

	Word	Meaning
01	flexible	
02	dictation	
03	generally	
04	immediate	
05	diminish	
06	graduate	
07	flush	
08	leak	
09	equality	
10	loaf	
11	invasion	
12	explorer	
13	grab	
14	employee	
15	invest	
16	gallon	
17	illustrate	
18	existence	

	Meaning	Word
01	구술, 받아쓰기	
02	줄어들다, 감소하다	
03	피고용자, 종업원	
04	평등, 같음	
05	존재, 생존	
06	탐험가, 조사자	
07	구부리기 쉬운, 유연성이 있는	
08	얼굴이 붉어지다, 분출하다	
09	갤런, 대량	
10	대개, 일반적으로	
11	붙잡다, 가로채다	
12	졸업하다, 학위를 수여하다	
13	설명하다, 삽화를 넣다	
14	즉석의, 가장 가까운	
15	침입, 침략	
16	투자하다, 돈을 쓰다	
17	새다, 새는 곳	
18	덩어리	

C. Listen, write the word and meaning. (Track 54)

	Word	Meaning		Word	Meaning
01			10		
02			11		
03			12		
04			13		
05			14		
06			15		
07			16		
08			17		
09			18		

Review 9

A. Read and fill in the word and meaning.

word	definition	meaning
	a written legal agreement	
	connected with the customs, ideas, etc of a society or country	
	without being affected by the thing mentioned	
	that you can get, buy, use, etc	
	one of the seven main areas of land on the Earth	
	wanting to know or learn something	
	to end a law or system officially	
	made up of several connected parts	
	a flower	
	a straight line that goes from one side to the other	
	to put information in order to persuade people	
	something that joins more people together such as a feeling of friendship	
	to come near to somebody/something	
	confident and not afraid	
	involving people or organizations competing against each other	
	to understand the value of somebody/something	
	a line that marks the limits and divides it from other things	
	to agree formally to something	

Hint

available   bold   curious   appreciate   approve   diameter   blossom   complex   boundary
approach   bond   despite   competitive   contract   cultural   advertise   abolish   continent

B. Read and fill in the word and meaning.

word	definition	meaning
	a person who works for somebody	
	to take something with a sudden movement	
	to put money into a bank, business to make a profit	
	to become or to make something smaller	
	to complete a course at a school, college, etc	
	the situation in which everyone has the same rights	
	to allow liquid or gas to get through a hole or crack	
	to explain or make something clear by using pictures, etc	
	to go red	
	the state of existing	
	happening or done without delay	
	a person who travels round a place	
	spoken words that somebody else must write	
	bread baked in one piece	
	a measure of liquid; 4.5 liters	
	the action of entering another country with your army	
	by most people, usually	
	able to bend or move easily without breaking	

Hint

explorer   dictation   employee   leak   invasion   flush   generally   illustrate   graduate
diminish   equality   immediate   grab   flexible   loaf   existence   gallon   invest

Unit 19

🎧 Listen and repeat. Track 55

01 march [mɑːrtʃ]
n 행진 / v 행진하다   an organized walk by a large group of people
They have been unable to get many students to take part in the protest **march**.
그들은 그 시위행진에 많은 학생들이 참가하도록 할 수가 없었다.

02 mass [mæs]
n 대중, 집단   ordinary people, a large number of people
This magazine is published not for a **mass** circulation but for a small audience of highly literate people.
이 잡지는 대중 구독이 아니라 학식이 높은 소수의 독자를 위해 출판된다.

03 meadow [médou]
n 풀밭, 목초지   a field of grass
The stream winds through the **meadow**.
시내는 목초지를 굽어져 흐르고 있다.

04 melt [melt]
v 녹다, 녹이다   to change something from a solid to a liquid
When we got up in the morning the snow had **melted**.
우리가 아침에 일어났을 때는 눈이 녹아 있었다.

05 misunderstand [mìsʌndəːrstǽnd]
v 오해하다, 진가를 못 알아보다   to understand somebody/something wrongly
I **misunderstand** the instructions and answered too many questions.
나는 지시사항을 오해하여 너무 많은 질문에 답을 했다.

06 mixture [míkstʃər]
n 혼합물, 혼합   a substance that is made by mixing other substances together
Mixtures of tantalum and other metals make strong, useful alloys.
탄탈과 다른 금속들의 혼합물은 강하고 유용한 합금들이 된다.

07 parliament [páːrləmənt]
n 의회, 국회   the group of people who are elected to make and change the laws of a country
In the Middle East, Israeli politicians never have to wear a tie in **parliament**.
중동지역에서, 이스라엘 정치가들은 국회에서 결코 타이를 메지 않는다.

08 particular [pərtíkjələr]
a 특별한, 특정한   special; greater than usual
This article is of **particular** interest to me.
이 기사는 나의 특별한 관심을 끌고 있다.

09 passive [pǽsiv]
a 소극적인, 수동의   not active; showing no reaction, feeling
Some people prefer to play a **passive** role in meetings.
어떤 사람들은 회의에서 소극적인 자세를 취하는 것을 좋아한다.

key words
protest n 항의 / circulation n 유통, 유포 / literate a 박식한, 지식이 있는 / alloy n 합금

🎧 Listen and repeat. Track 56

10 portrait
[pɔ́ːrtrit]
n 초상화   a picture, painting or photograph of a person
I am pleased with this vivid **portrait** in particular.
나는 특히 이 선명한 색채의 초상화가 마음에 든다.

11 pose
[pouz]
v 자세를 취하다, 제기하다   to sit or stand in a particular position for a painting, photograph, etc
After the wedding we all **posed** for photographs.
결혼식이 끝난 후 우리 모두는 사진을 찍기 위해 자세를 취했다.

12 possess
[pəzés]
v 소유하다, 지니다   to have or own something
The nearest approach to happiness for man in the life is to **possess** liberty, health and a peaceful mind.
삶에서 인간이 행복해지는 가장 가까운 길은 자유와 건강과 평화로운 마음을 소유하는 것이다.

13 rap
[ræp]
n 톡톡 두드림 / **v** 두드리다   a quick, sharp hit
There was a series of **raps** on the window.
창문을 톡톡 두드리는 소리가 여러 번 났다.

14 rarely
[rɛ́ərli]
ad 좀처럼 ~하지 않다   seldom, hardly
She may be lovable, but she **rarely** keeps her promise.
그녀는 사랑스럽지만 좀처럼 약속을 지키지 않는다.

15 realize
[ríːəlàiz]
v 깨닫다, 실현하다   became fully aware of something
I could not **realize** my situation it had happened so suddenly.
너무 갑작스러운 일이라서 내 상황을 깨달을 수 없었다.

16 revolution
[rèvəlúːʃən]
n 혁명, 회전   a complete change in methods, opinions, etc
Shopping malls have produced a **revolution** in the United States shopping in just 45 years.
쇼핑몰은 단 45년 만에 미국에서의 쇼핑생활에 혁명을 일으켰다.

17 riddle
[rídl]
n 수수께끼, 난문   a difficult question that has a clever or amusing answer
He got the answer to the **riddle** as quick as a flash.
그는 수수께끼의 답을 재빨리 알아냈다.

18 roast
[roust]
v 굽다, 볶다   to cook in an oven or over a fire
We **roasted** two wild boars in our garden.
우리는 정원에서 멧돼지 두 마리를 구웠다.

key words
vivid **a** 선명한 / seldom **ad** 좀처럼 ~않는 / boar **n** 멧돼지

Exercise

A. Complete the sentence.

1. In the Middle East, Israeli politicians never have to wear a tie in _____.
   중동지역에서, 이스라엘 정치가들은 국회에서 결코 타이를 메지 않는다.
2. He got the answer to the _____ as quick as a flash.
   그는 수수께끼의 답을 재빨리 알아냈다.
3. _____ of tantalum and other metals make strong, useful alloys.
   탄탈과 다른 금속들의 혼합물은 강하고 유용한 합금들이 된다.
4. She may be lovable, but she _____ keeps her promise.
   그녀는 사랑스럽지만 좀처럼 약속을 지키지 않는다.
5. They have been unable to get many students to take part in the protest _____.
   그들은 그 시위행진에 많은 학생들이 참가하도록 할 수가 없었다.
6. We _____ two wild boars in our garden.
   우리는 정원에서 멧돼지 두 마리를 구웠다.
7. I _____ the instructions and answered too many questions.
   나는 지시사항을 오해하여 너무 많은 질문에 답을 했다.
8. There was a series of _____ on the window.
   창문을 톡톡 두드리는 소리가 여러 번 났다.
9. This article is of _____ interest to me.
   이 기사는 나의 특별한 관심을 끌고 있다.
10. The stream winds through the _____.
    시내는 목초지를 굽어져 흐르고 있다.
11. Some people prefer to play a _____ role in meetings.
    어떤 사람들은 회의에서 소극적인 자세를 취하는 것을 좋아한다.
12. When we got up in the morning the snow had _____.
    우리가 아침에 일어났을 때는 눈이 녹아 있었다.
13. After the wedding we all _____ for photographs.
    결혼식이 끝난 후 우리 모두는 사직을 찍기 위해 자세를 취했다.
14. The nearest approach to happiness for man in the life is to _____ liberty, health and a peaceful mind.
    삶에서 인간이 행복해지는 가장 가까운 길은 자유와 건강과 평화로운 마음을 소유하는 것이다.
15. I am pleased with this vivid _____ in particular.
    나는 특히 이 선명한 색채의 초상화가 마음에 든다.
16. I could not _____ my situation it had happened so suddenly.
    너무 갑작스러운 일이라서 내 상황을 깨달을 수 없었다.
17. This magazine is published not for a _____ circulation but for a small audience of highly literate people.
    이 잡지는 대중 구독이 아니라 학식이 높은 소수의 독자를 위해 출판된다.
18. Shopping malls have produced a _____ in the United States shopping in just 45 years.
    쇼핑몰은 단 45년 만에 미국에서의 쇼핑생활에 혁명을 일으켰다.

Hint

| passive | misunderstand | particular | mass | roast | realize | mixture | portrait | rap |
| riddle | parliament | | meadow | rarely | march | possess | revolution | melt | pose |

Exercise

B. Fill in the word and meaning.

	Word	Meaning
01	particular	
02	march	
03	rap	
04	passive	
05	mass	
06	realize	
07	parliament	
08	riddle	
09	misunderstand	
10	roast	
11	possess	
12	meadow	
13	revolution	
14	portrait	
15	rarely	
16	melt	
17	pose	
18	mixture	

	Meaning	Word
01	행진, 행진하다	
02	대중, 집단	
03	풀밭, 목초지	
04	녹다, 녹이다	
05	오해하다, 진가를 못 알아보다	
06	혼합물, 혼합	
07	의회, 국회	
08	특별한, 특정한	
09	소극적인, 수동의	
10	초상화	
11	자세를 취하다, 제기하다	
12	소유하다, 지니다	
13	톡톡 두드림, 두드리다	
14	좀처럼 ~하지 않다	
15	깨닫다, 실현하다	
16	혁명, 회전	
17	수수께끼, 난문	
18	굽다, 볶다	

C. Listen, write the word and meaning. (Track 57)

	Word	Meaning		Word	Meaning
01			10		
02			11		
03			12		
04			13		
05			14		
06			15		
07			16		
08			17		
09			18		

Unit 20

🎧 Listen and repeat. Track 58

01 share [ʃɛəːr]
v 공유하다, 분배하다   to have, use, do something together with other people
I want a friend who can **share** my interest in books.
책에 대한 나의 관심사를 공유할 수 있는 친구를 원한다.

02 shave [ʃeiv]
v 깎다, 면도하다   to remove hair with an extremely sharp piece of metal
He decided to make a new beginning and **shaved** his head.
그는 새롭게 시작하기로 결심하고 머리를 빡빡 깎았다.

03 shed [ʃed]
v 떨어뜨리다, 뿌리다   to lose something because it falls off
Autumn is coming and the trees are beginning to **shed** their leaves.
가을이 다가오자 나무들은 잎들을 떨어뜨리기 시작하고 있다.

04 somewhat [sʌ́mhwàt]
ad 얼마간, 다소   rather; to some degree
Strictly speaking, his view differs **somewhat** from mine.
엄밀하게 말해서 그의 견해는 나의 것과 다소 다르다.

05 somewhere [sʌ́mhwɛ̀əːr]
ad 어딘가에   at, in, or to a place that you do not know or mention
He should be **somewhere** in the office, but he's not at his desk at the moment.
그는 회사 내 어딘가에 있을 겁니다만, 지금 자리에는 없습니다.

06 sorrow [sárou]
n 슬픔, 비애   a feeling of great sadness
The busy bee has no time for **sorrow**.
분주한 벌에게는 슬퍼할 시간이 없다.

07 suffer [sʌ́fər]
v 경험하다, 앓다, 괴로워하다   to experience something unpleasant like pain, sadness, etc
All children **suffer** a great deal when their parents divorce.
자식들은 부모들이 이혼을 하면 굉장히 괴로워한다.

08 sufficient [səfíənt]
a 충분한, 흡족한   as much as is necessary; enough
My allowance doesn't seem to be **sufficient**.
내 용돈이 충분치가 않은 것 같다.

09 suicide [súːəsàid]
n 자살   the act of killing yourself
Even more awful, he has been thinking of **suicide**.
더욱 끔찍스러운 것은 그가 자살을 생각하고 있다는 것이다.

key words
divorce v 이혼하다 / allowance n 용돈 / awful a 끔찍한, 무서운

🎧 Listen and repeat. Track 59

10 thrill
[θril]
n 스릴, 전율   a sudden strong feeling of pleasure or excitement
I was so **thrilled** that she was alive I could not speak.
나는 그녀가 살아 있다는 사실에 전율하여 말을 할 수가 없었다.

11 tighten
[táitn]
v 죄다, 단단하게 하다   to become or to make something tight
The arm of my glasses keeps wobbling, so I want to **tighten** the screw.
안경다리가 흔들흔들해서 나사를 조이고 싶다.

12 tremendous
[triméndəs]
a 거대한, 무서운   very large or great
The merchant accumulated **tremendous** fortune during the postwar era.
그 무역상은 전후 시대에 거대한 재산을 축적했다.

13 utilize
[júːtəlàiz]
v 활용하다, 이용하다   to make use of something
Many educators believe that TV can be **utilized** for education.
많은 교육자들은 텔레비전이 교육을 위해 활용 될 수 있다고 믿는다.

14 various
[vɛ́əriəs]
a 다양한, 다방면의   several different
Each school clubs prepared for **various** events.
각 동아리들이 다양한 행사를 준비했다.

15 vary
[vɛ́əri]
v 변화하다, 다양하게 하다   to be different or to change from each other
The charges **vary** according to the type of call you make.
요금은 거시는 전화 종류에 따라 다양합니다.

16 worsen
[wə́ːrsən]
v 악화되다, 악화시키다   to make something worse
Relations between the two countries have **worsened**.
두 나라의 관계는 악화되어 왔다.

17 wreck
[rek]
n 난파 / v 난파시키다   a ship that has sunk or been badly damaged
All attempts to salvage the **wreck** ship failed.
난파선을 구조하려는 모든 시도는 허사였다.

18 youth
[juːθ]
n 젊음, 청년   the state of being young, a young person
Keep in mind that **youth** is not eternal.
젊음은 영원하지 않다는 것을 항상 잊지 마라.

key words
wobbling a 흔들거리는 / accumulate v 모으다 / sink v 침몰하다 / salvage v 구조하다

Exercise

A. Complete the sentence.

1. Relations between the two countries have _____.
   두 나라의 관계는 악화되어 왔다.
2. Autumn is coming and the trees are beginning to _____ their leaves.
   가을이 다가오자 나무들은 잎들을 떨어뜨리기 시작하고 있다.
3. The merchant accumulated _____ fortune during the postwar era.
   그 무역상은 전후 시대에 거대한 재산을 축적했다.
4. Each school clubs prepared for _____ events.
   각 동아리들이 다양한 행사를 준비했다.
5. Keep in mind that _____ is not eternal.
   젊음은 영원하지 않다는 것을 항상 잊지 마라.
6. Strictly speaking, his view differs _____ from mine.
   엄밀하게 말해서 그의 견해는 나의 것과 다소 다르다.
7. I was so _____ that she was alive I could not speak.
   나는 그녀가 살아 있다는 사실에 전율하여 말을 할 수가 없었다.
8. All children _____ a great deal when their parents divorce.
   자식들은 부모들이 이혼을 하면 굉장히 괴로워한다.
9. My allowance doesn't seem to be _____.
   내 용돈이 충분치가 않은 것 같다.
10. Even more awful, he has been thinking of _____.
    더욱 끔찍스러운 것은 그가 자살을 생각하고 있다는 것이다.
11. The arm of my glasses keeps wobbling, so I want to _____ the screw.
    안경다리가 흔들흔들해서 나사를 조이고 싶다.
12. All attempts to salvage the _____ ship failed.
    난파선을 구조하려는 모든 시도는 허사였다.
13. I want a friend who can _____ my interest in books.
    책에 대한 나의 관심사를 공유할 수 있는 친구를 원한다.
14. Many educators believe that TV can be _____ for education.
    많은 교육자들은 텔레비전이 교육을 위해 활용 될 수 있다고 믿는다.
15. He should be _____ in the office, but he's not at his desk at the moment.
    그는 회사 내 어딘가에 있을 겁니다만, 지금 자리에는 없습니다.
16. He decided to make a new beginning and _____ his head.
    그는 새롭게 시작하기로 결심하고 머리를 빡빡 깎았다.
17. The charges _____ according to the type of call you make.
    요금은 거시는 전화 종류에 따라 다양합니다.
18. The busy bee has no time for _____.
    분주한 벌에게는 슬퍼할 시간이 없다.

Hint

| youth | suffer | suicide | worsen | tighten | shed | sufficient | somewhat | tremendous |
| share | wreck | shave | thrill | | sorrow | utilize | various | vary | somewhere |

Exercise

B. Fill in the word and meaning.

	Word	Meaning
01	somewhat	
02	thrill	
03	suicide	
04	share	
05	tighten	
06	suffer	
07	various	
08	shave	
09	wreck	
10	sufficient	
11	worsen	
12	shed	
13	tremendous	
14	youth	
15	somewhere	
16	vary	
17	utilize	
18	sorrow	

	Meaning	Word
01	공유하다, 분배하다	
02	깎다, 면도하다	
03	떨어뜨리다, 뿌리다	
04	얼마간, 다소	
05	어딘가에	
06	슬픔, 비애	
07	경험하다, 앓다, 괴로워하다	
08	충분한, 흡족한	
09	자살	
10	스릴, 전율	
11	죄다, 단단하게 하다	
12	거대한, 무서운	
13	활용하다, 이용하다	
14	다양한, 다방면의	
15	변화하다, 다양하게 하다	
16	악화되다, 악화시키다	
17	난파, 난파시키다	
18	젊음, 청년	

🎧 C. Listen, write the word and meaning. (Track 60)

	Word	Meaning		Word	Meaning
01			10		
02			11		
03			12		
04			13		
05			14		
06			15		
07			16		
08			17		
09			18		

Review 10

A. Read and fill in the word and meaning.

word	definition	meaning
	seldom, hardly	
	to cook in an oven or over a fire	
	became fully aware of something	
	ordinary people, a large number of people	
	special; greater than usual	
	a quick, sharp hit	
	an organized walk by a large group of people	
	to have or own something	
	the group of people who are elected to make and change the laws of a country	
	a field of grass	
	not active; showing no reaction, feeling	
	a complete change in methods, opinions, etc	
	to change something from a solid to a liquid	
	to sit or stand in a particular position for a painting, photograph, etc	
	a substance that is made by mixing other substances together	
	a picture, painting or photograph of a person	
	to understand somebody/something wrongly	
	a difficult question that has a clever or amusing answer	

Hint

passive   misunderstand   particular   mass   roast   realize   mixture   portrait   rap
riddle   parliament   meadow rarely march   possess   revolution melt   pose

B. Read and fill in the word and meaning.

word	definition	meaning
	to make use of something	
	the act of killing yourself	
	a sudden strong feeling of pleasure or excitement	
	several different	
	to have, use, do something together with other people	
	to become or to make something tight	
	to lose something because it falls off	
	to make something worse	
	to be different or to change from each other	
	to remove hair with an extremely sharp piece of metal	
	very large or great	
	at, in, or to a place that you do not know or mention	
	a ship that has sunk or been badly damaged	
	to experience something unpleasant like pain, sadness, etc	
	rather; to some degree	
	as much as is necessary; enough	
	the state of being young, a young person	
	a feeling of great sadness	

Hint

youth   suffer   suicide   worsen   tighten   shed   sufficient   somewhat   tremendous
share   wreck   shave   thrill   sorrow   utilize   various   vary   somewhere

Unit 21

🎧 Listen and repeat. Track 61

01 abandon [əbǽndən]
v 버리다, 포기하다   to stop doing something without finishing it
We had to **abandon** a picnic because of bad weather.
우리는 궂은 날씨 때문에 소풍을 포기해야 했다.

02 abruptly [əbrʌ́ptli]
ad 갑자기, 퉁명스럽게   suddenly
It ended **abruptly** after 37 episodes.
그것은 37회를 끝으로 갑자기 막을 내리고 말았다.

03 accurate [ǽkjərit]
a 정확한, 신중한   exact and correct
His answer was **accurate** in every detail.
그의 대답은 모든 점에서 정확했다.

04 afflict [əflíkt]
v 괴롭히다   to cause somebody/something to suffer pain
He had been **afflicted** with a serious illness since childhood.
그는 어린 시절부터 극심한 질병으로 괴롭힘 당했었다.

05 apparent [əpǽrənt]
a 명백한, 겉보기의   that seems to be real or true; clear
It quickly became **apparent** to us that our teacher could not speak French.
우리 선생님이 프랑스어를 못한다는 사실이 일순간에 명백해졌다.

06 applaud [əplɔ́ːd]
v 박수 갈채하다   to hit your hands together noisily
The audience **applauded** continually for about 5 minutes.
관객들은 약 5분 여간 계속 박수갈채를 보냈다.

07 banquet [bǽŋkwit]
n 연회, 진수성찬   a formal dinner for a large number of people
They should know which fork to use, for which course at a **banquet**.
그들은 연회장에서 어느 식사 코스에 어떤 포크를 사용하는지를 알아야 한다.

08 barrier [bǽriər]
n 장벽, 장애   an object that prevents something moving
The mountains form a natural **barrier** between the two countries.
그 산은 두 나라 사이에 자연적인 장벽을 이루고 있다.

09 beguile [bigáil]
v 현혹하다, 속이다   to make a trick to somebody
He **beguiled** her into a false sense of security.
그는 그녀를 속여서 잘못된 안전감을 갖게 했다.

---

key words
noisily ad 요란하게 / continually ad 계속해서 / prevent v 막다 / trick v 속이다

🎧 Listen and repeat. Track 62

10 burden [bə́:rdn]
n 부담, 짐 / v 짐을 지우다   a responsibility that causes a lot of work or worry
I don't want to be a **burden** to my children when I'm old.
내가 늙었을 때 아이들에게 부담이 되고 싶지는 않다.

11 comfort [kʌ́mfərt]
n 위로, 위안 / v 위로하다   help or kindness to somebody who is suffering
Her frequent visits gave me great **comfort** while I was ill in bed.
내가 병석에 있을 때 그녀가 자주 찾아온 것이 큰 위로가 되었다.

12 confide [kənfáid]
v 털어놓다, 맡기다   to tell somebody that is secret
She **confided** her troubles to a friend.
그녀는 자신의 문제를 친구에게 털어놓았다.

13 contribute [kəntríbju:t]
v 기부하다, 기여하다   to be one of the causes of something
He **contributed** toward the achievement of these results.
그는 이런 성과를 이루는 데 기여했다.

14 cooperate [kouápərèit]
v 협력하다, 협동하다   to be helpful by doing what somebody asks you to do
They agreed to **cooperate** in the fight against crime.
그들은 범죄와의 싸움에 협력하기로 동의했다.

15 debt [det]
n 은혜, 빚   an amount of money that you owe to somebody
With the appearance of credit cards more people got into **debt**.
신용 카드의 등장으로 더 많은 사람들이 빚을 지게 되었다.

16 declare [diklέər]
v 선언하다, 단언하다   to state publicly and officially
They **declared** themselves bankrupt.
그들은 파산을 선언했다.

17 disappoint [dìsəpɔ́int]
v 실망시키다, 좌절시키다   to make somebody sad what he/she had hoped is less good
We are indeed **disappointed** with the way this has all turned out.
결과가 이렇게 되어 우리는 정말 실망했다.

18 drown [draun]
v 물에 빠지다, 익사시키다   to die in water
The excellent swimmer **drowned** in the lake yesterday.
훌륭한 수영 선수가 어제 호수에서 익사했다.

---

key words
responsibility n 책임, 의무 / frequent a 자주 있는 / appearance n 출현 / indeed ad 정말

Unit 21 107

Exercise

A. Complete the sentence.

1. She _____ her troubles to a friend.
   그녀는 자신의 문제를 친구에게 털어놓았다.
2. The mountains form a natural _____ between the two countries.
   그 산은 두 나라 사이에 자연적인 장벽을 이루고 있다.
3. We had to _____ a picnic because of bad weather.
   우리는 궂은 날씨 때문에 소풍을 포기해야 했다.
4. The excellent swimmer _____ in the lake yesterday.
   훌륭한 수영 선수가 어제 호수에서 익사했다.
5. They _____ themselves bankrupt.
   그들은 파산을 선언했다.
6. He had been _____ with a serious illness since childhood.
   그는 어린 시절부터 극심한 질병으로 괴롭힘 당했었다.
7. They agreed to _____ in the fight against crime.
   그들은 범죄와의 싸움에 협력하기로 동의했다.
8. The audience _____ continually for about 5 minutes.
   관객들은 약 5분 여간 계속 박수갈채를 보냈다.
9. They should know which fork to use, for which course at a _____.
   그들은 연회장에서 어느 식사 코스에 어떤 포크를 사용하는지를 알아야 한다.
10. It ended _____ after 37 episodes.
    그것은 37회를 끝으로 갑자기 막을 내리고 말았다.
11. He _____ her into a false sense of security.
    그는 그녀를 속여서 잘못된 안전감을 갖게 했다.
12. Her frequent visits gave me great _____ while I was ill in bed.
    내가 병석에 있을 때 그녀가 자주 찾아온 것이 큰 위로가 되었다.
13. It quickly became _____ to us that our teacher could not speak French.
    우리 선생님이 프랑스어를 못한다는 사실이 일순간에 명백해졌다.
14. He _____ toward the achievement of these results.
    그는 이런 성과를 이루는 데 기여했다.
15. His answer was _____ in every detail.
    그의 대답은 모든 점에서 정확했다.
16. I don't want to be a _____ to my children when I'm old.
    내가 늙었을 때 아이들에게 부담이 되고 싶지는 않다.
17. With the appearance of credit cards more people got into _____.
    신용 카드의 등장으로 더 많은 사람들이 빚을 지게 되었다.
18. We are indeed _____ with the way this has all turned out.
    결과가 이렇게 되어 우리는 정말 실망했다.

Hint

| afflict | abandon | comfort | drown | applaud | confide | cooperate | abruptly | burden |
| debt | banquet | disappoint | barrier | contribute | beguile | apparent | declare | accurate |

 Unit 21

Exercise

B. Fill in the word and meaning.

	Word	Meaning
01	burden	
02	cooperate	
03	abandon	
04	debt	
05	accurate	
06	drown	
07	beguile	
08	abruptly	
09	declare	
10	comfort	
11	afflict	
12	confide	
13	applaud	
14	disappoint	
15	barrier	
16	apparent	
17	contribute	
18	banquet	

	Meaning	Word
01	버리다, 포기하다	
02	갑자기, 퉁명스럽게	
03	정확한, 신중한	
04	괴롭히다	
05	명백한, 겉보기의	
06	박수 갈채하다	
07	연회, 진수성찬	
08	장벽, 장애	
09	현혹하다, 속이다	
10	부담, 짐, 짐을 지우다	
11	위로, 위안, 위로하다	
12	털어놓다, 맡기다	
13	기부하다, 기여하다	
14	협력하다, 협동하다	
15	은혜, 빚	
16	선언하다, 단언하다	
17	실망시키다, 좌절시키다	
18	물에 빠지다, 익사시키다	

C. Listen, write the word and meaning. (Track 63)

	Word	Meaning		Word	Meaning
01			10		
02			11		
03			12		
04			13		
05			14		
06			15		
07			16		
08			17		
09			18		

Unit 22

🎧 Listen and repeat. Track 64

01 equipment [ikwípmənt]
n 장비, 설비 — the things that are needed to do a particular activity
She tested all her fire-fighting **equipment**.
그녀는 자신의 모든 소방 장비를 점검했다.

02 examine [igzǽmin]
v 조사하다, 시험하다 — to consider or study an idea, a subject, etc
Geologists **examined** moon rocks brought back by the Apollo 11 astronauts.
아폴로 11호 우주 비행사들이 가져온 달 암석을 지질학자들이 조사했다.

03 fierce [fiərs]
a 사나운, 격렬한 — angry, aggressive and frightening
The house was guarded by **fierce** dogs.
그 집은 사나운 개들이 지키고 있었다.

04 freeze [fri:z]
v 얼다, 얼게 하다 — to become hard because of extreme cold
Freeze this meat in the freezer compartment.
고기를 냉동 칸에 넣어 얼려라.

05 grace [greis]
n 우아, 은혜 — the ability to move in a smooth and controlled way
She danced with marvelous **grace**.
그녀는 놀랄 만큼 우아하게 춤을 추었다.

06 guarantee [gæ̀rəntí:]
v 보증하다 / n 보증 — to promise something
We want the quality of the goods **guaranteed** perfectly.
우리는 품질이 완전히 보증된 물품을 원합니다.

07 howl [haul]
v 짖다, 울부짖다 — to make a long loud sound
We don't have such time to listen to that **howling** sound.
우리는 그런 울부짖는 소리를 들을 시간이 없다.

08 hydrogen [háidrədʒən]
n 수소 — a light colorless gas
Hydrogen and oxygen combine to form water.
수소와 산소는 결합하여 물을 만든다.

09 hygiene [háidʒi:n]
n 위생, 위생법 — keeping yourself and things clean to prevent disease
High standards of **hygiene** are essential when you are preparing food.
음식을 준비할 때는 확실한 위생 규범이 필수적이다.

key words
geologist n 지질학자 / aggressive a 공격적인, 의욕적인 / compartment n 칸막이, 구획
marvelous a 놀라운, 훌륭한 / oxygen n 산소

🎧 Listen and repeat. Track 65

10 insert [insə́ːrt] v 삽입하다, 게재하다   to put something into something or between two things
I decided to **insert** an extra paragraph in the text.
나는 본문에 여분의 단락을 삽입하기로 결심했다.

11 insight [ínsàit] n 통찰, 통찰력   an understanding of what somebody/something is like
He has the **insight** to recognize people's talents.
그에게는 사람들의 재능을 알 수 있는 통찰력이 있다.

12 legacy [légəsi] n 유산, 물려받은 것   property that is given to you after someone you know dies
Part of **legacy** from my parents is an album of family photographs.
부모로부터 물려받은 유산의 일부는 가족사진이 담긴 앨범이다.

13 legend [lédʒənd] n 전설, 일화집   an old story that may or may not be true
There's a **legend** about a beautiful creature that lives in the deep ocean.
깊은 바다에 사는 아름다운 존재에 관한 전설이 있다.

14 magnitude [mǽgnətjùːd] n 크기, 중대함   the great size or importance of something
We simply don't have the resources to take on a project of that **magnitude**.
우리는 그 정도로 중대한 프로젝트를 맡을 자원이 없어요.

15 majority [mədʒɔ́(ː)rəti] n 대다수, 과반수, 다수파   the largest number or part of a group of people
The **majority** was in favor of the proposal.
대다수가 그 제안에 찬성했다.

16 meager [míːgər] a 적은, 빈약한   too small in amount
Moths may seem a **meager** meal for a bear, but their bodies are rich in fat.
곰에게 나방은 빈약한 먹이인 것 같지만 나방의 몸체에는 지방질이 풍부하다.

17 mend [mend] v 고치다, 수선하다   to repair something that is damaged or broken
It is never too late to **mend** something wrong.
잘못된 것을 고치는데 너무 늦다는 법은 없다.

18 minister [mínistər] n 장관, 목사   the head of a government department
The **minister** refused to comment on the rumors of his resignation.
그 장관은 자신의 사임과 관련된 소문에 대하여 언급하기를 거부했다.

key words
extra a 여분의 / resource n 자원, 재원 / moth n 나방 / resignation n 사직, 사임

Unit 22 111

Exercise

A. Complete the sentence.

1. _____ and oxygen combine to form water.
   수소와 산소는 결합하여 물을 만든다.
2. She danced with marvelous _____.
   그녀는 놀랄 만큼 우아하게 춤을 추었다.
3. Geologists _____ moon rocks brought back by the Apollo 11 astronauts.
   아폴로 11호 우주 비행사들이 가져온 달 암석을 지질학자들이 조사했다.
4. The _____ refused to comment on the rumors of his resignation.
   그 장관은 자신의 사임과 관련된 소문에 대하여 언급하기를 거부했다.
5. The house was guarded by _____ dogs.
   그 집은 사나운 개들이 지키고 있었다.
6. We simply don't have the resources to take on a project of that _____.
   우리는 그 정도로 중대한 프로젝트를 맡을 자원이 없어요.
7. We want the quality of the goods _____ perfectly.
   우리는 품질이 완전히 보증된 물품을 원합니다.
8. We don't have such time to listen to that _____ sound.
   우리는 그런 울부짖는 소리를 들을 시간이 없다.
9. High standards of _____ are essential when you are preparing food.
   음식을 준비할 때는 확실한 위생 규범이 필수적이다.
10. She tested all her fire-fighting _____.
    그녀는 자신의 모든 소방 장비를 점검했다.
11. Moths may seem a _____ meal for a bear, but their bodies are rich in fat.
    곰에게 나방은 빈약한 먹이인 것 같지만 나방의 몸체에는 지방질이 풍부하다.
12. I decided to _____ an extra paragraph in the text.
    나는 본문에 여분의 단락을 삽입하기로 결심했다.
13. Part of _____ from my parents is an album of family photographs.
    부모로부터 물려받은 유산의 일부는 가족사진이 담긴 앨범이다.
14. _____ this meat in the freezer compartment.
    고기를 냉동 칸에 넣어 얼려라.
15. There's a _____ about a beautiful creature that lives in the deep ocean.
    깊은 바다에 사는 아름다운 존재에 관한 전설이 있다.
16. The _____ was in favor of the proposal.
    대다수가 그 제안에 찬성했다.
17. He has the _____ to recognize people's talents.
    그에게는 사람들의 재능을 알 수 있는 통찰력이 있다.
18. It is never too late to _____ something wrong.
    잘못된 것을 고치는데 너무 늦다는 법은 없다.

Hint

| hydrogen | fierce | equipment | howl | magnitude | insight | freeze | meager | legacy |
| minister | grace | guarantee | insert | hygiene | | legend | majority | examine | mend |

Unit 22

Exercise

B. Fill in the word and meaning.

	Word	Meaning
01	howl	
02	insert	
03	equipment	
04	legend	
05	guarantee	
06	magnitude	
07	examine	
08	mend	
09	legacy	
10	fierce	
11	insight	
12	meager	
13	freeze	
14	minister	
15	hydrogen	
16	majority	
17	grace	
18	hygiene	

	Meaning	Word
01	장비, 설비	
02	조사하다, 시험하다	
03	사나운, 격렬한	
04	얼다, 얼게 하다	
05	우아, 은혜	
06	보증하다, 보증	
07	짖다, 울부짖다	
08	수소	
09	위생, 위생법	
10	삽입하다, 게재하다	
11	통찰, 통찰력	
12	유산, 물려받은 것	
13	전설, 일화집	
14	크기, 중대함	
15	대다수, 과반수, 다수파	
16	적은, 빈약한	
17	고치다, 수선하다	
18	장관, 목사	

C. Listen, write the word and meaning. (Track 66)

	Word	Meaning		Word	Meaning
01			10		
02			11		
03			12		
04			13		
05			14		
06			15		
07			16		
08			17		
09			18		

Review 11

A. Read and fill in the word and meaning.

word	definition	meaning
	to be helpful by doing what somebody asks you to do	
	to state publicly and officially	
	to stop doing something without finishing it	
	an amount of money that you owe to somebody	
	suddenly	
	to make somebody sad what he/she had hoped is less good	
	to cause somebody/something to suffer pain	
	to make a trick to somebody	
	to be one of the causes of something	
	to die in water	
	exact and correct	
	a responsibility that causes a lot of work or worry	
	to hit your hands together noisily	
	to tell somebody that is secret	
	that seems to be real or true; clear	
	a formal dinner for a large number of people	
	help or kindness to somebody who is suffering	
	an object that prevents something moving	

Hint

afflict   abandon   comfort   drown   applaud   confide   cooperate   abruptly   burden
debt   banquet   disappoint   barrier   contribute   beguile   apparent   declare   accurate

B. Read and fill in the word and meaning.

word	definition	meaning
	angry, aggressive and frightening	
	an understanding of what somebody/something is like	
	an old story that may or may not be true	
	the things that are needed to do a particular activity	
	property that is given to you after someone you know dies	
	to repair something that is damaged or broken	
	to consider or study an idea, a subject, etc	
	the head of a government department	
	to become hard because of extreme cold	
	the great size or importance of something	
	the ability to move in a smooth and controlled way	
	the largest number or part of a group of people	
	to make a long loud sound	
	too small in amount	
	to promise something	
	a light colorless gas	
	to put something into something or between two things	
	keeping yourself and things clean to prevent disease	

Hint

hydrogen fierce equipment howl magnitude insight freeze meager legacy
minister grace guarantee insert hygiene legend majority examine mend

Unit 23

🎧 Listen and repeat. Track 67

01 nourish [nə́:riʃ]
v (영양분을)주다, 기르다   to give the right kind food
This cream is supposed to help **nourish** your skin.
이 크림은 당신 피부에 영양분을 공급하는데 도움이 된다고 생각된다.

02 novelty [nάvəlti]
n 진기함, 새로운 것   the quality of being new and different
What I'm in the market for is an electronic toy that's got both **novelty** and appeal.
내가 구매하고자 하는 것은 신기하고 매력적인 전자식 장난감이다.

03 operator [άpərèitər]
n 교환수, 조작자   a person whose job is to connect telephone calls
If you require assistance, please dial 0 for the **operator**.
도움이 필요하시면, 0번을 돌려서 교환수를 찾으세요.

04 optimistic [àptəmístik]
a 낙천적인, 낙관적인   expecting good things to happen
The experts are **optimistic** about our chances of success.
전문가들은 우리의 성공 가능성에 대해 낙관적이다.

05 owe [ou]
v 빚지고 있다, 은혜를 입고 있다   to have to pay money to somebody
My brother denied that he **owed** me any money at all.
나의 동생은 그가 나에게 빚진 것을 완전히 부인했다.

06 paralyze [pǽrəlàiz]
v 마비시키다, 무력케하다   to make something unable to act or function properly
The heavy rains yesterday that have **paralyzed** the transportation services in the capital.
어제 내린 폭우는 도심의 교통수단을 마비시켰다.

07 persist [pə:rsíst]
v 고집하다, 지속하다   to continue doing something even though other people say that you are wrong
How can he **persist** in denying that he was at the scene?
어떻게 그가 현장에 없었다고 계속 고집할 수 있나요?

08 postpone [poustpóun]
v 연기하다, 차위에 두다   to arrange that something will happen at a later time
The expedition has **postponed** its departure to the Antarctic.
탐험대는 남극으로 출발하는 것을 연기했다.

09 posture [pάstʃər]
n 자세, 태도   the way that a person sits, stands, walks, etc
Good **posture** is important to health.
좋은 자세가 건강에 중요합니다.

---

key words
appeal n 매력 / assistance n 도움, 원조 / transportation n 운송, 수송
expedition n 탐험대 / departure n 출발

🎧 Listen and repeat. Track 68

10 pretend [priténd]
v ~인 체하다   to behave in a particular way in order to make other people believe something
I sat there **pretending** to listen but I was bored to death.
나는 거기에 앉아 듣는 척했지만 따분해 죽는 줄 알았다.

11 prevail [privéil]
v 우세하다, 보급되다   to win or be accepted
Although it is sometimes hard, we must have faith that justice will **prevail**.
때로는 어렵겠지만 우리는 정의가 우세하게 되리라는 신념을 가져야 한다.

12 profound [prəfáund]
a 깊이가 있는, 심오한   needing or showing a lot of knowledge or thought
The audience was impressed by his **profound** lecture.
청중은 그의 심오한 강연 내용에 감명을 받았다.

13 puzzle [pʌ́zl]
v 당황하게 하다, 이리 저리 생각하다   to make somebody feel confused
Her strange illness **puzzled** all the experts.
그녀의 이상한 병은 모든 전문가들을 당황하게 했다.

14 racial [réiʃəl]
a 인종의, 종족의   connected with people's race
Our goal is to free ourselves completely of the **racial** prejudice.
우리의 목표는 인종 편견으로부터 우리자신을 완전히 해방시키는 것이다.

15 recruit [rikrúːt]
v 채용하다, 모집하다   to find new people to join a company, etc
More staff will have to be **recruited** for the additional patients.
환자들을 더 받으려면 직원을 더 채용해야 할 것이다.

16 relate [riléit]
v 이야기하다, 관계 짓다   to tell a story to somebody
She **related** how it happened.
그녀는 그 일이 어떻게 일어났는지 이야기 했다.

17 reproduce [riːprədjúːs]
v 번식하다, 재생하다   to produce young
Although viruses can **reproduce**, they do not exhibit most of the other characteristics of life.
비록 바이러스는 번식을 할 수 있지만, 생명체의 다른 특성 대부분을 보여주지 못한다.

18 resentful [rizéntfəl]
a 분개한, 골을 잘 내는   connected with the angry about something
I grew **resentful** of his lack of sensitivity.
나는 그의 무신경함에 분개했다.

---

key words
faith n 신념 / lecture n 강의 / prejudice n 편견, 선입관 / exhibit v 나타내다 / characteristic n 특성, 특색

Unit 23

Exercise

A. Complete the sentence.

1. Although it is sometimes hard, we must have faith that justice will _____.
   때로는 어렵겠지만 우리는 정의가 우세하게 되리라는 신념을 가져야 한다.

2. This cream is supposed to help _____ your skin.
   이 크림은 당신 피부에 영양분을 공급하는데 도움이 된다고 생각된다.

3. I grew _____ of his lack of sensitivity.
   나는 그의 무신경함에 분개했다.

4. What I'm in the market for is an electronic toy that's got both _____ and appeal.
   내가 구매하고자 하는 것은 신기하고 매력적인 전자식 장난감이다.

5. The audience was impressed by his _____ lecture.
   청중은 그의 심오한 강연 내용에 감명을 받았다.

6. Although viruses can _____, they do not exhibit most of the other characteristics of life.
   비록 바이러스는 번식을 할 수 있지만, 생명체의 다른 특성 대부분을 보여주지 못한다.

7. The experts are _____ about our chances of success.
   전문가들은 우리의 성공 가능성에 대해 낙관적이다.

8. The heavy rains yesterday that have _____ the transportation services in the capital.
   어제 내린 폭우는 도심의 교통수단을 마비시켰다.

9. How can he _____ in denying that he was at the scene?
   어떻게 그가 현장에 없었다고 계속 고집할 수 있나요?

10. My brother denied that he _____ me any money at all.
    나의 동생은 그가 나에게 빚진 것을 완전히 부인했다.

11. The expedition has _____ its departure to the Antarctic.
    탐험대는 남극으로 출발하는 것을 연기했다.

12. If you require assistance, please dial 0 for the _____.
    도움이 필요하시면, 0번을 돌려서 교환수를 찾으세요.

13. More staff will have to be _____ for the additional patients.
    환자들을 더 받으려면 직원을 더 채용해야 할 것이다.

14. I sat there _____ to listen but I was bored to death.
    나는 거기에 앉아 듣는 척했지만 따분해 죽는 줄 알았다.

15. Our goal is to free ourselves completely of the _____ prejudice.
    우리의 목표는 인종 편견으로부터 우리자신을 완전히 해방시키는 것이다.

16. Good _____ is important to health.
    좋은 자세가 건강에 중요합니다.

17. She _____ how it happened.
    그녀는 그 일이 어떻게 일어났는지 이야기 했다.

18. Her strange illness _____ all the experts.
    그녀의 이상한 병은 모든 전문가들을 당황하게 했다.

Hint

| postpone | owe | posture | novelty | resentful | paralyze | relate | optimistic | pretend |
| reproduce | racial | nourish | persist | profound | operator | prevail | puzzle | recruit |

Exercise

B. Fill in the word and meaning.

	Word	Meaning
01	owe	
02	pretend	
03	nourish	
04	puzzle	
05	persist	
06	racial	
07	novelty	
08	prevail	
09	reproduce	
10	paralyze	
11	resentful	
12	operator	
13	profound	
14	relate	
15	postpone	
16	recruit	
17	posture	
18	optimistic	

	Meaning	Word
01	(영양분을)주다, 기르다	
02	진기함, 새로운 것	
03	교환수, 조작자	
04	낙천적인, 낙관적인	
05	빚지고 있다, 은혜를 입고 있다	
06	마비시키다, 무력케하다	
07	고집하다, 지속하다	
08	연기하다, 차위에 두다	
09	자세, 태도	
10	~인 체하다	
11	우세하다, 보급되다	
12	깊이가 있는, 심오한	
13	당황하게 하다, 이리 저리 생각하다	
14	인종의, 종족의	
15	채용하다, 모집하다	
16	이야기하다, 관계 짓다	
17	번식하다, 재생하다	
18	분개한, 골을 잘 내는	

C. Listen, write the word and meaning. (Track 69)

	Word	Meaning		Word	Meaning
01			10		
02			11		
03			12		
04			13		
05			14		
06			15		
07			16		
08			17		
09			18		

Unit 24

🎧 Listen and repeat. Track 70

01 ridiculous
[ridíkjələs]
a 우스꽝스러운, 어리석은   very silly or unreasonable
His imagination is able to convert the most **ridiculous** situation into high romance.
그의 상상력은 가장 우스꽝스런 상황을 거창한 낭만으로 바꿀 수 있다.

02 rigid
[rídʒid]
a 단단한, 엄격한   difficult to bend; strict
It goes without saying that military discipline is literally **rigid**.
군대 규율이 글자 그대로 엄격한 것은 말할 것도 없다.

03 seize
[si:z]
v (붙)잡다, 파악하다   to take hold of something suddenly and firmly
She **seized** me by the wrist.
그녀가 내 손목을 붙잡았다.

04 sequence
[sí:kwəns]
n 연속, 순서   the order in which a number of things are arranged
We as readers must rely on other clues to understand the true **sequence** of events.
독자로서 우리는 진정한 사건의 순서를 이해하기 위해 다른 단서들에 의존해야만 한다.

05 slip
[slip]
v 미끄러지다, 몰래 나오다   to slide accidentally
When it rains, a lot of cars **slip** on the wet road.
비가 오면 빗길에 미끄러지는 차가 많다.

06 slope
[sloup]
n 경사지, 비탈   a surface or piece of land that goes up or down
This mountain **slope** contains slides that will challenge even experts.
이 산의 경사지에는 전문가들에게 조차 힘든 비탈이 있다.

07 spectacular
[spektǽkjələːr]
a 장관의, 구경거리의   very impressive to see
The effect is so **spectacular** and extensive that it can be seen from space.
그 광경은 너무나 장관이고 광범위해서 우주에서도 볼 수 있다.

08 spectator
[spékteitəːr]
n 구경꾼, 관객   a person who is watching an event
The **spectators** were moved by her graceful performance.
관객은 그녀의 우아한 공연에 감동했다.

09 sting
[stiŋ]
v 찌르다, 괴롭히다 / **n** 찌름   to make a person feel a sudden pain by pushing something sharp
Be careful because those plants **sting** your body.
저 식물들은 몸을 찌르니까 조심하세요.

---

key words
unreasonable **a** 이성적이 아닌, 철없는 / convert **v** 변하게 하다 / discipline **n** 규율, 기강
literally **ad** 글자 그대로 / clue **n** 실마리, 단서

🎧 Listen and repeat. Track 71

10 strength [streŋkθ]
n 힘, 세기, 강점   the quality of being physically strong
He was my teacher, my idol, my symbol of **strength** and protection.
그는 나의 스승이자 우상이며 힘과 보호의 상징이었다.

11 temperate [témpərit]
a 절제하는, 온화한   not to get angry or lose one's temper easily
Temperate living will effect the recovery of his health.
절제하는 생활이 그의 건강을 회복하는데 영향을 미칠 것이다.

12 temporary [témpərèri]
a 임시의, 일시적인   lasting for a short time; not permanent
We usually take on **temporary** staff in the summer.
우리는 여름에 대개 임시 직원을 고용한다.

13 transform [trænsfɔ́:rm]
v 변형시키다, 변모시키다   to change somebody/something completely
It will **transform** the way we learn and the way we teach within a few decades.
이것은 수십 년 안에 배우고 가르치는 방법을 변형 시킬 것이다.

14 transplant [trænsplǽnt]
v 옮겨 심다, 이식하다 / n 이식   a operation in which an organ, etc is taken out and put into another person's body
The surgeon persuaded me to undergo an organ **transplant** operation.
외과 의사는 나를 설득하여 장기 이식 수술을 받도록 하였다.

15 utmost [ʌ́tmòust]
a 최고의, 최대의   greatest
I have used my **utmost** endeavors.
나는 최선의 노력을 다했다.

16 utter [ʌ́tər]
v 말하다 / a 완전한   to say something or make a sound with your voice
She didn't **utter** a word all night.
그녀는 밤새 한마디 말도 하지 않았다.

17 virtue [vǝ́:rtʃu:]
n 덕, 장점   moral excellence in general; a good quality or habit
Virtue is its own reward.
덕에 대한 보상은 바로 그 덕 자체이다.

18 voluntary [válǝntèri]
a 자발적인, 임의의   done because you want to do it, not because you have to do it
Many **voluntary** helpers were active in the Olympic Games.
많은 자발적인 봉사자들이 올림픽 경기에서 활동했었다.

---

key words
idol n 우상 / permanent a 불변의, 영구적인 / surgeon a 외과의 / undergo v 겪다, 견디다
endeavor n 노력

Unit 24

Exercise

A. Complete the sentence.

1. This mountain _____ contains slides that will challenge even experts.
   이 산의 경사지에는 전문가들에게 조차 힘든 비탈이 있다.

2. The surgeon persuaded me to undergo an organ _____ operation.
   외과 의사는 나를 설득하여 장기 이식 수술을 받도록 하였다.

3. He was my teacher, my idol, my symbol of _____ and protection.
   그는 나의 스승이자 우상이며 힘과 보호의 상징이었다.

4. His imagination is able to convert the most _____ situation into high romance.
   그의 상상력은 가장 우스꽝스런 상황을 거창한 낭만으로 바꿀 수 있다.

5. We as readers must rely on other clues to understand the true _____ of events.
   독자로서 우리는 진정한 사건의 순서를 이해하기 위해 다른 단서들에 의존해야만 한다.

6. When it rains, a lot of cars _____ on the wet road.
   비가 오면 빗길에 미끄러지는 차가 많다.

7. Many _____ helpers were active in the Olympic Games.
   많은 자발적인 봉사자들이 올림픽 경기에서 활동했었다.

8. The effect is so _____ and extensive that it can be seen from space.
   그 광경은 너무나 장관이고 광범위해서 우주에서도 볼 수 있다.

9. It goes without saying that military discipline is literally _____.
   군대 규율이 글자 그대로 엄격한 것은 말할 것도 없다.

10. The _____ were moved by her graceful performance.
    관객은 그녀의 우아한 공연에 감동했다.

11. _____ living will effect the recovery of his health.
    절제하는 생활이 그의 건강을 회복하는데 영향을 미칠 것이다.

12. She _____ me by the wrist.
    그녀가 내 손목을 붙잡았다.

13. It will _____ the way we learn and the way we teach within a few decades.
    이것은 수십 년 안에 배우고 가르치는 방법을 변형 시킬 것이다.

14. I have used my _____ endeavors.
    나는 최선의 노력을 다했다.

15. _____ is its own reward.
    덕에 대한 보상은 바로 그 덕 자체이다.

16. Be careful because those plants _____ your body.
    저 식물들은 몸을 찌르니까 조심하세요.

17. We usually take on _____ staff in the summer.
    우리는 여름에 대개 임시 직원을 고용한다.

18. She didn't _____ a word all night.
    그녀는 밤새 한마디 말도 하지 않았다.

Hint

spectator   utter   strength   temporary   utmost   slip   ridiculous   seize   spectacular
temperate   sting   voluntary   sequence   slope   rigid   transplant   virtue   transform

Exercise

B. Fill in the word and meaning.

	Word	Meaning
01	sting	
02	temporary	
03	ridiculous	
04	transplant	
05	slope	
06	transform	
07	rigid	
08	utmost	
09	spectacular	
10	virtue	
11	seize	
12	voluntary	
13	spectator	
14	utter	
15	sequence	
16	temperate	
17	strength	
18	slip	

	Meaning	Word
01	우스꽝스러운, 어리석은	
02	단단한, 엄격한	
03	(붙)잡다, 파악하다	
04	연속, 순서	
05	미끄러지다, 몰래 나오다	
06	경사지, 비탈	
07	장관의, 구경거리의	
08	구경꾼, 관객	
09	찌르다, 괴롭히다, 찌름	
10	힘, 세기, 강점	
11	절제하는, 온화한	
12	임시의, 일시적인	
13	변형시키다, 변모시키다	
14	옮겨 심다, 이식하다, 이식	
15	최고의, 최대의	
16	말하다, 완전한	
17	덕, 장점	
18	자발적인, 임의의	

C. Listen, write the word and meaning. Track 72

	Word	Meaning		Word	Meaning
01			10		
02			11		
03			12		
04			13		
05			14		
06			15		
07			16		
08			17		
09			18		

Review 12

A. Read and fill in the word and meaning.

word	definition	meaning
	to continue doing something even though other people say that you are wrong	
	connected with people's race	
	to tell a story to somebody	
	to make something unable to act or function properly	
	to win or be accepted	
	connected with the angry about something	
	to arrange that something will happen at a later time	
	to find new people to join a company, etc	
	expecting good things to happen	
	the way that a person sits, stands, walks, etc	
	the quality of being new and different	
	to behave in a particular way in order to make other people believe something	
	to produce young	
	to give the right kind food	
	to make somebody feel confused	
	a person whose job is to connect telephone calls	
	needing or showing a lot of knowledge or thought	
	to have to pay money to somebody	

Hint

postpone   owe   posture   novelty   resentful   paralyze   relate   optimistic   pretend
reproduce   racial   nourish   persist   profound   operator   prevail   puzzle   recruit

Review 12

B. Read and fill in the word and meaning.

word	definition	meaning
transplant	a operation in which an organ, etc is taken out and put into another person's body	
seize	to take hold of something suddenly and firmly	
spectacular	very impressive to see	
utter	to say something or make a sound with your voice	
spectator	a person who is watching an event	
transform	to change somebody/something completely	
strength	the quality of being physically strong	
ridiculous	very silly or unreasonable	
temporary	lasting for a short time; not permanent	
sting	to make a person feel a sudden pain by pushing something sharp	
virtue	moral excellence in general; a good quality or habit	
temperate	not to get angry or lose one's temper easily	
slope	a surface or piece of land that goes up or down	
utmost	greatest	
slip	to slide accidentally	
voluntary	done because you want to do it, not because you have to do it	
rigid	difficult to bend; strict	
sequence	the order in which a number of things are arranged	

Hint

spectator   utter   strength   temporary   utmost   slip   ridiculous   seize   spectacular
temperate   sting   voluntary   sequence   slope   rigid   transplant   virtue   transform

Unit 25

🎧 Listen and repeat. (Track 73)

01 absolutely [ǽbsəlúːtli]
ad 절대적으로, 완전히   completely; totally
It is **absolutely** our fault that we delivered you the parts of a different model.
다른 모델의 부품을 당신에게 전달한 것은 절대적으로 우리의 잘못입니다.

02 absurd [æbsə́ːrd]
a 부조리한, 불합리한   not at all logical or sensible
His **absurd** behavior made many people laugh at him.
그의 부조리한 행동은 모든 사람들이 그를 비웃게 만들었다.

03 aim [eim]
n 목표, 목적 / v 겨누다   something that you intend to do; a purpose
You've got to **aim** high if you want to succeed.
성공하려면 목표를 높이 잡아야 한다.

04 ally [əlái]
n 동맹국, 협력자   a country that has an agreement to support another country
In this exigency, we must look for aid from our **allies**.
이 위급한 시기에 우리는 우리의 동맹국들에게 원조를 구해야만 한다.

05 appliance [əpláiəns]
n 기구, 장치, 설비   a piece of equipment for a particular purpose in the house
There were no **appliances** back then so his mother had to do everything by hand.
그땐 설비가 하나도 없어서 그의 어머니는 손으로 모든 것을 다 해야 했어요.

06 astonish [əstániʃ]
v 놀라게 하다   to surprise somebody very much
The cook was **astonished** at his incredible appetite.
요리사는 그의 엄청난 식욕에 놀랐다.

07 beneath [biníːθ]
prep ~의 밑(아래)에   in, at or to a lower position; under
Beneath these desert slopes lies one of the longest, deepest and most surprising caves in the world.
이 사막의 경사면 밑에는 세계에서 가장 길고, 깊고, 놀라운 동굴이 하나 있다.

08 besides [bisáidz]
ad 게다가, 그 밖에 / prep ~외에도   in addition to or as well as somebody/something
What's the difference between the two **besides** the price?
가격이외에 그 둘 사이의 차이점은 무엇입니까?

09 canal [kənǽl]
n 운하, 수로   a deep cut that is made through land so that ships can travel
The **canal** connects the Atlantic with the Pacific.
그 운하는 대서양과 태평양을 연결하고 있다.

---

key words
exigency n 위급(한 때) / aid n 원조, 도움 / incredible a 놀라운 / appetite n 식욕

🎧 Listen and repeat. Track 74

10 colony [kάləni]
n 식민지, 집단 — a country that is ruled by another, more powerful country
The **colony** declared independence.
그 식민지는 독립을 선언했다.

11 column [kάləm]
n (신문의)란, 기둥 — one of the vertical sections into which a printed page is divided
I always read the baseball **column**.
나는 항상 야구 기사란을 읽는다.

12 comfortably [kʌ́mfərtəbəli]
ad 편안하게, 기분 좋게 — physically relaxed; easily
Why don't you lie on your back and sleep **comfortably**?
바로 누워서 편하게 주무시지 그러세요?

13 coordinate [kouɔ́:rdənèit]
v 조정하다, 조화시키다 — to organize different things or people so that they work together
It is her job to **coordinate** the various departments.
다양한 부서들을 조정하는 것이 그녀의 일이다.

14 correctly [kəréktli]
ad 정확히, 바르게 — in a correct way
The other children spelled all five words **correctly**, but she wrote only four.
다른 학생들은 모두 다섯 단어의 철자를 정확히 썼지만, 그녀는 네 단어만 썼다.

15 delegate [déligèit]
v 위임하다 / n 대표자 — to give somebody with a lower job or position a task to do
You can't do everything yourself so you must learn how to **delegate**.
너 혼자 모든 것을 다 할 수 없으니 위임하는 법을 배우도록 해.

16 delight [diláit]
n 기쁨, 기쁨을 주는 것 — great pleasured; something that gives great pleasure
He takes **delight** in teasing his younger sister.
그는 여동생을 괴롭히면서 즐거움을 찾는다.

17 dumb [dʌm]
a 벙어리의, 말을 하지 않는 — not able to speak
I have not known that he is **dumb** from birth.
나는 그가 태어날 때부터 벙어리라는 사실을 몰랐다.

18 dump [dʌmp]
v (쓰레기를)내버리다, 내려뜨리다 — throw something down; let something fall in a mass
Bill **dumped** his old car at the side of the road.
빌은 그의 낡은 차를 길가에 내버렸다.

key words
vertical a 세로의 / spell v 철자를 쓰다 / teasing a 괴롭히는, 들볶는

Unit 25

Exercise

A. Complete the sentence.

1. The other children spelled all five words _____, but she wrote only four.
   다른 학생들은 모두 다섯 단어의 철자를 정확히 썼지만, 그녀는 네 단어만 썼다.

2. It is _____ our fault that we delivered you the parts of a different model.
   다른 모델의 부품을 당신에게 전달한 것은 절대적으로 우리의 잘못입니다.

3. He takes _____ in teasing his younger sister.
   그는 여동생을 괴롭히면서 즐거움을 찾는다.

4. In this exigency, we must look for aid from our _____.
   이 위급한 시기에 우리는 우리의 동맹국들에게 원조를 구해야만 한다.

5. Bill _____ his old car at the side of the road.
   빌은 그의 낡은 차를 길가에 내버렸다.

6. The _____ declared independence.
   그 식민지는 독립을 선언했다.

7. There were no _____ back then so his mother had to do everything by hand.
   그땐 설비가 하나도 없어서 그의 어머니는 손으로 모든 것을 다 해야 했어요.

8. _____ these desert slopes lies one of the longest, deepest and most surprising caves in the world.
   이 사막의 경사면 밑에는 세계에서 가장 길고, 깊고, 놀라운 동굴이 하나 있다.

9. What's the difference between the two _____ the price?
   가격이외에 그 둘 사이의 차이점은 무엇입니까?

10. The _____ connects the Atlantic with the Pacific.
    그 운하는 대서양과 태평양을 연결하고 있다.

11. The cook was _____ at his incredible appetite.
    요리사는 그의 엄청난 식욕에 놀랐다.

12. Why don't you lie on your back and sleep _____?
    바로 누워서 편하게 자는게 어때?

13. You've got to _____ high if you want to succeed.
    성공하려면 목표를 높이 잡아야 한다.

14. It is her job to _____ the various departments.
    다양한 부서들을 조정하는 것이 그녀의 일이다.

15. You can't do everything yourself so you must learn how to _____.
    너 혼자 모든 것을 다 할 수 없으니 위임하는 법을 배우도록 해.

16. His _____ behavior made many people laugh at him.
    그의 부조리한 행동은 모든 사람들이 그를 비웃게 만들었다.

17. I have not known that he is _____ from birth.
    나는 그가 태어날 때부터 벙어리라는 사실을 몰랐다.

18. I always read the baseball _____.
    나는 항상 야구 기사란을 읽는다.

Hint

| canal | absolutely | besides | aim | beneath | appliance | colony | astonish | delight |
| dump | comfortably | column | dumb | delegate | coordinate | absurd | correctly | ally |

Unit 25

Exercise

B. Fill in the word and meaning.

	Word	Meaning
01	comfortably	
02	absolutely	
03	beneath	
04	delegate	
05	absurd	
06	canal	
07	delight	
08	aim	
09	coordinate	
10	astonish	
11	colony	
12	dumb	
13	ally	
14	dump	
15	besides	
16	correctly	
17	appliance	
18	column	

	Meaning	Word
01	절대적으로, 완전히	
02	부조리한, 불합리한	
03	목표, 목적, 겨누다	
04	동맹국, 협력자	
05	기구, 장치, 설비	
06	놀라게 하다	
07	~의 밑(아래)에	
08	게다가, 그 밖에, ~외에도	
09	운하, 수로	
10	식민지, 집단	
11	(신문의)란, 기둥	
12	편안하게, 기분 좋게	
13	조정하다, 조화시키다	
14	정확히, 바르게	
15	위임하다, 대표자	
16	기쁨, 기쁨을 주는 것	
17	벙어리의, 말을 하지 않는	
18	(쓰레기를)내버리다, 내려뜨리다	

C. Listen, write the word and meaning. Track 75

	Word	Meaning		Word	Meaning
01			10		
02			11		
03			12		
04			13		
05			14		
06			15		
07			16		
08			17		
09			18		

Unit 26

🎧 Listen and repeat. Track 76

01 explode [iksplóud]
v 폭발시키다, 격발하다   to burst with a loud noise
A bomb **exploded** at London's railway station this morning.
폭탄 하나가 오늘 아침 런던 역에서 폭발했다.

02 explore [ikspló:r]
v 탐험하다, 탐구하다   to travel around a place, etc in order to learn about it
The scientist **explored** the bottom of the ocean with help of a hydroscope.
그 과학자는 수중안경의 도움으로 해저를 탐험했다.

03 firm [fə:rm]
a 굳은, 확고한   strong and steady or not likely to change
He gave me a **firm** handshake.
그는 나와 굳은 악수를 하였다.

04 flee [fli:]
v 달아나다, 도망치다   to run away or escape from something
Most of the nobility **fled** during the revolution.
혁명 중에 대부분의 귀족들이 도망쳤다.

05 frost [fro:st]
n 서리 / v 서리로 덮다   a thin layer of ice forms on the ground
Frost is possible at this time of year.
연중 이맘때면 서리가 올 수도 있다.

06 further [fə́:rðə:r]
ad 더욱이, 더 먼   more; to a greater distance in time or space
I felt it useless to say anything **further**.
나는 더 먼 이야기를 하는 것이 소용없다고 느꼈다.

07 guardian [gá:rdiən]
n 보호자, 후견인   a person who guards or protects
The police are the **guardians** of law and order.
경찰은 법과 질서의 보호자들이다.

08 halt [ho:lt]
n 정지 / v 정지하다   a stop
The elevator creaked to a **halt** at the second floor.
엘리베이터가 삐걱거리며 2층에서 정지했다.

09 iceberg [áisbə:rg]
n 빙산   a very large block of ice that floats in the sea
When the Titanic hit an **iceberg**, it carried enough lifeboats for about half of its approximately 2,200 passengers and crew.
타이타닉이 빙산에 충돌했을 때, 그 배의 약 2,200명의 승객과 승무원 중의 반 정도만을 위한 구명보트를 가지고 있었다.

---

key words
burst v 폭발하다 / hydroscope n 수중투시경 / nobility n 귀족계급
creak v 삐걱거리다 / approximately ad 대략, 거의

🎧 Listen and repeat. Track 77

10 immediately [imíːdiːtli]
ad 곧, 즉시   at once; without delay
Because I fell into a faint, I was **immediately** taken to a hospital.
내가 기절을 해서 즉시 병원으로 옮겨졌다.

11 indigenous [indídʒənəs]
a 토착의, 원산의   living or growing in the place where they are from originally
Tobacco is one of the **indigenous** plants which the early explorers found in this country.
담배는 초기 탐험가들이 이 나라에서 발견한 고유한 토착 식물 중의 하나다.

12 insist [insíst]
v 주장하다, 강력히 요구하다   to say strongly
I **insisted** that he should come with us.
나는 그가 우리와 함께 올 것을 강력히 요구했다.

13 instrument [ínstrəmənt]
n 기계, 기구, 도구   a tool that is used for doing a particular job
The men are carrying medical **instruments**.
남자들이 의료 기구들을 나르고 있습니다.

14 legislate [lédʒislèit]
v 법률을 제정하다   to make a law or laws
He promised to **legislate** against abortion but he couldn't do that.
그는 낙태를 금하는 법을 제정하겠다고 약속했지만 지키지 못했다.

15 liberal [líbərəl]
a 너그러운, 자유주의의   accepting different opinions or kinds of behavior
She's very **liberal** with her money but not her time.
그녀는 돈에 대해서는 매우 너그럽지만 시간에 대해서는 그렇지 않다.

16 manipulate [mənípjəlèit]
v 조작하다, (기계) 잘 다루다   to use, move or control something with skill
How do you **manipulate** these puppets?
당신은 이 꼭두각시 인형들을 어떻게 조작합니까?

17 monument [mánjəmənt]
n 기념비, 기념물   a statue that is built to remind people of a famous person or event
A beautiful **monument** was built to honor Abraham Lincoln.
아브라함 링컨을 기리기 위해 아름다운 기념비가 건립되었다.

18 mutual [mjúːtʃuəl]
a 서로의, 공동의   felt or done equally by both people involved
Our friendship has proved to be durable because it is based on **mutual** respect.
우리의 우정은 상호 간의 존경에 바탕을 두기 때문에 견고하다는 사실이 입증 되었다.

key words
faint **v** 기절하다 / abortion **n** 낙태, 유산 / puppet **n** 꼭두각시 / durable **a** 영속성이 있는, 오래 버티는

Unit 26 131

Exercise

A. Complete the sentence.

1. Most of the nobility _____ during the revolution.
   혁명 중에 대부분의 귀족들이 도망쳤다.
2. The scientist _____ the bottom of the ocean with help of a hydroscope.
   그 과학자는 수중안경의 도움으로 해저를 탐험했다.
3. How do you _____ these puppets?
   당신은 이 꼭두각시 인형들을 어떻게 조작합니까?
4. He gave me a _____ handshake.
   그는 나와 굳은 악수를 하였다.
5. A bomb _____ at London's railway station this morning.
   폭탄 하나가 오늘 아침 런던 역에서 폭발했다.
6. I felt it useless to say anything _____.
   나는 더 먼 이야기를 하는 것이 소용없다고 느꼈다.
7. The police are the _____ of law and order.
   경찰은 법과 질서의 보호자들이다.
8. A beautiful _____ was built to honor Abraham Lincoln.
   아브라함 링컨을 기리기 위해 아름다운 기념비가 건립되었다.
9. The elevator creaked to a _____ at the second floor.
   엘리베이터가 삐걱거리며 2층에서 정지했다.
10. When the Titanic hit an _____, it carried enough lifeboats for about half of its approximately 2,200 passengers and crew.
    타이타닉이 빙산에 충돌했을 때, 그 배의 약 2,200명의 승객과 승무원 중의 반 정도만을 위한 구명보트를 가지고 있었다.
11. _____ is possible at this time of year.
    연중 이맘때면 서리가 올 수도 있다.
12. Tobacco is one of the _____ plants which the early explorers found in this country.
    담배는 초기 탐험가들이 이 나라에서 발견한 고유한 토착 식물 중의 하나다.
13. I _____ that he should come with us.
    나는 그가 우리와 함께 올 것을 강력히 요구했다.
14. The men are carrying medical _____.
    남자들이 의료 기구들을 나르고 있습니다.
15. She's very _____ with her money but not her time.
    그녀는 돈에 대해서는 매우 너그럽지만 시간에 대해서는 그렇지 않다.
16. Because I fell into a faint, I was _____ taken to a hospital.
    내가 기절을 해서 즉시 병원으로 옮겨졌다.
17. Our friendship has proved to be durable because it is based on _____ respect.
    우리의 우정은 상호 간의 존경에 바탕을 두기 때문에 견고하다는 사실이 입증 되었다.
18. He promised to _____ against abortion but he couldn't do that.
    그는 낙태를 금하는 법을 제정하겠다고 약속했지만 지키지 못했다.

Hint

| guardian | frost | instrument | monument | halt | liberal | flee | explode | indigenous |
| iceberg | further | manipulate | immediately | firm | mutual | explore | insist | legislate |

Exercise

B. Fill in the word and meaning.

	Word	Meaning
01	further	
02	iceberg	
03	explode	
04	insist	
05	halt	
06	legislate	
07	explore	
08	manipulate	
09	immediately	
10	firm	
11	mutual	
12	instrument	
13	frost	
14	monument	
15	indigenous	
16	flee	
17	liberal	
18	guardian	

	Meaning	Word
01	폭발시키다, 격발하다	
02	탐험하다, 탐구하다	
03	굳은, 확고한	
04	달아나다, 도망치다	
05	서리, 서리로 덮다	
06	더욱이, 더 먼	
07	보호자, 후견인	
08	정지, 정지하다	
09	빙산	
10	곧, 즉시	
11	토착의, 원산의	
12	주장하다, 강력히 요구하다	
13	기계, 기구, 도구	
14	법률을 제정하다	
15	너그러운, 자유주의의	
16	조작하다, (기계) 잘 다루다	
17	기념비, 기념물	
18	서로의, 공동의	

🎧 **C. Listen, write the word and meaning.** (Track 78)

	Word	Meaning		Word	Meaning
01			10		
02			11		
03			12		
04			13		
05			14		
06			15		
07			16		
08			17		
09			18		

Review 13

A. Read and fill in the word and meaning.

word	definition	meaning
	not able to speak	
	completely; totally	
	throw something down; let something fall in a mass	
	to organize different things or people so that they work together	
	not at all logical or sensible	
	in a correct way	
	a country that is ruled by another, more powerful country	
	to give somebody with a lower job or position a task to do	
	something that you intend to do; a purpose	
	in addition to or as well as somebody/something	
	great pleasured; something that gives great pleasure	
	a deep cut that is made through land so that ships can travel	
	a country that has an agreement to support another country	
	in, at or to a lower position; under	
	to surprise somebody very much	
	one of the vertical sections into which a printed page is divided	
	a piece of equipment for a particular purpose in the house	
	physically relaxed; easily	

Hint

canal   absolutely   besides   aim   beneath   appliance   colony   astonish   delight
dump   comfortably   column   dumb   delegate   coordinate   absurd   correctly   ally

B. Read and fill in the word and meaning.

word	definition	meaning
	a thin layer of ice forms on the ground	
	a person who guards or protects	
	more; to a greater distance in time or space	
	to make a law or laws	
	to run away or escape from something	
	felt or done equally by both people involved	
	a tool that is used for doing a particular job	
	a stop	
	strong and steady or not likely to change	
	accepting different opinions or kinds of behavior	
	to say strongly	
	to travel around a place, etc in order to learn about it	
	a very large block of ice that floats in the sea	
	to use, move or control something with skill	
	at once; without delay	
	to burst with a loud noise	
	a statue that is built to remind people of a famous person or event	
	living or growing in the place where they are from originally	

Hint

guardian   frost   instrument   monument   halt   liberal   flee   explode   indigenous
iceberg   further   manipulate   immediately   firm   mutual   explore   insist   legislate

Unit 27

🎧 Listen and repeat. Track 79

01 nursery
[nə́ːrsəri]
n 육아실, 탁아소   place where babies are looked after
Her company runs its own workplace **nursery**.
그녀의 회사는 직장 내 육아실을 운영하고 있다.

02 nurture
[nə́ːrtʃəːr]
v 양육하다, 교육하다   to care a young child while it is growing and developing
My grandmother stayed at our home and **nurtured** me.
할머니는 우리 집에 계시면서 나를 길러 주셨다.

03 outlet
[áutlet]
n 배출구, 판매 대리점, 콘센트   a way of expressing strong feelings or energy
Like her mother, she found no **outlet** for her passion in the cold, severe New England society.
그녀의 어머니처럼 그녀 역시 춥고 모진 뉴잉글랜드의 사회에서 열정의 배출구를 찾지 못했다.

04 outstanding
[àutstǽndiŋ]
a 눈에 띄는, 현저한   extremely good; excellent
He is one of the most **outstanding** musicians of our time.
그는 우리 시대에서 가장 눈에 띄는 음악가 중 한 사람이다.

05 parcel
[páːrsəl]
n 소포 / v 꾸러미로 하다   something that is covered in brown paper and sent to somebody
How much will it cost to send this **parcel** to the U.S.?
이 소포를 미국에 보내는데 얼마가 듭니까?

06 patriotism
[péitriətizəm]
n 애국심   love for one's country and loyalty towards it
He knows the best way to impart a spirit of **patriotism** to young people.
그는 젊은이들에게 애국심을 전파하는 최선의 방법을 알고 있다.

07 pliable
[pláiəbəl]
a 유연한, 융통성이 있는   easy to influence
His **pliable** outlook on life seems to me a lack of responsibility.
그의 유연한 인생관은 내게 책임감의 부족으로 보인다.

08 poverty
[pávərti]
n 가난, 결핍   the state of being poor
When **poverty** comes in at door, love flies out of window.
가난이 문 안으로 들어서면, 애정은 창 밖으로 달아난다.

09 prairie
[préəri]
n 대초원, 목초지   a very large area of flat land covered in grass
Two species of large mammals once dominated the North American **prairies**.
두 종의 큰 포유동물들이 한때 북미의 대초원을 지배했었다.

key words
severe a 엄한, 모진 / impart v 전하다, 가르치다 / dominate v 지배하다

🎧 Listen and repeat. Track 80

10 preview [príːvjùː]
n 미리 보기, 시사회   a chance to see something before it is shown
The exhibition is a **preview** of what life may be like 20 years from now.
그 전시회는 지금부터 20년 후의 생활을 미리 보여준다.

11 primary [práiməri]
a 주요한, 본래의, 첫째의   most important; main
Language has **primary** purposes, expression and communication.
언어는 표현과 의사소통이라는 주요한 목적을 가지고 있다.

12 prohibit [prouhíbit]
v 금지하다, 방해하다   to say that something is not allowed by law
The bill would **prohibit** any activities in human cloning.
이 법안에 따르면 인간 복제와 관련된 어떠한 행동도 금지된다.

13 pronunciation [prənʌ̀nsiéiʃən]
n 발음, 발음표기   the way in which a language or sound is said
I practice **pronunciation** with a tape recorder.
나는 녹음기를 가지고 발음을 연습한다.

14 radical [rǽdikəl]
a 근본적인, 근본의   basic; of or from a roots
My theme is about the possibility of a **radical** reform of industrial society.
나의 주제는 산업사회의 근본적인 개혁의 가능성에 대한 것이다.

15 random [rǽndəm]
a 임의의, 되는 대로   chosen by chance
She started reading a magazine here and there at **random**.
그녀는 잡지를 여기저기 닥치는 대로 읽기 시작했다.

16 relay [ríːlei]
v 전달하다, 중계하다   to receive and then pass on a signal or message
I'll leave it with my secretary, and she'll **relay** it to you.
제가 비서한테 그것을 맡기면 그녀가 당신에게 전달할 것이다.

17 residence [rézidəns]
n 거주, 주거   the state of having home in a particular place
All citizens shall enjoy freedom of **residence** and movement.
모든 국민은 거주와 이전의 자유를 누립니다.

18 resist [rizíst]
v 견디다, 저항하다   to try to stop something happening
He was so childish that he couldn't **resist** temptation.
그는 너무 어린애 같아서 유혹을 견딜 수 없었다.

key words
bill n 법안 / reform n 개혁, 개정 / signal n 신호 / childish a 어린이 같은 / temptation n 유혹

Unit 27 137

Exercise

A. Complete the sentence.

1. He was so childish that he couldn't _____ temptation.
   그는 너무 어린애 같아서 유혹을 견딜 수 없었다.

2. Her company runs its own workplace _____.
   그녀의 회사는 직장 내 육아실을 운영하고 있다.

3. Language has _____ purposes, expression and communication.
   언어는 표현과 의사소통이라는 주요한 목적을 가지고 있다.

4. Like her mother, she found no _____ for her passion in the cold, severe New England society.
   그녀의 어머니처럼 그녀 역시 춥고 모진 뉴잉글랜드의 사회에서 열정의 배출구를 찾지 못했다.

5. How much will it cost to send this _____ to the U.S.?
   이 소포를 미국에 보내는데 얼마가 듭니까?

6. I'll leave it with my secretary, and she'll _____ it to you.
   제가 비서한테 그것을 맡기면 그녀가 당신에게 전달할 것이다.

7. Two species of large mammals once dominated the North American _____.
   두 종의 큰 포유동물들이 한때 북미의 대초원을 지배했었다.

8. He knows the best way to impart a spirit of _____ to young people.
   그는 젊은이들에게 애국심을 전파하는 최선의 방법을 알고 있다.

9. My grandmother stayed at our home and _____ me.
   할머니는 우리 집에 계시면서 나를 길러 주셨다.

10. The exhibition is a _____ of what life may be like 20 years from now.
    그 전시회는 지금부터 20년 후의 생활을 미리 보여준다.

11. The bill would _____ any activities in human cloning.
    이 법안에 따르면 인간 복제와 관련된 어떠한 행동도 금지된다.

12. I practice _____ with a tape recorder.
    나는 녹음기를 가지고 발음을 연습한다.

13. My theme is about the possibility of a _____ reform of industrial society.
    나의 주제는 산업사회의 근본적인 개혁의 가능성에 대한 것이다.

14. He is one of the most _____ musicians of our time.
    그는 우리 시대에서 가장 눈에 띄는 음악가 중 한 사람이다.

15. She started reading a magazine here and there at _____.
    그녀는 잡지를 여기저기 닥치는 대로 읽기 시작했다.

16. When _____ comes in at door, love flies out of window.
    가난이 문 안으로 들어서면, 애정은 창 밖으로 달아난다.

17. All citizens shall enjoy freedom of _____ and movement.
    모든 국민은 거주와 이전의 자유를 누립니다.

18. His _____ outlook on life seems to me a lack of responsibility.
    그의 유연한 인생관은 내게 책임감의 부족으로 보인다.

Hint

| outstanding | prairie | relay | primary | radical | random | outlet | poverty | pronunciation |
| residence | nurture | pliable | nursery | parcel | patriotism | prohibit | resist | preview |

Exercise

B. Fill in the word and meaning.

	Word	Meaning
01	patriotism	
02	prohibit	
03	nursery	
04	poverty	
05	radical	
06	nurture	
07	prairie	
08	relay	
09	outlet	
10	primary	
11	preview	
12	residence	
13	outstanding	
14	pronunciation	
15	pliable	
16	resist	
17	parcel	
18	random	

	Meaning	Word
01	육아실, 탁아소	
02	양육하다, 교육하다	
03	배출구, 판매 대리점, 콘센트	
04	눈에 띄는, 현저한	
05	소포, 꾸러미로 하다	
06	애국심	
07	유연한, 융통성이 있는	
08	가난, 결핍	
09	대초원, 목초지	
10	미리 보기, 시사회	
11	주요한, 본래의, 첫째의	
12	금지하다, 방해하다	
13	발음, 발음표기	
14	근본적인, 근본의	
15	임의의, 되는 대로	
16	전달하다, 중계하다	
17	거주, 주거	
18	견디다, 저항하다	

🎧 **C. Listen, write the word and meaning.** (Track 81)

	Word	Meaning		Word	Meaning
01			10		
02			11		
03			12		
04			13		
05			14		
06			15		
07			16		
08			17		
09			18		

Unit 28

🎧 Listen and repeat. Track 82

01 roar [rɔːr]
v 으르렁거리다, 울부짖다   to make a loud, deep sound
The boys held their breath at the **roaring** of a lion.
그 소년들은 사자의 으르렁거리는 소리에 숨을 죽였다.

02 sacrifice [sǽkrəfàis]
n 희생 / v 희생하다   giving up something important
He sees her act not as a **sacrifice** but as a betrayal.
그는 그녀의 행위를 희생이 아니라 배신으로 여긴다.

03 servant [sə́ːrvənt]
n 하인, 봉사자   a person who is paid to work in somebody's house
He showed no mercy to his **servants**.
그는 자기 하인들에게 자비를 전혀 베풀지 않았다.

04 settle [sétl]
v 결정하다, 이주하다   to decide or arrange something finally
When everything is **settled**, I'll give you a call.
모든 것이 결정이 되면 전화를 할 것이다.

05 sniff [snif]
v 냄새 맡다   to smell something
She **sniffed** the perfume, and then bought it.
그녀는 향수의 냄새 맡고 나서 그것을 샀다.

06 sob [sab]
v 흐느껴 울다 / n 흐느낌   to cry while taking in sudden, sharp breaths
Someone kept **sobbing** throughout the whole movie.
누군가가 영화를 보는 내내 흐느껴 울었다.

07 splash [splæʃ]
v 튀기다, 첨벙거리다   to make liquid fall fly drops onto a person or thing
That taxi **splashed** muddy water on my new clothes.
저 택시가 새 옷에 흙탕물을 튀겼다.

08 spot [spat]
n 장소, 반점 / v 더럽히다   a particular place or area
I'd like to see historic **spots** like palaces, temples and shrines.
고궁이나 사원, 성지 같은 역사적인 장소를 구경하고 싶다.

09 struggle [strʌ́gəl]
v 투쟁하다, 애쓰다   to fight in order to prevent or escape from something
Women are **struggling** for their economic, social, and sexual liberation.
여성들은 그들의 경제적, 사회적, 성적 자유를 위해 투쟁하고 있다.

---

key words
betrayal n 배신, 배반 / mercy n 자비 / shrine n 성지, 성당 / liberation n 해방

🎧 Listen and repeat. (Track 83)

10 superb [suːpə́ːrb]
a 뛰어난, 멋진   extremely good; excellent
The **superb** bird of paradise calls to attract a female.
멋진 극락조가 암컷을 유혹하는 노래를 부른다.

11 tempt [tempt]
v 유혹하다, 꾀다   to try to persuade or attract somebody to do something
They tried to **tempt** her with offers of promotion.
그들은 승진시켜 주겠다는 제의를 하며 그녀를 유혹하려고 애썼다.

12 tense [tens]
a 긴장한 / **n** 시제   tight; not relaxed
It's from being too **tense** while talking with buyer.
바이어와 상담을 하느라고 너무 긴장해서 그래요.

13 triumph [tráiəmf]
n 승리 / **v** 승리하다   a great success or victory
His rival was discouraged by his **triumph**.
그의 승리에 경쟁 상대는 낙담했다.

14 ultimate [ʌ́ltəmit]
a 최후의, 궁극적인   being at the end; last or final
The **ultimate** goal of the United Nations is to achieve a lasting peace among all nations.
국제 연합의 궁극적인 목표는 모든 국가들 사이에 영구적인 평화를 이룩하는 것이다.

15 vague [veig]
a 막연한, 모호한, 희미한   not clear or definite
She felt a sudden **vague** malaise when she heard sounds at the door.
문간에서 소리를 들었을 때 그녀는 갑작스럽게 막연한 불쾌감을 느꼈다.

16 vain [vein]
a 헛된, 허영심이 강한   useless; failing to produce the result you want
People tried in **vain** to prevent flu from spreading.
사람들이 유행성 감기의 확산을 막으려고 했으나 그 노력은 헛되어 버렸다.

17 voyage [vɔ́idʒ]
n 여행, 항해 / **v** 여행하다   a long journey by sea or in space
The crew prepared for the **voyage** to outer space.
승무원들은 우주를 향한 항해 준비를 했다.

18 whisker [hwískəːr]
n 구레나룻   one of the long thick hairs that grow near the mouth
She cuts the **whiskers** of her husband every night.
그녀는 매일 밤마다 남편의 구레나룻을 깎아 준다.

key words
paradise **n** 극락, 지상 낙원 / malaise **n** 불쾌(감) / flu **n** 유행성 감기

Unit 28

Exercise

A. Complete the sentence.

1. His rival was discouraged by his _____.
   그의 승리에 경쟁 상대는 낙담했다.

2. She _____ the perfume, and then bought it.
   그녀는 향수의 냄새 맡고 나서 그것을 샀다.

3. The crew prepared for the _____ to outer space.
   승무원들은 우주를 향한 항해 준비를 했다.

4. He showed no mercy to his _____.
   그는 자기 하인들에게 자비를 전혀 베풀지 않았다.

5. That taxi _____ muddy water on my new clothes.
   저 택시가 새 옷에 흙탕물을 튀겼다.

6. The _____ goal of the United Nations is to achieve a lasting peace among all nations.
   국제 연합의 궁극적인 목표는 모든 국가들 사이에 영구적인 평화를 이룩하는 것이다.

7. I'd like to see historic _____ like palaces, temples and shrines.
   고궁이나 사원, 성지 같은 역사적인 장소를 구경하고 싶다.

8. The boys held their breath at the _____ of a lion.
   그 소년들은 사자의 으르렁거리는 소리에 숨을 죽였다.

9. Women are _____ for their economic, social, and sexual liberation.
   여성들은 그들의 경제적, 사회적, 성적 자유를 위해 투쟁하고 있다.

10. They tried to _____ her with offers of promotion.
    그들은 승진시켜 주겠다는 제의를 하며 그녀를 유혹하려고 애썼다.

11. It's from being too _____ while talking with buyer.
    바이어와 상담을 하느라고 너무 긴장해서 그래요.

12. He sees her act not as a _____ but as a betrayal.
    그는 그녀의 행위를 희생이 아니라 배신으로 여긴다.

13. She felt a sudden _____ malaise when she heard sounds at the door.
    문간에서 소리를 들었을 때 그녀는 갑작스럽게 막연한 불쾌감을 느꼈다.

14. Someone kept _____ throughout the whole movie.
    누군가가 영화를 보는 내내 흐느껴 울었다.

15. People tried in _____ to prevent flu from spreading.
    사람들이 유행성 감기의 확산을 막으려고 했으나 그 노력은 헛되어 버렸다.

16. When everything is _____, I'll give you a call.
    모든 것이 결정이 되면 전화를 할 것이다.

17. The _____ bird of paradise calls to attract a female.
    멋진 극락조가 암컷을 유혹하는 노래를 부른다.

18. She cuts the _____ of her husband every night.
    그녀는 매일 밤마다 남편의 구레나룻을 깎아 준다.

Hint

| servant | struggle | voyage | spot | sob | triumph | settle | superb | vague |
| whisker | tense | sacrifice | tempt | vain | splash | roar | ultimate | sniff |

Unit 28

Exercise

B. Fill in the word and meaning.

	Word	Meaning
01	sacrifice	
02	triumph	
03	struggle	
04	roar	
05	spot	
06	vain	
07	servant	
08	vague	
09	tense	
10	sob	
11	voyage	
12	settle	
13	whisker	
14	ultimate	
15	splash	
16	tempt	
17	sniff	
18	superb	

	Meaning	Word
01	으르렁거리다, 울부짖다	
02	희생, 희생하다	
03	하인, 봉사자	
04	이주하다, 결정하다	
05	냄새 맡다	
06	흐느껴 울다, 흐느낌	
07	튀기다, 첨벙거리다	
08	장소, 반점, 더럽히다	
09	투쟁하다, 애쓰다	
10	뛰어난, 멋진	
11	유혹하다, 꾀다	
12	긴장한, 시제	
13	승리, 승리하다	
14	최후의, 궁극적인	
15	막연한, 모호한, 희미한	
16	헛된, 허영심이 강한	
17	여행, 항해, 여행하다	
18	구레나룻	

C. Listen, write the word and meaning. (Track 84)

	Word	Meaning		Word	Meaning
01			10		
02			11		
03			12		
04			13		
05			14		
06			15		
07			16		
08			17		
09			18		

Review 14

A. Read and fill in the word and meaning.

word	definition	meaning
	the state of being poor	
	to care a young child while it is growing and developing	
	the state of having home in a particular place	
	a very large area of flat land covered in grass	
	place where babies are looked after	
	to try to stop something happening	
	a chance to see something before it is shown	
	to receive and then pass on a signal or message	
	a way of expressing strong feelings or energy	
	basic; of or from a roots	
	the way in which a language or sound is said	
	most important; main	
	love for one's country and loyalty towards it	
	extremely good; excellent	
	easy to influence	
	chosen by chance	
	something that is covered in brown paper and sent to somebody	
	to say that something is not allowed by law	

Hint

outstanding   prairie   relay   primary   radical   random   outlet   poverty   pronunciation
residence   nurture   pliable   nursery   parcel   patriotism   prohibit   resist   preview

B. Read and fill in the word and meaning.

word	definition	meaning
struggle	to fight in order to prevent or escape from something	
sob	to cry while taking in sudden, sharp breaths	
sacrifice	giving up something important	
whisker	one of the long thick hairs that grow near the mouth	
superb	extremely good; excellent	
roar	to make a loud, deep sound	
spot	a particular place or area	
voyage	a long journey by sea or in space	
sniff	to smell something	
ultimate	being at the end; last or final	
splash	to make liquid fall fly drops onto a person or thing	
vague	not clear or definite	
tense	tight; not relaxed	
tempt	to try to persuade or attract somebody to do something	
vain	useless; failing to produce the result you want	
settle	to decide or arrange something finally	
triumph	a great success or victory	
servant	a person who is paid to work in somebody's house	

Hint

servant   struggle   voyage   spot   sob   triumph   settle   superb   vague
whisker   tense   sacrifice   tempt   vain   splash   roar   ultimate   sniff

Review 14

Unit 29

🎧 Listen and repeat. (Track 85)

01 abuse [əbjúːz]
v 학대하다, 남용하다 — to treat somebody badly
Several of the children had been physically **abused**.
그 아이들 중 몇 명은 신체적 학대를 받았었다.

02 accent [ǽksent]
n 강세, 강조 — the particular importance that is given to something
The belt of her dress gives an **accent** to the outfit.
그녀 드레스의 벨트가 의상을 강조한다.

03 amazing [əméiziŋ]
a 놀랄 만한, 굉장한 — very surprising and difficult to believe
Do you know what an **amazing** gift that is?
당신은 그것이 얼마나 놀랄 만한 선물인지 아는가?

04 analyze [ǽnəlàiz]
v 분석하다, 분해하다 — to think about the details of something carefully
The left brain **analyzes** the parts while the right brain looks at the whole.
왼쪽 뇌가 부분을 분석하는 반면에 오른쪽 뇌는 전체를 본다.

05 attempt [ətémpt]
v 시도하다 / **n** 시도 — to try to do something that is difficult
She was charged with **attempting** to bribe a policeman.
그녀는 경찰관에게 뇌물을 주려고 시도한 혐의로 고발되었다.

06 attendant [əténdənt]
n 시중드는 사람, 참석자 — a person whose job is to serve people
If your head still aches, shall I call a flight **attendant** and ask for some aspirin?
머리가 계속 아프면 승무원을 불러 아스피린 좀 달라고 할까?

07 beyond [bijánd]
prep ~의 저편에, ~을 넘어서 — used to say that something is not possible
We knew we'd won a prize but winning first prize was **beyond** all our expectations.
우리가 상을 타리라는 것은 알고 있었지만 1등 상을 탄 것은 기대를 넘어선 것이었다.

08 biography [baiágrəfi]
n 전기, 일대기 — the story of a person's life written by somebody else
The relationship of **biography** and history is clear.
전기와 역사의 관계는 분명하다.

09 carve [kaːrv]
v 새기다, 조각하다 — to cut wood or stone to make an object
The faces of four Presidents are **carved** into Mount Rushmore.
Rushmore 산에 4명의 대통령 얼굴이 새겨져 있다.

---

key words
charge **v** 고발하다 / bribe **v** 뇌물을 주다 / expectation **n** 기대, 예상

🎧 Listen and repeat. Track 86

10 cemetery [sémətèri]
n 묘지   a place where dead people are buried
We visit the National **Cemetery** on Memorial Day every year.
우리는 매년 현충일마다 국립묘지에 간다.

11 communicate [kəmjúːnəkèit]
v 의사소통하다, 전달하다   give or exchange messages talking, writing, etc.
I feel frustrated because I can't **communicate** well with my American clients.
미국인 고객들과 의사소통을 할 수 없어서 답답하다.

12 comparison [kəmpǽrisən]
n 비교, 유사   an act of comparing
It's **comparison** that makes men happy or miserable.
행복과 불행은 비교에서 시작된다.

13 costume [kάstjuːm]
n 복장, 의상   a set or style of clothes worn by people
Because of his **costume**, he was denied entrance into the dining room.
그는 복장 때문에 식당에 입장하는 것을 거부당했다.

14 crew [kruː]
n 승무원   all the people who work on a ship, aircraft, etc
The lifeboat ferried the **crew** and passengers to safety.
구명보트는 승무원과 승객들을 안전한 곳으로 운반했다.

15 deserve [dizə́ːrv]
v 받을 가치가 있다, ~할 만하다   to earn something because of something that you have done
On holidays and birthdays, they **deserve** separate gifts, cards and recognition.
명절이나 생일에 그들은 각각 선물, 카드 그리고 인사를 받을 만하다.

16 desire [dizáiər]
n 바램, 소망   the feeling of wanting something very much
Because she felt no **desire** to marry, she refused his proposal.
그녀는 결혼하고 싶은 소망이 없었기 때문에 그의 청혼을 거절했다.

17 elaborate [ilǽbərèit]
a 정교한 / **v** 공들여 만들다   very complicated
A more thorough coverage would call for a far more **elaborate** curriculum as well as time.
더 자세한 내용을 다루고자 할 경우에는 훨씬 더 많은 시간과 정교한 커리큘럼이 필요할 것이다.

18 election [ilékʃən]
n 선거, 투표   choosing a member of parliament, president, etc by voting
The government announced the date of the next **election**.
정부는 다음 선거의 날짜를 발표했다.

key words
deny **v** 부인하다 / ferry **v** (사람 등을) 나르다 / recognition **n** 인사 / coverage **n** 범위
announce **v** 발표하다, 공고하다

Exercise

A. Complete the sentence.

1. A more thorough coverage would call for a far more _____ curriculum as well as time.
   더 자세한 내용을 다루고자 할 경우에는 훨씬 더 많은 시간과 정교한 커리큘럼이 필요할 것이다.

2. We knew we'd won a prize but winning first prize was _____ all our expectations.
   우리가 상을 타리라는 것은 알고 있었지만 1등 상을 탄 것은 기대를 넘어선 것이었다.

3. Do you know what an _____ gift that is?
   당신은 그것이 얼마나 놀랄 만한 선물인지 아는가?

4. The relationship of _____ and history is clear.
   전기와 역사의 관계는 분명하다.

5. The left brain _____ the parts while the right brain looks at the whole.
   왼쪽 뇌가 부분을 분석하는 반면에 오른쪽 뇌는 전체를 본다.

6. If your head still aches, shall I call a flight _____ and ask for some aspirin?
   머리가 계속 아프면 승무원을 불러 아스피린 좀 달라고 할까?

7. The faces of four Presidents are _____ into Mount Rushmore.
   Rushmore 산에 4명의 대통령 얼굴이 새겨져 있다.

8. Several of the children had been physically _____.
   그 아이들 중 몇 명은 신체적 학대를 받았었다.

9. We visit the National _____ on Memorial Day every year.
   우리는 매년 현충일마다 국립묘지에 간다.

10. She was charged with _____ to bribe a policeman.
    그녀는 경찰관에게 뇌물을 주려고 시도한 혐의로 고발되었다.

11. The belt of her dress gives an _____ to the outfit.
    그녀 드레스의 벨트가 의상을 강조한다.

12. It's _____ that makes men happy or miserable.
    행복과 불행은 비교에서 시작된다.

13. Because of his _____, he was denied entrance into the dining room.
    그는 복장 때문에 식당에 입장하는 것을 거부당했다.

14. The lifeboat ferried the _____ and passengers to safety.
    구명보트는 승무원과 승객들을 안전한 곳으로 운반했다.

15. On holidays and birthdays, they _____ separate gifts, cards and recognition.
    명절이나 생일에 그들은 각각 선물, 카드 그리고 인사를 받을 만하다.

16. I feel frustrated because I can't _____ well with my American clients.
    미국인 고객들과 의사소통을 할 수 없어서 답답하다.

17. Because she felt no _____ to marry, she refused his proposal.
    그녀는 결혼하고 싶은 소망이 없었기 때문에 그의 청혼을 거절했다.

18. The government announced the date of the next _____.
    정부는 다음 선거의 날짜를 발표했다.

Hint

elaborate   abuse   election   analyze   crew   amazing   cemetery   beyond   communicate
attendant   desire   deserve   costume   accent   biography   attempt   carve   comparison

Exercise

B. Fill in the word and meaning.

	Word	Meaning
01	deserve	
02	carve	
03	abuse	
04	crew	
05	attendant	
06	comparison	
07	accent	
08	cemetery	
09	elaborate	
10	attempt	
11	election	
12	amazing	
13	desire	
14	biography	
15	costume	
16	analyze	
17	beyond	
18	communicate	

	Meaning	Word
01	학대하다, 남용하다	
02	강세, 강조	
03	놀랄 만한, 굉장한	
04	분석하다, 분해하다	
05	시도하다, 시도	
06	시중드는 사람, 참석자	
07	~의 저편에, ~을 넘어서	
08	전기, 일대기	
09	새기다, 조각하다	
10	묘지	
11	의사소통하다, 전달하다	
12	비교, 유사	
13	복장, 의상	
14	승무원	
15	받을 가치가 있다, ~할 만하다	
16	바램, 소망	
17	정교한, 공들여 만들다	
18	선거, 투표	

C. Listen, write the word and meaning. Track 87

	Word	Meaning		Word	Meaning
01			10		
02			11		
03			12		
04			13		
05			14		
06			15		
07			16		
08			17		
09			18		

Unit 29

Unit 30

🎧 Listen and repeat.   Track 88

01 extract   v 추출하다, 뽑다   obtain by boiling, pressing ; pull out or take out something
[ekstrǽkt]
They boiled or crushed the grapes to **extract** their juice.
그들은 즙을 추출하기 위해 포도를 삶거나 으깼다.

02 extracurricular   a 과외의, 정식 과목이외   not part of the normal course of studies
[èkstrəkəríkjələr]
We hope to vitalize our **extracurricular** program by introducing many new activities.
우리는 많은 새로운 활동을 도입함으로써 우리의 과외활동 계획을 활성화하기를 희망한다.

03 fluent   a 유창한, 능변의   able to speak or write a foreign language easily
[flúːənt]
The linguist is **fluent** in several Chinese dialects.
그 언어학자는 여러 가지 중국어 사투리를 유창하게 구사한다.

04 foremost   a 최고의, 맨 처음의   most famous or important; best
[fɔ́ːrmòust]
Did you know that Benjamin Franklin was one of the **foremost** inventors of the eighteenth century?
벤자민 프랭클린이 18세기 최고의 발명가 중 한 사람이라는 사실을 알았니?

05 garment   n 의류, 옷가지   one piece of clothing
[gáːrmənt]
She always discarded all **garments** which were no longer modish.
그녀는 더 이상 유행하지 않는 옷들은 항상 갖다 버렸다.

06 gay   a 명랑한, 화려한   happy and full of fun
[gei]
To think that only yesterday I was cheerful bright and **gay**.
바로 어제까지만 하더라도 나는 무척 즐겁고 밝고 명랑했었다.

07 hardship   n 고난, 역경   the fact of not having enough money, food, etc
[háːrdʃip]
There will always be someone who benefits from **hardship**.
고난 속에서도 이득을 보는 사람이 있기 마련이다.

08 immigrant   n 이민자 / a 이주하는   a person who has come into a foreign country to live there
[ímigrənt]
The United States consists of many different **immigrant** groups.
미국은 여러 다른 이민자의 그룹으로 구성되어 있다.

09 import   v 수입하다, ~의 뜻을 내포하다   bring in goods or services from another country; mean
[impɔ́ːrt]
This is **imported** from China and is currently out of stock.
이것은 중국에서 수입하는 것인데, 현재 재고가 하나도 없다.

---

key words
crush v 눌러 부수다 / vitalize v 활력을 주다 / linguist n 언어학자 / dialect n 사투리
modish a 유행을 따르는 / stock n 재고품

🎧 Listen and repeat. Track 89

10 intelligent [intélədʒənt]
a 이해력 있는, 지적인, 총명한 — having the ability to understand, learn and think
Not only are whales among the largest animals, but they are also among the most **intelligent**.
고래는 가장 큰 동물 중에 속할 뿐만 아니라, 가장 총명한 동물 중에도 속한다.

11 interfere [ìntərfíər]
v 간섭하다, 방해하다 — to prevent something from succeeding
Alcoholism **interferes** with an individual's health and work behavior.
알코올 중독은 개인의 건강과 직장생활을 방해한다.

12 intimate [íntəmit]
a 친밀한, 깊은 — having a very close relationship
Two women seldom grow **intimate** but at the expense of a third person.
제3자의 희생이 없이는 여자 둘이 친밀해지는 법은 거의 없다.

13 likewise [láikwàiz]
ad 마찬가지로, 똑같이 — the same; in a similar way
Likewise, goods made in Korea and sold overseas bring money into Korea.
마찬가지로, 한국에서 만들어져 해외에서 팔리는 상품들은 한국에 돈을 가져다 준다.

14 literature [lítərətʃər]
n 문학, 문헌 — writing that is considered to be a work of art including novels and poetry
You can't fully appreciate foreign **literature** in translation.
번역으로는 외국 문학을 제대로 감상할 수 없다.

15 mandatory [mǽndətɔ̀:ri]
a 명령의, 강제의 — that you must do, have, obey, etc
They can do a **mandatory** drug test wherever there has been an accident.
그들은 사건 현장이라면 어디에서든 강제로 마약검사를 할 수 있다.

16 minority [minɔ́:rəti]
n 소수, 소수파 — the smaller number or part of a group
Ethnic **minorities** struggle against prejudice, poverty and so on.
소수 민족들은 편견과 빈곤 등의 문제와 싸우고 있다.

17 myth [miθ]
n 신화, 전설 — a story from past time, especially one about gods and men of courage
The **myth** offers insights into the ancient civilization.
신화는 고대 문명에 대한 통찰력을 제공한다.

18 needy [ní:di]
a 매우 가난한 — not having enough money, food, clothes, etc
They helped **needy** people by the provision of food, clothing and shelter.
그들은 의식주를 제공하여 매우 가난한 사람들을 도왔다.

---

key words
alcoholism **n** 알코올 중독(증) / translatione **n** 번역 / ethnic **a** 민족의
prejudice **n** 편견, 선입관 / provision **n** 공급, 제공

Exercise

A. Complete the sentence.

1. They boiled or crushed the grapes to _____ their juice.
   그들은 즙을 추출하기 위해 포도를 삶거나 으깬다.
2. Alcoholism _____ with an individual's health and work behavior.
   알코올 중독은 개인의 건강과 직장생활을 방해한다.
3. To think that only yesterday I was cheerful bright and _____.
   바로 어제까지만 하더라도 나는 무척 즐겁고 밝고 명랑했었다.
4. The linguist is _____ in several Chinese dialects.
   그 언어학자는 여러 가지 중국어 사투리를 유창하게 구사한다.
5. Two women seldom grow _____ but at the expense of a third person.
   제3자의 희생이 없이는 여자 둘이 친밀해지는 법은 거의 없다.
6. We hope to vitalize our _____ program by introducing many new activities.
   우리는 많은 새로운 활동을 도입함으로써 우리의 과외활동 계획을 활성화하기를 희망한다.
7. Did you know that Benjamin Franklin was one of the _____ inventors of the eighteenth century?
   벤자민 프랭클린이 18세기 최고의 발명가 중 한 사람이라는 사실을 알았었나?
8. The United States consists of many different _____ groups.
   미국은 여러 다른 이민자의 그룹으로 구성되어 있다.
9. She always discarded all _____ which were no longer modish.
   그녀는 더 이상 유행하지 않는 옷들은 항상 갖다 버렸다.
10. There will always be someone who benefits from _____.
    고난 속에서도 이득을 보는 사람이 있기 마련이다.
11. This is _____ from China and is currently out of stock.
    이것은 중국에서 수입하는 것인데, 현재 재고가 하나도 없다.
12. Ethnic _____ struggle against prejudice, poverty and so on.
    소수 민족들은 편견과 빈곤 등의 문제와 싸우고 있다.
13. You can't fully appreciate foreign _____ in translation.
    번역으로는 외국 문학을 제대로 감상할 수 없다.
14. The _____ offers insights into the ancient civilization.
    신화는 고대 문명에 대한 통찰력을 제공한다.
15. Not only are whales among the largest animals, but they are also among the most _____.
    고래는 가장 큰 동물 중에 속할 뿐만 아니라, 가장 총명한 동물 중에도 속한다.
16. _____, goods made in Korea and sold overseas bring money into Korea.
    마찬가지로, 한국에서 만들어져 해외에서 팔리는 상품들은 한국에 돈을 가져다 준다.
17. They helped _____ people by the provision of food, clothing and shelter.
    그들은 의식주를 제공하여 매우 가난한 사람들을 도왔다.
18. They can do a _____ drug test wherever there has been an accident.
    그들은 사건 현장이라면 어디에서든 강제로 마약검사를 할 수 있다.

Hint

literature   intimate   fluent   extract   import   myth   garment   mandatory   extracurricular
immigrant   hardship   needy   minority   likewise   gay   foremost   interfere   intelligent

Exercise

B. Fill in the word and meaning.

	Word	Meaning
01	import	
02	likewise	
03	extract	
04	fluent	
05	interfere	
06	extracurricular	
07	myth	
08	hardship	
09	needy	
10	intelligent	
11	garment	
12	literature	
13	intimate	
14	foremost	
15	mandatory	
16	immigrant	
17	minority	
18	gay	

	Meaning	Word
01	추출하다, 뽑다	
02	과외의, 정식 과목이외	
03	유창한, 능변의	
04	최고의, 맨 처음의	
05	의류, 옷가지	
06	명랑한, 화려한	
07	고난, 역경	
08	이민자, 이주하는	
09	수입하다, ~의 뜻을 내포하다	
10	이해력 있는, 지적인, 총명한	
11	간섭하다, 방해하다	
12	친밀한, 깊은	
13	마찬가지로, 똑같이	
14	문학, 문헌	
15	명령의, 강제의	
16	소수, 소수파	
17	신화, 전설	
18	매우 가난한	

C. Listen, write the word and meaning. (Track 90)

	Word	Meaning		Word	Meaning
01			10		
02			11		
03			12		
04			13		
05			14		
06			15		
07			16		
08			17		
09			18		

Review 15

A. Read and fill in the word and meaning.

word	definition	meaning
	to cut wood or stone to make an object	
	very complicated	
	to treat somebody badly	
	the story of a person's life written by somebody else	
	a place where dead people are buried	
	the feeling of wanting something very much	
	the particular importance that is given to something	
	choosing a member of parliament, president, etc by voting	
	give or exchange messages talking, writing, etc.	
	very surprising and difficult to believe	
	used to say that something is not possible	
	to earn something because of something that you have done	
	to try to do something that is difficult	
	an act of comparing	
	to think about the details of something carefully	
	a set or style of clothes worn by people	
	a person whose job is to serve people	
	all the people who work on a ship, aircraft, etc	

Hint

elaborate abuse election analyze crew amazing cemetery beyond communicate
attendant desire deserve costume accent biography attempt carve comparison

B. Read and fill in the word and meaning.

word	definition	meaning
	to prevent something from succeeding	
	obtain by boiling, pressing ; pull out or take out something	
	not having enough money, food, clothes, etc	
	having a very close relationship	
	the fact of not having enough money, food, etc	
	having the ability to understand, learn and think	
	the same; in a similar way	
	not part of the normal course of studies	
	the smaller number or part of a group	
	happy and full of fun	
	a story from past time, especially one about gods and men of courage	
	a person who has come into a foreign country to live there	
	writing that is considered to be a work of art including novels and poetry	
	able to speak or write a foreign language easily	
	one piece of clothing	
	bring in goods or services from another country; mean	
	that you must do, have, obey, etc	
	most famous or important; best	

Hint
literature   intimate   fluent   extract   import   myth   garment   mandatory   extracurricular
immigrant   hardship   needy   minority   likewise   gay   foremost   interfere   intelligent

Review 15

Unit 31

🎧 Listen and repeat. Track 91

01 nutrition [njuːtríʃən]
n 영양(분), 영양 공급   the food that affects your health when you eat
The body requires proper **nutrition** in order to maintain it.
신체는 몸을 유지하는데 필요한 알맞은 영양분을 요구한다.

02 oath [ouθ]
n 맹세, 선서   a formal promise
The Student **Oath** teaches students discipline and awareness.
학생 선서는 학생들에게 규율과 자각을 가르친다.

03 overall [óuvərɔ̀ːl]
ad 전체적으로 / a 전체의   including everything; generally
Overall, she learns well from her teachers and is happy with her studies.
전체적으로 그녀는 선생님들한테서 잘 배우고 있으며 공부과목들에 만족하고 있다.

04 overhear [óuvərhìər]
v 엿듣다, 우연히 듣다   to hear what somebody is saying by accident
One of the experienced lawyers **overheard** and stopped to offer his support.
경험 있는 변호사 중 한 명이 우연히 듣고 도움을 주기 위해 멈춰 섰다.

05 pessimistic [pèsəmístik]
a 비관적인, 염세적인   a person who always thinks that bad things will happen
I'm sure you have the picture by now that I'm a rather **pessimistic**.
분명 이 정도면 당신은 내가 다소 비관적이라는 생각을 가질 것이다.

06 petal [pétl]
n 꽃잎   one of the thin soft coloured parts of a flower
You were pulling **petals** off a flower at that time.
당신은 그 때 꽃잎을 한 장씩 떼고 있었다.

07 precaution [prikɔ́ːʃən]
n 조심, 예방책   something that you do to avoid danger or problems
Visitors to the park are urged to take **precautions** to avoid encounters with bears.
공원에 방문하는 사람들은 곰과 마주치지 않도록 각별한 조심이 요구된다.

08 prime [praim]
a 첫째의, 주요한   the first example of something; main
A **prime** reason for our economic decline is lack of investment.
경기 하락의 첫째의 이유는 투자 부족이다.

09 principal [prínsəpəl]
n 교장, 장 / a 주요한   the head of some schools, colleges, etc
The **principal** reproved the students when they became unruly in the auditorium.
강당에서 학생들은 제멋대로였기 때문에 교장 선생님이 그들을 야단쳤다.

key words
discipline n 규율, 훈련 / urge v 요구하다, 설득하다 / encounter n 마주침
reprove v 꾸짖다, 나무라다 / unruly a 제멋대로 하는 / auditorium n 강당, 회관

🎧 Listen and repeat. (Track 92)

10 proceed
[prousí:d]
v 계속하다, 나아가다   to continue doing something
We would appreciate some indication as to how you would like to **proceed**.
어떻게 계속하실 것인지를 알려주시면 감사하겠어요.

11 prosperity
[praspérəti]
n 번영, 부유   the state of being successful
You must realize that **prosperity** does not last forever.
번영이 영원히 계속되지 않는다는 사실을 깨달아야 한다.

12 protest
[prətést]
v 항의하다, 주장하다   to say that you do not approve of or agree with something
A lot of people **protested** about the new working hours.
많은 사람들이 새로운 근무 시간에 대해 항의했다.

13 rare
[rɛə:r]
a 드문, 희귀한   not done, seen, etc very often
This is a shopping search engine to find **rare** books.
이것은 희귀한 책들을 찾기 위한 쇼핑 검색엔진이다.

14 rear
[riə:r]
n 뒤쪽 / a 후방의   the back part
Our car is waiting at our company's reserved parking space in the **rear** of this building.
치는 이 건물 뒤쪽에 있는 회사지정주차구역에 대기시켜 놓았습니다.

15 release
[rilí:s]
v 놓아주다, 공개하다, 개봉하다   to allow somebody/something to be free
The animal doctor gave it time to recover and then **released** it.
그 수의사는 그 새가 회복할 시간을 준 다음 그 새를 놓아주었다.

16 relieve
[rilí:v]
v 구원하다, 덜다   to make an unpleasant feeling stop or get better
I needed some medicine to **relieve** my pain but I was not strong to call somebody.
고통을 덜어 줄 약이 필요했으나 누군가를 부를 힘이 없었다.

17 resource
[rí:sɔ:rs]
n 자원, 재료   a supply of something, a piece of equipment, etc
I do not feel that your limited **resources** will permit you to carry out such a great program.
나는 당신의 제한된 자원으로는 그렇게 대단한 계획을 수행할 수 없으리라 생각한다.

18 responsible
[rispánsəbəl]
a 책임이 있는, 신뢰 할 수 있는   having duty of dealing with somebody/something
Is this a realistic salary for such a **responsible** job?
그처럼 책임이 큰 직업에 이것이 적절한 봉급인가?

---

key words
appreciate v 고맙게 생각하다 / reserved a 지정의 / realistic a 실질적인

Unit 31 157

Exercise

A. Complete the sentence.

1. You were pulling _____ off a flower at that time.
   당신은 그 때 꽃잎을 한 장씩 떼고 있었다.

2. We would appreciate some indication as to how you would like to _____.
   어떻게 계속하실 것인지를 알려주시면 감사하겠어요.

3. The body requires proper _____ in order to maintain it.
   신체는 몸을 유지하는데 필요한 알맞은 영양분을 요구한다.

4. _____, she learns well from her teachers and is happy with her studies.
   전체적으로 그녀는 선생님들한테서 잘 배우고 있으며 공부과목들에 만족하고 있다.

5. This is a shopping search engine to find _____ books.
   이것은 희귀한 책들을 찾기 위한 쇼핑 검색엔진이다.

6. Is this a realistic salary for such a _____ job?
   그처럼 책임이 큰 직업에 이것이 적절한 봉급인가?

7. I'm sure you have the picture by now that I'm a rather _____.
   분명 이 정도면 당신은 내가 다소 비관적이라는 생각을 가질 것이다.

8. The _____ reproved the students when they became unruly in the auditorium.
   강당에서 학생들은 제멋대로였기 때문에 교장 선생님이 그들을 야단쳤다.

9. The Student _____ teaches students discipline and awareness.
   학생 선서는 학생들에게 규율과 자각을 가르친다.

10. You must realize that _____ does not last forever.
    번영이 영원히 계속되지 않는다는 사실을 깨달아야 한다.

11. A lot of people _____ about the new working hours.
    많은 사람들이 새로운 근무 시간에 대해 항의했다.

12. Our car is waiting at our company's reserved parking space in the _____ of this building.
    차는 이 건물 뒤쪽에 있는 회사지정주차구역에 대기시켜 놓았습니다.

13. The animal doctor gave it time to recover and then _____ it.
    그 수의사는 그 새가 회복할 시간을 준 다음 그 새를 놓아주었다.

14. A _____ reason for our economic decline is lack of investment.
    경기 하락의 첫째 이유는 투자 부족이다.

15. Visitors to the park are urged to take _____ to avoid encounters with bears.
    공원에 방문하는 사람들은 곰과 마주치지 않도록 각별한 조심이 요구된다.

16. One of the experienced lawyers _____ and stopped to offer his support.
    경험 있는 변호사 중 한 명이 우연히 듣고 도움을 주기 위해 멈춰 섰다.

17. I needed some medicine to _____ my pain but I was not strong to call somebody.
    고통을 덜어 줄 약이 필요했으나 누군가를 부를 힘이 없었다.

18. I do not feel that your limited _____ will permit you to carry out such a great program.
    나는 당신의 제한된 자원으로는 그렇게 대단한 계획을 수행할 수 없으리라 생각한다.

Hint

precaution resource release prime overall prosperity rear nutrition petal
responsible principal protest relieve proceed overhear oath pessimistic rare

Exercise

B. Fill in the word and meaning.

	Word	Meaning
01	oath	
02	prosperity	
03	principal	
04	rear	
05	nutrition	
06	proceed	
07	resource	
08	overall	
09	relieve	
10	petal	
11	responsible	
12	overhear	
13	protest	
14	prime	
15	rare	
16	precaution	
17	release	
18	pessimistic	

	Meaning	Word
01	영양(분), 영양 공급	
02	맹세, 선서	
03	전체적으로, 전체의	
04	엿듣다, 우연히 듣다	
05	비관적인, 염세적인	
06	꽃잎	
07	조심, 예방책	
08	첫째의, 주요한	
09	교장, 장, 주요한	
10	계속하다, 나아가다	
11	번영, 부유	
12	항의하다, 주장하다	
13	드문, 희귀한	
14	뒤쪽, 후방의	
15	놓아주다, 공개하다, 개봉하다	
16	구원하다, 덜다	
17	자원, 재료	
18	책임이 있는, 신뢰 할 수 있는	

C. Listen, write the word and meaning. (Track 93)

	Word	Meaning		Word	Meaning
01			10		
02			11		
03			12		
04			13		
05			14		
06			15		
07			16		
08			17		
09			18		

Unit 32

🎧 Listen and repeat. Track 94

01 satellite
[sǽtəlàit]
n (인공)위성 / n (인공)위성의   a natural object that moves round a bigger object
The moon we see at night is the only **satellite** in the Earth.
우리가 밤에 보는 달은 지구의 유일한 위성이다.

02 scar
[skaːr]
n 상처, 흔적   a mark on the skin
When I pop the pimples, it'll leave **scars**.
여드름을 짜면, 흉터가 남을 것이다.

03 shift
[ʃift]
v 옮기다, 이동시키다   to move or be moved from one position to another
She complained without breaking to **shift** furniture from this room to the other.
가구를 이 방에서 저 방으로 옮겨달라고 그녀는 쉬지 않고 불평했다.

04 shrug
[ʃrʌg]
v 으쓱하다 / n 어깨를 으쓱하기   to lift your shoulders
Shrug my shoulders and hope I'll have better luck at the next store.
나는 어깨를 으쓱하고는 다음 가게에서는 운이 따르기를 기대해 본다.

05 solemn
[sάləm]
a 엄숙한, 근엄한, 중대한   very serious; pompous
She held a **solemn** expression on her face.
그녀는 엄숙한 표정을 지었다.

06 solitary
[sάlitèri]
a 혼자의, 외로운   done alone, without other people
One reason why I like the beach is its **solitary** atmosphere.
내가 해변을 좋아하는 한 가지 이유는 외로운 분위기 때문이다.

07 stare
[stɛəːr]
v 응시하다, 빤히 보다   to look at somebody or something for a long time
My mother **stared** at me, her eyes widening.
나의 어머니는 눈을 동그랗게 뜨고 나를 응시하셨다.

08 startle
[stάːrtl]
v 깜짝 놀라게 하다   to surprise somebody in a way that slightly shocks him/her
Yesterday the emergency alarm rang and **startled** me terribly.
어제 비상벨이 울려서 정말로 나를 깜짝 놀라게 했다.

09 suspend
[səspénd]
v 보류하다, 매달다, 중지하다   to stop or delay something for a time
Decision on the matter has been **suspended** by our manager.
그 문제에 대한 결정은 매니저에 의해 보류 되었다.

---

key words
pimple n 여드름 / pompous a 점잔 빼는 / atmosphere n 분위기, 대기 / widening n 확대, 확장

🎧 Listen and repeat. (Track 95)

10 transition [trænzíʃən]
n 변천(기), 변이   a change from one state or form to another
His life was the **transition** from poverty to power.
그의 인생은 가난으로부터 권력으로 넘어가는 과도기였다.

11 transmit [trænsmít]
v 전송하다, 전도하다   to send out television programs, electronic signals, etc
How wonderful it is to **transmit** colored images over thousands of miles!
천연색 영상을 수천 마일 저쪽으로 전송하는 것이 얼마나 놀라운 일인가!

12 unity [júːnəti]
n 통일, 일치   the state of different things being joined together
The figure on the left spoils the **unity** of the painting.
왼쪽에 있는 무늬가 그 그림의 통일성을 망친다.

13 unlettered [ʌnlétərd]
a 문맹의, 무학의   not know how to read or write
In the United States, numberless people are **unlettered** for a variety of reasons.
미국에서는 많은 사람들이 다양한 이유로 글을 알지 못한다.

14 unwind [ʌnwáind]
v 풀리다, 풀다   to relax, especially after working hard
A hot bath is a good way to **unwind** your tired body.
뜨거운 목욕은 당신의 지친 몸을 풀리게 하는 좋은 방법이다.

15 vain [vein]
a 헛된, 무익한   useless, fruitless
He made a **vain** resolution never to repeat the act.
그는 다시는 그런 행위를 되풀이하지 않겠다고 결심했으나 헛일이었다.

16 valid [vælid]
a 타당한, 유효한   that is legally or officially acceptable
Because her argument was **valid**, the judge accepted it.
그녀의 주장은 타당했기 때문에 판사는 그것을 받아들였다.

17 whistle [hwísəl]
n 휘파람 / v 휘파람을 불다   the sound made by blowing air out between your lips
Researchers say dolphins' **whistles** have meaning.
연구자들은 돌고래의 휘파람 소리에 의미가 있다고 말합니다.

18 wilderness [wíldərnis]
n 황야, 미개지   a large area of land that has never been used for growing things
The snow leopard is an almost mythical creature, an icon of the **wilderness**.
눈표범은 거의 신화적인 존재이며 황야의 표상이다.

---

key words
spoil v 망치다 / resolution n 결심, 결의 / leopard n 표범 / mythical a 신화의, 신화를 쓰는

Exercise

A. Complete the sentence.

1. When I pop the pimples, it'll leave _____.
   여드름을 짜면, 흉터가 남을 것이다.

2. How wonderful it is to _____ colored images over thousands of miles!
   천연색 영상을 수천 마일 저쪽으로 전송하는 것이 얼마나 놀라운 일인가!

3. Decision on the matter has been _____ by our manager.
   그 문제에 대한 결정은 매니저에 의해 보류 되었다.

4. She complained without breaking to _____ furniture from this room to the other.
   가구를 이 방에서 저 방으로 옮겨달라고 그녀는 쉬지 않고 불평했다.

5. Because her argument was _____, the judge accepted it.
   그녀의 주장은 타당했기 때문에 판사는 그것을 받아들였다.

6. My mother _____ at me, her eyes widening.
   나의 어머니는 눈을 동그랗게 뜨고 나를 응시하셨다.

7. His life was the _____ from poverty to power.
   그의 인생은 가난으로부터 권력으로 넘어가는 과도기였다.

8. The figure on the left spoils the _____ of the painting.
   왼쪽에 있는 무늬가 그 그림의 통일성을 망친다.

9. The moon we see at night is the only _____ in the Earth.
   우리가 밤에 보는 달은 지구의 유일한 위성이다.

10. In the United States, numberless people are _____ for a variety of reasons.
    미국에서는 많은 사람들이 다양한 이유로 글을 알지 못한다.

11. She held a _____ expression on her face.
    그녀는 엄숙한 표정을 지었다.

12. A hot bath is a good way to _____ your tired body.
    뜨거운 목욕은 당신의 지친 몸을 풀리게 하는 좋은 방법이다.

13. One reason why I like the beach is its _____ atmosphere.
    내가 해변을 좋아하는 한 가지 이유는 외로운 분위기 때문이다.

14. He made a _____ resolution never to repeat the act.
    그는 다시는 그런 행위를 되풀이하지 않겠다고 결심했으나 헛일이었다.

15. Researchers say dolphins' _____ have meaning.
    연구자들은 돌고래의 휘파람 소리에 의미가 있다고 말합니다.

16. Yesterday the emergency alarm rang and _____ me terribly.
    어제 비상벨이 울려서 정말로 나를 깜짝 놀라게 했다.

17. _____ my shoulders and hope I'll have better luck at the next store.
    나는 어깨를 으쓱하고는 다음 가게에서는 운이 따르기를 기대해 본다.

18. The snow leopard is an almost mythical creature, an icon of the _____.
    눈표범은 거의 신화적인 존재이며 황야의 표상이다.

Hint

| satellite | valid | whistle | solemn | startle | wilderness | unlettered | unity | scar |
| transmit | stare | suspend | unwind | vain | transition | solitary | shrug | shift |

Unit 32

Exercise

B. Fill in the word and meaning.

	Word	Meaning
01	shift	
02	unity	
03	suspend	
04	satellite	
05	transition	
06	vain	
07	scar	
08	transmit	
09	whistle	
10	solemn	
11	wilderness	
12	startle	
13	valid	
14	shrug	
15	unwind	
16	solitary	
17	unlettered	
18	stare	

	Meaning	Word
01	(인공)위성, (인공)위성의	
02	상처, 흔적	
03	옮기다, 이동시키다	
04	으쓱하다, 어깨를 으쓱하기	
05	엄숙한, 근엄한, 중대한	
06	혼자의, 외로운	
07	응시하다, 빤히 보다	
08	깜짝 놀라게 하다	
09	보류하다, 매달다, 중지하다	
10	변천(기), 변이	
11	전송하다, 전도하다	
12	통일, 일치	
13	문맹의, 무학의	
14	풀리다, 풀다	
15	헛된, 무익한	
16	타당한, 유효한	
17	휘파람, 휘파람을 불다	
18	황야, 미개지	

C. Listen, write the word and meaning. Track 96

	Word	Meaning		Word	Meaning
01			10		
02			11		
03			12		
04			13		
05			14		
06			15		
07			16		
08			17		
09			18		

Review 16

A. Read and fill in the word and meaning.

word	definition	meaning
	something that you do to avoid danger or problems	
	having duty of dealing with somebody/something	
	a formal promise	
	one of the thin soft coloured parts of a flower	
	a supply of something, a piece of equipment, etc	
	to hear what somebody is saying by accident	
	the first example of something; main	
	the food that affects your health when you eat	
	to allow somebody/something to be free	
	a person who always thinks that bad things will happen	
	the state of being successful	
	the head of some schools, colleges, etc	
	to make an unpleasant feeling stop or get better	
	including everything; generally	
	not done, seen, etc very often	
	to continue doing something	
	the back part	
	to say that you do not approve of or agree with something	

Hint

precaution　resource　release　prime　overall　prosperity　rear　nutrition　petal
responsible　principal　protest　relieve　proceed　overhear　oath　pessimistic　rare

B. Read and fill in the word and meaning.

word	definition	meaning
stare	to look at somebody or something for a long time	
unlettered	not know how to read or write	
shift	to move or be moved from one position to another	
transmit	to send out television programs, electronic signals, etc	
unity	the state of different things being joined together	
satellite	a natural object that moves round a bigger object	
solemn	very serious; pompous	
transition	a change from one state or form to another	
shrug	to lift your shoulders	
wilderness	a large area of land that has never been used for growing things	
unwind	to relax, especially after working hard	
scar	a mark on the skin	
whistle	the sound made by blowing air out between your lips	
suspend	to stop or delay something for a time	
solitary	done alone, without other people	
vain	useless, fruitless	
startle	to surprise somebody in a way that slightly shocks him/her	
valid	that is legally or officially acceptable	

Hint

satellite valid whistle solemn startle wilderness unlettered unity scar
transmit stare suspend unwind vain transition solitary shrug shift

Unit 33

🎧 Listen and repeat. Track 97

01 accuse [əkjúːz]
v 고발하다, 비난하다 to say that somebody has broken the law
The politician was **accused** of accepting bribes from the company.
그 정치인은 회사로부터 뇌물을 받아 고발당했다.

02 acquire [əkwáiər]
v 얻다, 취득하다 to obtain or buy something
The most valuable skill one can **acquire** is the ability to think for oneself.
사람이 얻을 수 있는 가장 가치 있는 기능은 스스로 생각하는 능력이다.

03 announcement [ənáunsmənt]
n 공고, 발표 an act of telling people about something
What did you do when you heard the **announcement**?
그 발표 듣고 당신은 어떻게 했나요?

04 anthem [ǽnθəm]
n 성가, 찬송가 a song, especially one that is sung on special occasions
I stood singing the **anthem** but he kept directing nervous glances toward me.
나는 서서 찬송가를 불렀지만 그는 근심스런 시선을 내게 계속 보냈다.

05 attract [ətrǽkt]
v (주의, 흥미 등을) 끌다, 매혹하다 to cause somebody give attention to something
A dark, pessimistic attitude toward technology is **attracting** more and more people.
기술에 대한 어둡고 비관적인 태도는 점점 더 많은 사람들의 주의를 끌고 있다.

06 awfully [ɔ́ːfəli]
ad 아주, 몹시 very much
He seems **awfully** quiet today, don't you think?
그가 오늘따라 아주 조용한 거 같지 않아요?

07 biology [baiálədʒi]
n 생물학, 생물학 책 the scientific study of living things
We learned in our **biology** class that all living things carry on the same vital functions.
모든 생물은 똑같이 중요한 기능을 한다고 우리는 생물학 수업에서 배웠다.

08 bother [báðər]
v 괴롭히다, 귀찮게 하다 to disturb, annoy or worry somebody
I don't want to **bother** you, but can you read this for me?
귀찮게 하고 싶지는 않지만 이것 좀 읽어주실 수 있나요?

09 charming [tʃáːrmiŋ]
a 매력적인, 매우 재미있는 very attractive or pleasing
I had a **charming** conversation with a young lady I met in the lobby.
로비에서 한 아가씨를 만나 재미있는 대화를 나눴다.

key words
bribe n 뇌물 / glance n 흘긋 봄 / vital a 절대 필요한 / disturb v 어지럽히다, 혼란시키다

🎧 Listen and repeat. (Track 98)

10 clamor [klǽmər]
n 아우성 / v 시끄럽게 요구하다   a loud or angry sound for demanding what you want
The **clamor** awakened the whole neighborhood.
그 아우성이 모든 이웃의 잠을 깨웠다.

11 competent [kámpətənt]
a 유능한, 능력이 있는   having the ability or skill needed for something
The **competent** teachers are respected by the students.
유능한 교사는 학생으로부터 존경을 받는다.

12 compliment [kámpləmənt]
n 칭찬, 찬사   a statement or action that shows admiration for somebody
One likes to hear **compliments** on one's appearance.
사람은 자기 외모를 칭찬하는 말을 듣기 좋아한다.

13 cruel [krúːəl]
a 잔인한, 참혹한   causing physical or mental pain or suffering
I think it is **cruel** to kill animals for sport.
오락으로 동물을 살해하는 것은 잔인한 짓이라고 생각한다.

14 damage [dǽmidʒ]
n 손해, 피해 / v 손해(피해)를 입다   harm or injury caused when something is spoiled
The storm caused extensive **damage**.
폭풍이 넓은 지역에 걸쳐 피해를 가져왔다.

15 despise [dispáiz]
v 경멸하다, 싫어하다   to hate somebody/something very much
Don't **despise** others because they are poor.
가난하다고 해서 남을 경멸하지 마라.

16 detective [ditéktiv]
n 탐정 / a 탐정의   a person who tries to solve crimes
The **detective** chases the criminal and there's always a shootout.
늘 탐정은 범인을 쫓고 총격전은 언제나 벌어진다.

17 elementary [èləméntəri]
a 초보의, 기본의   connected with the first stages of learning something
I got an **elementary** course in salsa dance, but it was not easy to me.
나는 살사 댄스의 초보자 과정을 들었는데 그것도 내게는 쉽지 않았다.

18 encourage [enkə́ːridʒ]
v 격려하다, 촉진하다   to give hope, support or confidence to somebody
My teacher always **encourages** me to make my dream come true.
나의 선생님은 나의 꿈을 실현하도록 항상 격려 해주신다.

---

key words
awaken v 깨우다 / appearance n 외관, 겉모습 / injury n 상해, 손상
chase v 추적하다 / shootout n 총격전

Exercise

A. Complete the sentence.

1. He seems _____ quiet today, don't you think?
   그가 오늘따라 아주 조용한 거 같지 않아요?
2. I had a _____ conversation with a young lady I met in the lobby.
   로비에서 한 아가씨를 만나 재미있는 대화를 나눴다.
3. The politician was _____ of accepting bribes from the company.
   그 정치인은 회사로부터 뇌물을 받아 고발당했다.
4. We learned in our _____ class that all living things carry on the same vital functions.
   모든 생물은 똑같이 중요한 기능을 한다고 우리는 생물학 수업에서 배웠다.
5. The storm caused extensive _____.
   폭풍이 넓은 지역에 걸쳐 피해를 가져왔다.
6. My teacher always _____ me to make my dream come true.
   나의 선생님은 나의 꿈을 실현하도록 항상 격려 해주신다.
7. What did you do when you heard the _____?
   그 발표 듣고 당신은 어떻게 했나요?
8. I think it is _____ to kill animals for sport.
   오락으로 동물을 살해하는 것은 잔인한 짓이라고 생각한다.
9. I stood singing the _____ but he kept directing nervous glances toward me.
   나는 서서 찬송가를 불렀지만 그는 근심스런 시선을 내게 계속 보냈다.
10. I don't want to _____ you, but can you read this for me?
    귀찮게 하고 싶지는 않지만 이것 좀 읽어주실 수 있나요?
11. The most valuable skill one can _____ is the ability to think for oneself.
    사람이 얻을 수 있는 가장 가치 있는 기능은 스스로 생각하는 능력이다.
12. The _____ awakened the whole neighborhood.
    그 아우성이 모든 이웃의 잠을 깨웠다.
13. One likes to hear _____ on one's appearance.
    사람은 자기 외모를 칭찬하는 말을 듣기 좋아한다.
14. A dark, pessimistic attitude toward technology is _____ more and more people.
    기술에 대한 어둡고 비관적인 태도는 점점 더 많은 사람들의 주의를 끌고 있다.
15. Don't _____ others because they are poor.
    가난하다고 해서 남을 경멸하지 마라.
16. The _____ teachers are respected by the students.
    유능한 교사는 학생으로부터 존경을 받는다.
17. I got an _____ course in salsa dance, but it was not easy to me.
    나는 살사 댄스의 초보자 과정을 들었는데 그것도 내게는 쉽지 않았다.
18. The _____ chases the criminal and there's always a shootout.
    늘 탐정은 범인을 쫓고 총격전은 언제나 벌어진다.

Hint

compliment   detective   accuse   damage   despise   clamor   attract   bother   announcement
elementary   encourage   biology   charming   acquire   anthem   awfully   cruel   competent

Exercise

B. Fill in the word and meaning.

	Word	Meaning
01	bother	
02	compliment	
03	accuse	
04	damage	
05	competent	
06	acquire	
07	despise	
08	awfully	
09	elementary	
10	announcement	
11	encourage	
12	charming	
13	anthem	
14	biology	
15	detective	
16	cruel	
17	attract	
18	clamor	

	Meaning	Word
01	고발하다, 비난하다	
02	얻다, 취득하다	
03	공고, 발표	
04	성가, 찬송가	
05	(주의, 흥미 등을) 끌다, 매혹하다	
06	아주, 몹시	
07	생물학, 생물학 책	
08	괴롭히다, 귀찮게 하다	
09	매력적인, 매우 재미있는	
10	아우성, 시끄럽게 요구하다	
11	유능한, 능력이 있는	
12	칭찬, 찬사	
13	잔인한, 참혹한	
14	손해, 피해, 손해(피해)를 입다	
15	경멸하다, 싫어하다	
16	탐정, 탐정의	
17	초보의, 기본의	
18	격려하다, 촉진하다	

🎧 **C. Listen, write the word and meaning.** (Track 99)

	Word	Meaning		Word	Meaning
01			10		
02			11		
03			12		
04			13		
05			14		
06			15		
07			16		
08			17		
09			18		

Unit 33

Unit 34

🎧 Listen and repeat. (Track 100)

01 extraordinary **a** 특별한, 범상치 않은   very unusual
[ekstrɔ́:rdənèri]
He has always shown himself to be an **extraordinary** athlete.
그는 항상 자신이 특별한 선수임을 보여 주었다.

02 extrovert **n** 외향적인 사람   a person who prefers being with other people
[ékstrouvə̀:rt]
A good salesman is usually an **extrovert**, who likes to talk with people.
훌륭한 외판원은 대개 사람들과 이야기하길 좋아하는 외향적인 사람이다.

03 foresee **v** 예견하다, 예지하다   to know that something is going to happen in the future
[fɔ:rsí:]
He **foresaw** the troubles ahead and took steps to avoid them.
그는 문제를 예견하고 그것을 피하고자 조치를 취했다.

04 formal **a** 형식적인, 정규의   very correct and serious rather than relaxed and friendly
[fɔ́:rməl]
The letter was stiff and **formal**.
그 편지는 딱딱하고 형식적이었다.

05 gaze **v** 응시하다, 바라보다   to look steadily for a long time
[geiz]
He was sitting on the rock, **gazing** at the sea.
그는 바다를 바라보면서 바위에 앉아 있었다.

06 generate **v** 생산하다, 발생하다   to produce or create something
[dʒénərèit]
If you burn wood, it **generates** carbon dioxide.
나무를 태우면 이산화탄소가 발생한다.

07 hardworking **a** 부지런한, 열심히 일하는   working with effort and energy
[há:rdwə̀:rkiŋ]
There is no denying that the Koreans feel proud of being said to be the most **hardworking** people in the world.
한국인은 세계에서 가장 부지런한 국민이라고 말하여 지는 것에 대해 자부심을 갖고 있음에 틀림없다.

08 haste **n** 급함, 서두름   the act of hurrying ; quickness of action
[heist]
Make **haste**, or you will miss the train.
서둘러라, 그렇지 않으면 기차를 놓친다.

09 heritage **n** 전통문화, 유산   the traditions of a country that have existed for a long time
[héritidʒ]
The State shall strive to sustain and develop cultural **heritages**.
국가는 전통문화의 계승과 발전에 노력해야 한다.

---

key words

stiff **a** 딱딱한 / carbon **n** 탄소 / dioxide **n** 이산화물 / strive **v** 노력하다 / sustain **v** 계속하다, 지속하다

🎧 Listen and repeat. Track 101

10 independent [ìndipéndənt]
a 독립의, 자주의   free from and not controlled by another person, country, etc
I like working because it makes me feel **independent**.
독립심을 느끼게 해 주기 때문에 나는 일하는 것을 좋아한다.

11 industrial [indʌ́striəl]
a 산업의, 공업의   connected with industry
The factory produces three tons of **industrial** waste a day.
그 공장에서는 하루 3톤의 산업 쓰레기를 쏟아낸다.

12 invader [invéidər]
n 침입자, 침략자   a person who enters somewhere in order to attack
I had a fight with him because he treated me as an **invader**.
그는 나를 침입자처럼 대했기 때문에 그와 싸움을 벌였다.

13 locate [lóukeit]
v 위치하다, 위치를 정하다   to put or build something in a particular place
The house was **located** in the heart of the city.
그 집은 그 도시의 심장부에 위치해 있었다.

14 luxurious [lʌgʒúəriəs]
a 사치스러운, 호화로운   full of expensive and beautiful things
Do you agree that the interior is very **luxurious**?
그 실내장식이 매우 사치스럽다는데 동의하나요?

15 master [mǽstəːr]
v 숙달하다 / n 주인, 대가   to learn how to do something well
Most things are easy to learn, but hard to **master**.
모든 것이 배우기는 쉬우나 숙달하기는 어렵다.

16 mediate [míːdièit]
v 조정하다, 화해시키다   to try to end a disagreement between more people or groups
As a supervisor she had to **mediate** between her colleagues and the boss.
감독자로서 그녀는 동료들과 상사의 관계를 조정해야만 했다.

17 norm [nɔːrm]
n 표준, 평균   a situation or way of behaving that is usual or expected
In every society there are **norms** that tell people how they are supposed to behave.
모든 사회에는, 사람들이 어떻게 행동해야 되는가를 말해주는 표준들이 있다.

18 notable [nóutəbl]
a 주목할 만한, 유명한   important enough to receive attention
He is a **notable** figure in baseball circles.
그는 야구계에서는 주목할 만한 존재이다.

key words
supervisor n 감독자, 지휘자 / colleague n 동료

Unit 34 171

Exercise

A. Complete the sentence.

1. If you burn wood, it _____ carbon dioxide.
   나무를 태우면 이산화탄소가 발생한다.

2. He has always shown himself to be an _____ athlete.
   그는 항상 자신이 특별한 선수임을 보여 주었다.

3. Most things are easy to learn, but hard to _____.
   모든 것이 배우기는 쉬우나 숙달하기는 어렵다.

4. The letter was stiff and _____.
   그 편지는 딱딱하고 형식적이었다.

5. He is a notable _____ in baseball circles.
   그는 야구계에서는 주목할 만한 존재이다.

6. He was sitting on the rock, _____ at the sea.
   그는 바다를 바라보면서 바위에 앉아 있었다.

7. There is no denying that the Koreans feel proud of being said to be the most _____ people in the world.
   한국인은 세계에서 가장 부지런한 국민이라고 말하여 지는 것에 대해 자부심을 갖고 있음에 틀림없다.

8. He _____ the troubles ahead and took steps to avoid them.
   그는 문제를 예견하고 그것을 피하고자 조치를 취했다.

9. The State shall strive to sustain and develop cultural _____.
   국가는 전통문화의 계승과 발전에 노력해야 한다.

10. A good salesman is usually an _____, who likes to talk with people.
    훌륭한 외판원은 대개 사람들과 이야기하길 좋아하는 외향적인 사람이다.

11. I like working because it makes me feel _____.
    독립심을 느끼게 해 주기 때문에 나는 일하는 것을 좋아한다.

12. Make _____, or you will miss the train.
    서둘러라. 그렇지 않으면 기차를 놓친다.

13. I had a fight with him because he treated me as an _____.
    그는 나를 침입자처럼 대했기 때문에 그와 싸움을 벌였다.

14. The house was _____ in the heart of the city.
    그 집은 그 도시의 심장부에 위치해 있었다.

15. As a supervisor she had to _____ between her colleagues and the boss.
    감독자로서 그녀는 동료들과 상사의 관계를 조정해야만 했다.

16. In every society there are _____ that tell people how they are supposed to behave.
    모든 사회에는, 사람들이 어떻게 행동해야 되는가를 말해주는 표준들이 있다.

17. The factory produces three tons of _____ waste a day.
    그 공장에서는 하루 3톤의 산업 쓰레기를 쏟아낸다.

18. Do you agree that the interior is very _____?
    그 실내장식이 매우 사치스럽다는데 동의하나요?

Hint

| master | norm | locate | haste | generate | extrovert | mediate | independent | hardworking |
| foresee | gaze | industrial | formal | luxurious | heritage | invader | extraordinary | notable |

Exercise

B. Fill in the word and meaning.

	Word	Meaning
01	extraordinary	
02	industrial	
03	heritage	
04	extrovert	
05	independent	
06	gaze	
07	master	
08	foresee	
09	locate	
10	mediate	
11	formal	
12	luxurious	
13	haste	
14	norm	
15	generate	
16	notable	
17	invader	
18	hardworking	

	Meaning	Word
01	특별한, 범상치 않은	
02	외향적인 사람	
03	예견하다, 예지하다	
04	형식적인, 정규의	
05	응시하다, 바라보다	
06	생산하다, 발생하다	
07	부지런한, 열심히 일하는	
08	급함, 서두름	
09	전통문화, 유산	
10	독립의, 자주의	
11	산업의, 공업의	
12	침입자, 침략자	
13	위치하다, 위치를 정하다	
14	사치스러운, 호화로운	
15	숙달하다, 주인, 대가	
16	조정하다, 화해시키다	
17	표준, 평균	
18	주목할 만한, 유명한	

🎧 C. Listen, write the word and meaning. (Track 102)

	Word	Meaning		Word	Meaning
01			10		
02			11		
03			12		
04			13		
05			14		
06			15		
07			16		
08			17		
09			18		

Review 17

A. Read and fill in the word and meaning.

word	definition	meaning
	very attractive or pleasing	
	harm or injury caused when something is spoiled	
	connected with the first stages of learning something	
	to disturb, annoy or worry somebody	
	to say that somebody has broken the law	
	a loud or angry sound for demanding what you want	
	a person who tries to solve crimes	
	to hate somebody/something very much	
	to obtain or buy something	
	a statement or action that shows admiration for somebody	
	very much	
	having the ability or skill needed for something	
	an act of telling people about something	
	to give hope, support or confidence to somebody	
	to cause somebody give attention to something	
	the scientific study of living things	
	a song, especially one that is sung on special occasions	
	causing physical or mental pain or suffering	

Hint

compliment   detective   accuse   damage   despise   clamor   attract   bother   announcement
elementary   encourage   biology   charming   acquire   anthem   awfully   cruel   competent

B. Read and fill in the word and meaning.

word	definition	meaning
locate	to put or build something in a particular place	
notable	important enough to receive attention	
extraordinary	very unusual	
industrial	connected with industry	
foresee	to know that something is going to happen in the future	
master	to learn how to do something well	
hardworking	working with effort and energy	
extrovert	a person who prefers being with other people	
invader	a person who enters somewhere in order to attack	
luxurious	full of expensive and beautiful things	
formal	very correct and serious rather than relaxed and friendly	
independent	free from and not controlled by another person, country, etc	
heritage	the traditions of a country that have existed for a long time	
gaze	to look steadily for a long time	
mediate	to try to end a disagreement between more people or groups	
generate	to produce or create something	
haste	the act of hurrying ; quickness of action	
norm	a situation or way of behaving that is usual or expected	

Hint

master norm locate   haste generate extrovert mediate independent hardworking
foresee gaze industrial formal luxurious heritage invader extraordinary notable

Unit 35

🎧 Listen and repeat. Track 103

01 oblige [əbláidʒ]
v 강요하다, 고맙게 여기다   to force somebody to do something
I was **obliged** to go to the dance party.
나는 댄스파티에 가야만 했다.

02 observe [əbzə́ːrv]
v 관찰하다, (규칙 등을)준수하다   to watch somebody/something carefully
He is better at **observing** looks than at reading hearts.
그는 마음을 읽기보다는 외모를 더 잘 관찰한다.

03 overlook [òuvərlúk]
v 간과하다, 내려다보다   fail to see; to have a view over something
I **overlooked** the fact that the house could be easily damaged by strong winds.
나는 그 집이 강풍의 피해를 받기 쉽다는 사실은 미처 고려하지 못했다.

04 overtake [òuvərtéik]
v 따라 잡다, 덮치다   come up or catch up with; to happen unexpectedly or suddenly
Did you manage to **overtake** them?
당신은 그들을 따라잡기는 했나?

05 physical [fízikəl]
a 신체의, 물질의   connected with your body
Westerners enjoy the mental and **physical** health taekwondo gives them.
서양 사람들은 태권도가 가져다 주는 정신적, 신체적 건강을 즐긴다.

06 physicist [fízisist]
n 물리학자   a person who studies or is an expert in physics
The **physicist** was aware of the danger of nuclear weapons.
그 물리학자는 핵무기의 위험성을 알고 있었다.

07 precise [prisáis]
a 정확한, 정밀한   accurate; exact
Above all, scientific terms need for **precise** definitions.
특히 과학용어는 정확한 정의를 필요로 한다.

08 preference [préfərəns]
n 선호, 좋아하는 물건   an interest in one thing more that another
Of the two, my **preference** is for the smaller car.
둘 중에 내가 선호하는 것은 더 작은 차다.

09 pervade [pərvéid]
v 널리 퍼지다, 충만하다   to spread through every part of something
Sweet odors of flowers **pervaded** the garden.
정원에는 달콤한 꽃 향기가 가득했다.

key words
mental a 정신의 / term n 말, 용어 / odor n 향기, 냄새

Listen and repeat. Track 104

10 private [práivit]
a 개인적인, 사적인   belonging to one particular person or group
He talks a lot about others' **private** business.
그는 남의 사적인 일에 대한 이야기를 잘 한다.

11 privilege [prívəlidʒ]
n 특권 / v 특권을 주다   a special right or advantage that
Prisoners who behave well enjoy special **privileges**.
행동이 바른 수감자들은 특권을 누린다.

12 proudly [práudli]
ad 자랑스럽게, 거만하게   used to express the feeling satisfied about something
He **proudly** showed us through his palatial home.
그는 우리들에게 그의 궁전 같은 집을 자랑스럽게 보여주었다.

13 recently [ríːsəntli]
ad 최근에, 요즈음   not long ago
That's how we've been handling all our contracts **recently**.
그것이 우리가 최근까지 계약을 다루어왔던 방법이다.

14 recite [risáit]
v 낭송하다, 말하다   to say aloud a piece of writing from memory
I was asked to **recite** a rather lengthy poem for a school event.
나는 학교 행사에서 다소 긴 시를 낭송하도록 요청 받았다.

15 rely [rilái]
v 의지하다, 믿다   to trust somebody/something to work or behave well
Nowadays we **rely** increasingly on computers.
요즘 우리는 점점 더 컴퓨터에 의지하고 있다.

16 remain [riméin]
v 남다, ~인 상태로 있다 / n 유적   to stay or continue in the same place or condition
The very rich cannot **remain** very rich for more than three generations.
부자는 3세대 이상 부유한 상태로 남지 못한다.

17 reveal [rivíːl]
v 드러내다, 폭로하다   to show something that was hidden before
He was worried about **revealing** the sources of his information.
그는 그의 정보의 출처를 폭로하는 것에 대해 염려했다.

18 revive [riváiv]
v 소생하다, 부활하다   come back to life or consciousness
The patient has begun to **revive**, but his revival may be temporary.
그 환자는 소생하기 시작했지만, 그의 회복이 일시적일지도 모른다.

---

key words
palatial a 궁전의, 호화로운 / lengthy a 긴, 오랜 / increasingly ad 점점, 더욱 더
temporary a 일시적인, 임시의

Unit 35

Exercise

A. Complete the sentence.

1. The patient has begun to _____, but his revival may be temporary.
   그 환자는 소생하기 시작했지만, 그의 회복이 일시적일지도 모른다.

2. He is better at _____ looks than at reading hearts.
   그는 마음을 읽기보다는 외모를 더 잘 관찰한다.

3. He was worried about _____ the sources of his information.
   그는 그의 정보의 출처를 폭로하는 것에 대해 염려했다.

4. Above all, scientific terms need for _____ definitions.
   특히 과학용어는 정확한 정의를 필요로 한다.

5. I was asked to _____ a rather lengthy poem for a school event.
   나는 학교 행사에서 다소 긴 시를 낭송하도록 요청 받았다.

6. Westerners enjoy the mental and _____ health taekwondo gives them.
   서양 사람들은 태권도가 가져다 주는 정신적, 신체적 건강을 즐긴다.

7. I was _____ to go to the dance party.
   나는 댄스파티에 가야만 했다.

8. Of the two, my _____ is for the smaller car.
   둘 중에 내가 선호하는 것은 더 작은 차다.

9. Did you manage to _____ them?
   당신은 그들을 따라잡기는 했나?

10. Sweet odors of flowers _____ the garden.
    정원에는 달콤한 꽃 향기가 가득했다.

11. Prisoners who behave well enjoy special _____.
    행동이 바른 수감자들은 특권을 누린다.

12. Nowadays we _____ increasingly on computers.
    요즘 우리는 점점 더 컴퓨터에 의지하고 있다.

13. He _____ showed us through his palatial home.
    그는 우리들에게 그의 궁전 같은 집을 자랑스럽게 보여주었다.

14. I _____ the fact that the house could be easily damaged by strong winds.
    나는 그 집이 강풍의 피해를 받기 쉽다는 사실은 미처 고려하지 못했다.

15. He talks a lot about others' _____ business.
    그는 남의 사적인 일에 대한 이야기를 잘 한다.

16. The very rich cannot _____ very rich for more than three generations.
    부자는 3세대 이상을 부유한 상태로 남지 못한다.

17. The _____ was aware of the danger of nuclear weapons.
    그 물리학자는 핵무기의 위험성을 알고 있었다.

18. That's how we've been handling all our contracts _____.
    그것이 우리가 최근까지 계약을 다루어왔던 방법이다.

Hint

| remain | precise | observe | preference | oblige | reveal | privilege | rely | physicist |
| proudly | revive | pervade | overtake | recite | physical | recently | private | overlook |

Unit 35

Exercise

B. Fill in the word and meaning.

	Word	Meaning
01	proudly	
02	oblige	
03	physical	
04	recite	
05	pervade	
06	observe	
07	rely	
08	preference	
09	overlook	
10	revive	
11	private	
12	remain	
13	overtake	
14	privilege	
15	reveal	
16	precise	
17	recently	
18	physicist	

	Meaning	Word
01	강요하다, 고맙게 여기다	
02	관찰하다, (규칙 등을)준수하다	
03	간과하다, 내려다보다	
04	따라 잡다, 덮치다	
05	신체의, 물질의	
06	물리학자	
07	정확한, 정밀한	
08	선호, 좋아하는 물건	
09	널리 퍼지다, 충만하다	
10	개인적인, 사적인	
11	특권, 특권을 주다	
12	자랑스럽게, 거만하게	
13	최근에, 요즈음	
14	낭송하다, 말하다	
15	의지하다, 믿다	
16	남다, ~인 상태로 있다, 유적	
17	드러내다, 폭로하다	
18	소생하다, 부활하다	

🎧 **C. Listen, write the word and meaning.** Track 105

	Word	Meaning		Word	Meaning
01			10		
02			11		
03			12		
04			13		
05			14		
06			15		
07			16		
08			17		
09			18		

Unit 36

🎧 Listen and repeat. Track 106

01 scarcely
[skéərsli]
ad 거의 ~않다, 간신히   almost not
He can **scarcely** tell fact from fiction.
그는 현실과 허구를 거의 구별하지 못한다.

02 scholar
[skálər]
n 학자, 고전학자   a person who studies and has a lot of knowledge
How unfortunate that hopeful **scholar** was to fall ill before completing his studies!
그 전도 유망한 학자가 연구를 마치지 못하고 병이 들었다니 정말 불운하구나!

03 significant
[signífikənt]
a 중요한, 의미 있는, 상당한   important or large enough to be noticed
Small company plays a **significant** role in the life of our communities.
소규모의 회사는 우리의 사회생활에서 중요한 역할을 한다.

04 similarity
[sìməlǽrəti]
n 비슷함, 유사점   a characteristic that people or things have which makes them similar
The article discussed at length the **similarities** between the two sports.
그 기사에서 그 두 스포츠의 유사점에 대해 자세하게 다루었다.

05 solution
[səlúːʃən]
n 해결, 용해   a way of solving a problem, dealing with a difficult situation
We must apply our minds to finding a **solution**.
우리는 해결책을 찾는데 마음을 모아야 한다.

06 sophomore
[sáfəmɔ̀ːr]
n 2학년생 / **a** 2학년생의   a student in the second year of college or high school
We will be promoted to the **sophomores** next year.
우리들은 내년에 2학년으로 진급한다.

07 steady
[stédi]
a 확고한, 착실한, 한결같은   firmly fixed; staying the same
We look forward to a **steady** growth in our dealings.
우리는 거래관계가 한결같은 성장을 이룰 수 있길 기대합니다.

08 steep
[stiːp]
a 가파른 / **v** 적시다   rising or falling quickly; at a sharp angle
The road is too **steep** to ride up on a bike.
그 길은 너무 가파른 곳이라 자전거를 타고 올라갈 수 없다.

09 suspicion
[səspíʃən]
n 의심, 혐의   a feeling that somebody has done something wrong
After a crime, **suspicion** naturally falls on the person who has a motive for it.
범죄가 일어난 후엔, 그 일을 할 동기를 가진 사람에게로 자연스럽게 혐의가 돌아간다.

key words
characteristic **n** 특성, 특질 / at length 상세히 / angle **n** 각도 / motive **n** 동기

🎧 Listen and repeat. Track 107

10	**swear**	v 맹세하다, 선서하다	to make a serious promise
	[swɛər]		I **swear** I will never leave you.
			결코 너를 떠나지 않을 것을 맹세할 것이다.

11	**tough**	a 강인한, 질긴, 힘든	difficult to cut, break, or bend
	[tʌf]		This meat is so **tough** that I can hardly chew it.
			이 고기는 너무 질겨서 거의 씹을 수가 없다.

12	**tradition**	n 전통, 전설	a custom, way of doing something that has continued from the past
	[trədíʃən]		In the West, women by **tradition** wear white dresses when they get married.
			서양에서는 전통에 따라 여자들이 결혼식을 할 때 하얀 드레스를 입는다.

13	**urgent**	a 긴급한, 절박한	needing immediate attention
	[ə́ːrdʒənt]		I've got an **urgent** problem, and was wondering if you could help me.
			긴급한 일이 생겨서 그러는데 혹시 나를 도와줄 수 있나요?

14	**useless**	a 쓸모 없는, 무익한	of no use; worthless
	[júːslis]		Don't expend all your energy on such a **useless** work.
			그처럼 쓸모 없는 일에 너의 힘을 모두 쓰지 마라.

15	**vanish**	v 사라지다, 희미해지다	to disappear suddenly; to stop existing
	[vǽniʃ]		Eventually the event **vanished** from memory.
			결국 그 사건은 사람들의 기억에서 사라져 갔다.

16	**vapor**	n 증기 / v 증발하다	a mass of very small drops of liquid in the air, for example steam
	[véipər]		Much of water turns into **vapor**, forming mist and clouds.
			많은 물이 증발하여 안개와 구름을 형성 한다.

17	**wireless**	a 무선의 / n 무선전신	not require any wires
	[wáiərlis]		In **wireless** systems, antennas and towers are also part of the network.
			무선 시스템에서는 안테나와 타워도 네트워크의 일부분이다.

18	**witness**	n 증거, 목격자	something to testify the crime or accident
	[wítnis]		History is the **witness** that testifies to the passing of time.
			역사란 시간의 경과를 입증하는 증거이다.

key words
chew v 씹다 / eventually ad 결국 / mist n 안개 / testify v 증명하다

Unit 36 181

Exercise

A. Complete the sentence.

1. The article discussed at length the _____ between the two sports.
   그 기사에서 그 두 스포츠의 유사점에 대해 자세하게 다루었다.

2. This meat is so _____ that I can hardly chew it.
   이 고기는 너무 질겨서 거의 씹을 수가 없다.

3. He can _____ tell fact from fiction.
   그는 현실과 허구를 거의 구별하지 못한다.

4. We will be promoted to the _____ next year.
   우리들은 내년에 2학년으로 진급한다.

5. In _____ systems, antennas and towers are also part of the network.
   무선 시스템에서는 안테나와 타워도 네트워크의 일부분이다.

6. After a crime, _____ naturally falls on the person who has a motive for it.
   범죄가 일어난 후엔, 그 일을 할 동기를 가진 사람에게로 자연스럽게 혐의가 돌아간다.

7. In the West, women by _____ wear white dresses when they get married.
   서양에서는 전통에 따라 여자들이 결혼식을 할 때 하얀 드레스를 입는다.

8. Small company plays a _____ role in the life of our communities.
   소규모의 회사는 우리의 사회생활에서 중요한 역할을 한다.

9. I've got an _____ problem, and was wondering if you could help me.
   긴급한 일이 생겨서 그러는데 혹시 나를 도와줄 수 있나요?

10. We look forward to a _____ growth in our dealings.
    우리는 거래관계가 한결같은 성장을 이룰 수 있길 기대합니다.

11. Don't expend all your energy on such a _____ work.
    그처럼 쓸모 없는 일에 너의 힘을 모두 쓰지 마라.

12. How unfortunate that hopeful _____ was to fall ill before completing his studies!
    그 전도 유망한 학자가 연구를 마치지 못하고 병이 들었다니 정말 불운하구나!

13. I _____ I will never leave you.
    결코 너를 떠나지 않을 것을 맹세할 것이다.

14. Much of water turns into _____, forming mist and clouds.
    많은 물이 증발하여 안개와 구름을 형성 한다.

15. We must apply our minds to finding a _____.
    우리는 해결책을 찾는데 마음을 모아야 한다.

16. History is the _____ that testifies to the passing of time.
    역사란 시간의 경과를 입증하는 증거이다.

17. Eventually the event _____ from memory.
    결국 그 사건은 사람들의 기억에서 사라져 갔다.

18. The road is too _____ to ride up on a bike.
    그 길은 너무 가파른 곳이라 자전거를 타고 올라갈 수 없다.

Hint

solution wireless scarcely witness suspicion sophomore tradition steep swear
urgent scholar vanish steady useless significant similarity tough vapor

Exercise

B. Fill in the word and meaning.

	Word	Meaning
01	significant	
02	swear	
03	tough	
04	scarcely	
05	suspicion	
06	useless	
07	scholar	
08	urgent	
09	vanish	
10	solution	
11	witness	
12	sophomore	
13	wireless	
14	steep	
15	vapor	
16	similarity	
17	tradition	
18	steady	

	Meaning	Word
01	거의 ~않다, 간신히	
02	학자, 고전학자	
03	중요한, 의미 있는, 상당한	
04	비슷함, 유사점	
05	해결, 용해	
06	2학년생, 2학년	
07	확고한, 착실한, 한결같은	
08	가파른, 적시다	
09	의심, 혐의	
10	맹세하다, 선서하다	
11	강인한, 질긴, 힘든	
12	전통, 전설	
13	긴급한, 절박한	
14	쓸모 없는, 무익한	
15	사라지다, 희미해지다	
16	증기, 증발하다	
17	무선의, 무선전신	
18	증거, 목격자	

🎧 **C. Listen, write the word and meaning.** (Track 108)

	Word	Meaning		Word	Meaning
01			10		
02			11		
03			12		
04			13		
05			14		
06			15		
07			16		
08			17		
09			18		

Review 18

A. Read and fill in the word and meaning.

word	definition	meaning
	belonging to one particular person or group	
	to force somebody to do something	
	come back to life or consciousness	
	a special right or advantage that	
	to watch somebody/something carefully	
	not long ago	
	to show something that was hidden before	
	an interest in one thing more that another	
	fail to see; to have a view over something	
	connected with your body	
	to trust somebody/something to work or behave well	
	to spread through every part of something	
	come up or catch up with; to happen unexpectedly or suddenly	
	to stay or continue in the same place or condition	
	a person who studies or is an expert in physics	
	to say aloud a piece of writing from memory	
	accurate; exact	
	used to express the feeling satisfied about something	

Hint

remain   precise   observe   preference   oblige   reveal   privilege   rely   physicist
proudly   revive   pervade   overtake   recite   physical   recently   private   overlook

B. Read and fill in the word and meaning.

word	definition	meaning
	a mass of very small drops of liquid in the air, for example steam	
	of no use; worthless	
	rising or falling quickly; at a sharp angle	
	a person who studies and has a lot of knowledge	
	not require any wires	
	a feeling that somebody has done something wrong	
	a custom, way of doing something that has continued from the past	
	to disappear suddenly; to stop existing	
	important or large enough to be noticed	
	firmly fixed; staying the same	
	almost not	
	a way of solving a problem, dealing with a difficult situation	
	difficult to cut, break, or bend	
	needing immediate attention	
	a student in the second year of college or high school	
	something to testify the crime or accident	
	a characteristic that people or things have which makes them similar	
	to make a serious promise	

Hint

solution   wireless   scarcely   witness   suspicion   sophomore   tradition   steep   swear
urgent   scholar   vanish   steady   useless   significant   similarity   tough   vapor

Review 18

Unit 37

🎧 Listen and repeat. Track 109

01 additional **a** 부가된, 추가의   added; extra
[ədíʃənəl]
Please write if you require **additional** information.
그밖에 추가적인 정보가 필요하면 적어주세요.

02 affection **n** 애정, 감동   a feeling of loving or liking somebody/something
[əfékʃən]
The **affections** are the noblest parts in human nature.
애정은 인간의 본성 중 가장 숭고한 부분이다.

03 anxiety **n** 걱정, 불안   a feeling of worry or fear
[æŋzáiəti]
We waited for news with a growing sense of **anxiety**.
우리는 점점 더 불안을 느끼며 소식을 기다렸다.

04 apology **n** 사과, 변명   a spoken or written statement that you are sorry for something
[əpálədʒi]
She accepted blame and sent me profuse **apologies**.
그녀는 비난을 받아들이고 나에게 거듭 사과했다.

05 banish **v** 추방하다, 내쫓다   to make somebody go away
[bǽniʃ]
The **banished** king was restored to the throne after 10 years.
추방되었던 왕은 10년 후에 왕권을 회복하였다.

06 bark **v** 짖다, 소리치며 말하다   to make a loud, aggressive noise
[ba:rk]
My dog always **barks** loudly when he sees a stranger.
나의 개는 낯선 사람을 보면 항상 큰 소리로 짖는다.

07 breakdown **n** 쇠약, 고장   a feeling that somebody cannot continue living and working normally
[bréikdàun]
The financial worry gave her nervous **breakdown**.
재정적인 걱정으로 그녀는 신경 쇠약에 걸렸다.

08 breakthrough **n** 중요한 성과, 획기적 발전   an important discovery or development
[bréikθrù:]
His research led to a major **breakthrough** in the fight against cancer.
그의 연구는 암 퇴치에 관한 중요한 성과를 이룩했다.

09 cleave **v** 쪼개다, 찢다   to split or divide something into two separate parts
[kli:v]
He ordered his servants to **cleave** these blocks of wood in two.
그는 하인들에게 이 나무토막들을 두 개로 쪼개라고 명령했다.

---

key words
profuse **a** 수없이 많은 / restore **v** 회복시키다 / throne **n** 왕권, 왕위 / aggressive **a** 공격적인

🎧 Listen and repeat. Track 110

10 coeducation [kòuedʒukéiʃən]
n 남녀 공학   a school teaching both boy and girl students
They have argued whether **coeducation** is proper or improper for two hours.
그들은 남녀 공학이 적절한지 부적절한지를 두 시간 째 논쟁하고 있다.

11 compulsory [kəmpʌ́lsəri]
a 의무적인, 강제적인   that must be done, by law, rules, etc
He regards so-called **compulsory** education as useless.
그는 소위 의무교육을 쓸모 없는 것으로 여긴다.

12 consist [kənsíst]
v 이루어지다, ~에 있다   to be formed from particular things or people
The human body **consists** of billions of tiny cells.
인간의 신체는 수십 억 개의 자그마한 세포들로 이루어져 있다.

13 deal [di:l]
n 거래 / v 다루다, 거래하다   an arrangement, especially in business
I'd like to firm up this **deal** as soon as possible.
가능한 한 빨리 이 거래를 확정짓고 싶다.

14 directly [diréktli]
ad 곧장, 직접, 즉시   in a direct line or way
The storekeeper said that they were brought **directly** from the farm.
가게 주인이 그것들은 농장에서 직접 가져오는 것이라 했다.

15 discharge [distʃɑ́:rdʒ]
v 이행하다, 해임하다, 방출하다   to do something that you have to do
The crowd obstructed the police to **discharge** their duties.
군중은 경찰이 자신들의 의무를 이행하는 것을 방해했다.

16 donation [dounéiʃən]
n 기부, 기증   money, etc that is given to a person or an organization to help people
Volunteers collected **donations** for the benefit of the handicapped.
자원 봉사자들이 장애자 복지를 위한 기부금을 모았다.

17 endurance [indjúərəns]
n 인내, 지구력, 내구성   the ability to continue doing something
I work out every day to increase muscle and develop **endurance**.
나는 근육을 늘리고 지구력을 키우기 위해 매일 운동을 한다.

18 engage [engéidʒ]
v 고용하다, 약속하다   to give work to somebody
She **engaged** the leading lawyer for her son.
그녀는 아들을 위해서 일류 변호사를 고용했다.

---

key words
so-called a 소위 / **obstruct v** 차단하다, 방해하다 / **handicapped a** 신체적 장애가 있는
leading a 일류의, 손꼽히는

Exercise

A. Complete the sentence.

1. He regards so-called _____ education as useless.
   그는 소위 의무교육을 쓸모 없는 것으로 여긴다.
2. My dog always _____ loudly when he sees a stranger.
   나의 개는 낯선 사람을 보면 항상 큰 소리로 짖는다.
3. The _____ are the noblest parts in human nature.
   애정은 인간의 본성 중 가장 숭고한 부분이다.
4. The storekeeper said that they were brought _____ from the farm.
   가게 주인이 그것들은 농장에서 직접 가져오는 것이라 했다.
5. She accepted blame and sent me profuse _____.
   그녀는 비난을 받아들이고 나에게 거듭 사과했다.
6. She _____ he leading lawyer for her son.
   그녀는 아들을 위해서 일류 변호사를 고용했다.
7. The _____ king was restored to the throne after 10 years.
   추방되었던 왕은 10년 후에 왕권을 회복하였다.
8. His research led to a major _____ in the fight against cancer.
   그의 연구는 암 퇴치에 관한 중요한 성과를 이룩했다.
9. He ordered his servants to _____ these blocks of wood in two.
   그는 하인들에게 이 나무토막들을 두 개로 쪼개라고 명령했다.
10. They have argued whether _____ is proper or improper for two hours.
    그들은 남녀 공학이 적절한지 부적절한지를 두 시간 째 논쟁하고 있다.
11. Volunteers collected _____ for the benefit of the handicapped.
    자원 봉사자들이 장애자 복지를 위한 기부금을 모았다.
12. Please write if you require _____ information.
    그밖에 추가적인 정보가 필요하면 적어주세요.
13. The human body _____ of billions of tiny cells.
    인간의 신체는 수십 억 개의 자그마한 세포들로 이루어져 있다.
14. We waited for news with a growing sense of _____.
    우리는 점점 더 불안을 느끼며 소식을 기다렸다.
15. The financial worry gave her nervous _____.
    재정적인 걱정으로 그녀는 신경 쇠약에 걸렸다.
16. I'd like to firm up this _____ as soon as possible.
    가능한 한 빨리 이 거래를 확정짓고 싶다.
17. I work out every day to increase muscle and develop _____.
    나는 근육을 늘리고 지구력을 키우기 위해 매일 운동을 한다.
18. The crowd obstructed the police to _____ their duties.
    군중은 경찰이 자신들의 의무를 이행하는 것을 방해했다.

Hint

additional   compulsory   consist   engage   bark   directly   banish   discharge   coeducation
endurance   breakdown   apology   cleave   deal   anxiety   donation   affection   breakthrough

Unit 37

Exercise

B. Fill in the word and meaning.

	Word	Meaning
01	bark	
02	consist	
03	additional	
04	donation	
05	breakthrough	
06	affection	
07	endurance	
08	deal	
09	banish	
10	discharge	
11	breakdown	
12	engage	
13	anxiety	
14	compulsory	
15	directly	
16	cleave	
17	apology	
18	coeducation	

	Meaning	Word
01	부가된, 추가의	
02	애정, 감동	
03	걱정, 불안	
04	사과, 변명	
05	추방하다, 내쫓다	
06	짖다, 소리치며 말하다	
07	쇠약, 고장	
08	중요한 성과, 획기적 발전	
09	쪼개다, 찢다	
10	남녀 공학	
11	의무적인, 강제적인	
12	이루어지다, ~에 있다	
13	거래, 다루다, 거래하다	
14	곧장, 직접, 즉시	
15	이행하다, 해임하다, 방출하다	
16	기부, 기증	
17	인내, 지구력, 내구성	
18	고용하다, 약속하다	

🎧 C. Listen, write the word and meaning. (Track 111)

	Word	Meaning		Word	Meaning
01			10		
02			11		
03			12		
04			13		
05			14		
06			15		
07			16		
08			17		
09			18		

Unit 38

🎧 Listen and repeat. Track 112

01 faint [feint] — v 기절하다 / a 희미한, 어질어질한 — to lose consciousness
Because I **fainted**, I was immediately taken to a hospital.
내가 기절을 해서 즉시 병원으로 옮겨졌다.

02 fate [feit] — n 운명, 숙명 — your future; something that happens to you
It's certain that more bears will share this **fate**.
더 많은 곰들이 이러한 운명을 맞게 될 것이 분명하다.

03 flagrant [fléigrənt] — a 악명 높은, 극악한 — scandalous; very wicked
Are you a **flagrant** criminal or wanted?
당신은 악명 높은 범죄자입니까 아니면 지명수배자입니까?

04 fortunately [fɔ́:rtʃənətli] — ad 운 좋게, 다행히 — by good luck; luckily
He was **fortunately** immune from the disease and could take care of the sick.
다행스럽게도 그는 그 병에 면역되어 있어서 환자들을 돌볼 수가 있었다.

05 genetic [dʒinétik] — a 유전의, 유전학의 — connected with the units in the cells of living things
Fortunately, scientists have developed some **genetic** treatments for these problems.
다행히도, 과학자들이 이러한 문제를 위한 어떤 유전자 치료를 개발하였다.

06 guild [gild] — n 동업 조합, 연맹 — an organization of people who do the same job
This **guild** of bank clerk supplied stories to a hundred newspapers.
이 은행원 조합은 많은 신문사에 기사를 공급했다.

07 hesitate [hézətèit] — v 주저하다, 망설이다 — to pause before you do something
I'm glad you didn't **hesitate** too long.
당신이 너무 오래 망설이지 않아서 다행이다.

08 hollow [hálou] — n 구멍, 우묵한 곳 — an area that is lower than the land around it
The ground is washed out in little **hollows** all over from the rain.
비 때문에 마당에 패어져서 우묵한 곳들이 생겼다.

09 infant [ínfənt] — n 유아 / a 유아의 — a baby or very young child
In the few weeks after birth, the **infant** is not able to see properly.
태어나서 몇 주 동안에 유아는 제대로 볼 수가 없다.

---

key words
scandalous a 악명 높은 / wicked a 사악한, 악질인 / immune a 면한, 면역의

🎧 Listen and repeat. Track 113

10 infect [infékt]
v 전염시키다, 영향을 미치다   to cause somebody/something to have a disease or illness
About one million Americans are now **infected** with the HIV virus.
현재 백만 명 정도의 미국인이 HIV 바이러스에 전염 되었다.

11 laboratory [lǽbərətɔ̀:ri]
n 실험실, 실습실   a room or building that is used for scientific research
The blood samples were sent to the **laboratory** for analysis.
그 혈액 샘플은 분석하기 위해 실험실로 보내졌다.

12 lecture [léktʃə:r]
n 강의, 훈계   a talk to teach people about a particular subject
His **lectures** are interesting but he never seems to come to the point.
그의 강의는 재미있지만 결코 핵심에 이르지는 못하는 것 같다.

13 magnificent [mægnífəsənt]
a 웅대한, 장엄한   extremely impressive and attractive
A sacred ritual took place in the **magnificent** temple.
신성한 의식이 그 장엄한 사원에서 거행되었다.

14 magnify [mǽgnəfài]
v 확대하다, 과장하다   make something look larger than its real size
The microscope **magnifies** objects three hundred times.
그 현미경은 물체를 3백배로 확대한다.

15 medieval [mì:dií:vəl]
a 중세의, 중고의   of the Middle Ages
Its use in business actually goes back to late **medieval** times.
그것이 비즈니스에서 실제로 사용되기 시작한 것은 중세말로 거슬러 올라간다.

16 Mediterranean [mèdətəréiniən]
n 지중해   a large inland sea between Africa and Europe
The ship vanished in the **Mediterranean** without trace.
그 배는 지중해에서 흔적도 없이 사라졌다.

17 notify [nóutəfài]
v 알리다, 신고하다   make known
Do you want me to **notify** you when that book is returned?
그 책이 반납되면 제가 당신에게 알려드릴까요?

18 notion [nóuʃən]
n 개념, 생각, 의견   a general idea; an intention
The postmodern feminists reject the **notion**, which they call ' grand theory .'
포스트모더니즘 여성학자들은 그들이' 웅대한 이론 이라고 부르는 그 개념에 반대한다.

---

key words
analysis n 분석 / sacred a 신성한, 성스러운 / ritual n 종교적인 의식 / inland a 내의
feminist n 여권 주장자

Unit 38 191

Exercise

A. Complete the sentence.

1. The blood samples were sent to the _____ for analysis.
   그 혈액 샘플은 분석하기 위해 실험실로 보내졌다.

2. Because I _____, I was immediately taken to a hospital.
   내가 기절을 해서 즉시 병원으로 옮겨졌다.

3. The postmodern feminists reject the _____, which they call ' grand theory .'
   포스트모더니즘 여성학자들은 그들이 웅대한 이론 이라고 부르는 그 개념에 반대한다.

4. He was _____ immune from the disease and could take care of the sick.
   다행스럽게도 그는 그 병에 면역되어 있어서 환자들을 돌볼 수가 있었다.

5. The microscope _____ objects three hundred times.
   그 현미경은 물체를 3백배로 확대한다.

6. Fortunately, scientists have developed some _____ treatments for these problems.
   다행히도, 과학자들이 이러한 문제를 위한 어떤 유전자 치료를 개발하였다.

7. I'm glad you didn't _____ too long.
   당신이 너무 오래 망설이지 않아서 다행이다.

8. In the few weeks after birth, the _____ is not able to see properly.
   태어나서 몇 주 동안에 유아는 제대로 볼 수가 없다.

9. It's certain that more bears will share this _____.
   더 많은 곰들이 이러한 운명을 맞게 될 것이 분명하다.

10. About one million Americans are now _____ with the HIV virus.
    현재 백만 명 정도의 미국인이 HIV 바이러스에 전염 되었다.

11. His _____ are interesting but he never seems to come to the point.
    그의 강의는 재미있지만 결코 핵심에 이르지는 못하는 것 같다.

12. Are you a _____ criminal or wanted?
    당신은 악명 높은 범죄자입니까 아니면 지명수배자입니까?

13. A sacred ritual took place in the _____ temple.
    신성한 의식이 그 장엄한 사원에서 거행되었다.

14. This _____ of bank clerk supplied stories to a hundred newspapers.
    이 은행원 조합은 많은 신문사에 기사를 공급했다.

15. Its use in business actually goes back to late _____ times.
    그것이 비즈니스에서 실제로 사용되기 시작한 것은 중세말로 거슬러 올라간다.

16. The ground is washed out in little _____ all over from the rain.
    비 때문에 마당에 패어져서 우묵한 곳들이 생겼다.

17. The ship vanished in the _____ without trace.
    그 배는 지중해에서 흔적도 없이 사라졌다.

18. Do you want me to _____ you when that book is returned?
    그 책이 반납되면 제가 당신에게 알려드릴까요?

Hint

hollow   faint   Mediterranean   genetic   lecture   notion   fate   magnify   magnificent
notify   infect   laboratory   medieval   hesitate   infant   guild   flagrant   fortunately

Unit 38

Exercise

B. Fill in the word and meaning.

	Word	Meaning
01	guild	
02	infect	
03	faint	
04	hesitate	
05	magnificent	
06	fate	
07	lecture	
08	laboratory	
09	flagrant	
10	medieval	
11	infant	
12	Mediterranean	
13	fortunately	
14	notify	
15	magnify	
16	genetic	
17	notion	
18	hollow	

	Meaning	Word
01	기절하다, 희미한, 어질어질한	
02	운명, 숙명	
03	악명 높은, 극악한	
04	운 좋게, 다행히	
05	유전의, 유전학의	
06	동업 조합, 연맹	
07	주저하다, 망설이다	
08	구멍, 우묵한 곳	
09	유아, 유아의	
10	전염시키다, 영향을 미치다	
11	실험실, 실습실	
12	강의, 훈계	
13	웅대한, 장엄한	
14	확대하다, 과장하다	
15	중세의, 중고의	
16	지중해	
17	알리다, 신고하다	
18	개념, 생각, 의견	

C. Listen, write the word and meaning. Track 114

	Word	Meaning		Word	Meaning
01			10		
02			11		
03			12		
04			13		
05			14		
06			15		
07			16		
08			17		
09			18		

Review 19

A. Read and fill in the word and meaning.

word	definition	meaning
	a feeling that somebody cannot continue living and working normally	
	in a direct line or way	
	to give work to somebody	
	an important discovery or development	
	added; extra	
	to do something that you have to do	
	a school teaching both boy and girl students	
	to make somebody go away	
	to split or divide something into two separate parts	
	money, etc that is given to a person or an organization to help people	
	a feeling of loving or liking somebody/something	
	to make a loud, aggressive noise	
	the ability to continue doing something	
	that must be done, by law, rules, etc	
	an arrangement, especially in business	
	a feeling of worry or fear	
	to be formed from particular things or people	
	a spoken or written statement that you are sorry for something	

Hint

additional   compulsory   consist   engage   bark   directly   banish   discharge   coeducation
endurance   breakdown   apology   cleave   deal   anxiety   donation   affection   breakthrough

B. Read and fill in the word and meaning.

word	definition	meaning
	a baby or very young child	
	by good luck; luckily	
	an area that is lower than the land around it	
	make known	
	connected with the units in the cells of living things	
	to pause before you do something	
	a large inland sea between Africa and Europe	
	to cause somebody/something to have a disease or illness	
	a general idea; an intention	
	an organization of people who do the same job	
	a talk to teach people about a particular subject	
	scandalous; very wicked	
	extremely impressive and attractive	
	a room or building that is used for scientific research	
	to lose consciousness	
	of the Middle Ages	
	your future; something that happens to you	
	make something look larger than its real size	

Hint

hollow　faint　Mediterranean　genetic　lecture　notion　fate　magnify　magnificent
notify　infect　laboratory　　　medieval　hesitate　infant　guild　flagrant　fortunately

Review 19

Unit 39

🎧 Listen and repeat. (Track 115)

01 obtain [əbtéin]
v 얻다, 획득하다   to get something
It will take about three months to **obtain** approval from the government.
정부로부터 승인을 얻는 데는 세 달 가량 걸린다.

02 offensive [əfénsiv]
a 무례한, 불쾌한, 공격의   unpleasant; insulting
Your **offensive** and insulting behavior hurted her.
당신의 무례하고 모욕적인 행동이 그녀에게 상처를 주었다.

03 overwhelm [òuvərhwélm]
v 압도하다, 질리게 하다   to be so powerful, etc that somebody cannot deal with it
The department store guards were nearly **overwhelmed** by the crowds of shoppers waiting for the sale to begin.
그 백화점 경비원들은 세일이 시작되기를 기다리는 손님들의 무리에 거의 압도되었다.

04 overwork [òuvərwə́:rk]
v 과로하다 / n 과로, 초과 노동   to work too hard
I was so **overworked** this week, what with all the script changes that you demanded.
당신이 요구한 대로 대본을 바꾸느라 이번 주에 너무 과로했다.

05 pilgrim [pílgrim]
n 순례자, 나그네   a person who travels a long way to visit a religious place
Christian **pilgrims** were travelling to Jerusalem.
기독교 순례자들이 예루살렘으로 가고 있었다.

06 positive [pázətiv]
a 명확한, 적극적인   certain; sure
I'm **positive** there was no defect when the item left the factory.
그 제품이 공장에서 떠날 때는 전혀 하자가 없었음이 확실하다.

07 prejudice [prédʒudis]
n 편견, 선입관   a strong unreasonable feeling of not liking somebody/something
She will need a reeducation to get rid of her **prejudices** against people of other races.
그녀는 다른 인종의 사람들에 대한 그녀의 편견을 제거하기 위해 재교육이 필요할 것이다.

08 premature [prì:mətjúər]
a 시기상조의, 조기의   happening before the normal or expected time
Although his death was **premature**, I am confident that he completed his life with great satisfaction.
비록 그의 죽음이 시기상조이기 하였으나 그가 참으로 만족스러운 인생을 마쳤다고 확신한다.

09 prior [práiər]
a 먼저의, ~에 우선하는   coming before or earlier
You should arrive at least one hour **prior** to boarding.
탑승에 앞서 최소한 한 시간 먼저 도착하셔야 합니다.

---

key words
approval n 승인력 / defect n 결함, 결점 / reeducation n 재교육

🎧 Listen and repeat. Track 116

10 produce [prədjúːs]   v 생산하다, 제작하다   to grow or make something by a natural process
It takes most fruit trees about 7 years before they are mature enough to **produce** good fruit.
대부분의 과실나무들은 훌륭한 열매를 생산해 낼 만큼 충분히 자라는 데 약 7년이 걸린다.

11 punish [pʌ́niʃ]   v 벌주다, 응징하다   to make somebody suffer because he/she has done wrong
Their mother **punished** them for their rudeness.
그들의 어머니는 그들이 무례한 행동에 대해 벌을 주었다.

12 pursue [pərsúː]   v 추적하다, 추구하다   follow to catch
The soldier **pursued** the fleeing enemy.
군인은 달아나는 적을 추적했다.

13 recover [rikʌ́vər]   v 회복하다, 되찾다   to become well again after you have been ill
When sick people become despondent about their health, it is more difficult for them to **recover**.
환자들이 그들의 건강에 관해서 낙담할 때 그들은 회복하기가 더 어렵다.

14 rein [rein]   n 고삐 / v 억제하다, 지배하다   a long thin piece of leather that is held by the rider
If a coachman found that his horses ran too fast, he had to hold back on the **reins**.
마부는 말들이 너무 빨리 달린다는 것을 알게 되면 그는 고삐를 잡아당겨야만 했다.

15 remove [rimúːv]   v 제거하다, 이동하다   to take somebody/something off or away
I'll **remove** plaque on my teeth in the summer vacation.
나는 여름휴가 동안 치석을 제거할 것이다.

16 republic [ripʌ́blik]   n 공화국   a country that has an elected government and leader
As for the standard of living, the **republic** has caught up with the West.
생활수준에 있어서는, 그 공화국이 서구의 국가들을 따라잡았다.

17 restrict [ristríkt]   v 제한하다, 한정하다   to put a limit on somebody/something
The United States has laws that **restrict** the numbers and kinds of immigrants allowed to enter this country.
미국에는 이 나라에 들어올 이민의 수와 종류를 제한하는 법이 있다.

18 revival [riváivəl]   n 부활, 재상영   the act of becoming strong or popular again
The Australian economy is experiencing a long awaited **revival** after enduring several years of recession.
호주 경제는 여러 해 동안의 경기 침체 후 오랜만에 부활되고 있다.

key words
mature **a** 성숙한, 잘 발육한 / flee **v** 달아나다 / despondent **a** 낙담한, 기가 죽은
coachman **n** 마부 / plaque **n** 치석

Unit 39

Exercise

A. Complete the sentence.

1. You should arrive at least one hour _____ to boarding.
   탑승에 앞서 최소한 한 시간 먼저 도착하셔야 합니다.
2. It will take about three months to _____ approval from the government.
   정부로부터 승인을 얻는 데는 세 달 가량 걸린다.
3. As for the standard of living, the _____ has caught up with the West.
   생활수준에 있어서는, 그 공화국이 서구의 국가들을 따라잡았다.
4. If a coachman found that his horses ran too fast, he had to hold back on the _____.
   마부는 말들이 너무 빨리 달린다는 것을 알게 되면 그는 고삐를 잡아당겨야만 했다.
5. The department store guards were nearly _____ by the crowds of shoppers waiting for the sale to begin.
   그 백화점 경비원들은 세일이 시작되기를 기다리는 손님들의 무리에 거의 압도되었다.
6. Christian _____ were travelling to Jerusalem.
   기독교 순례자들이 예루살렘으로 가고 있었다.
7. I was so _____ this week, what with all the script changes that you demanded.
   당신이 요구한 대로 대본을 바꾸느라 이번 주에 너무 과로했다.
8. Although his death was _____, I am confident that he completed his life with great satisfaction.
   비록 그의 죽음이 시기상조이기 하였으나 그가 참으로 만족스러운 인생을 마쳤다고 확신한다.
9. Your _____ and insulting behavior hurted her.
   당신의 무례하고 모욕적인 행동이 그녀에게 상처를 주었다.
10. It takes most fruit trees about 7 years before they are mature enough to _____ good fruit.
    대부분의 과실나무들은 훌륭한 열매를 생산해 낼 만큼 충분히 자라는 데 약 7년이 걸린다.
11. She will need a reeducation to get rid of her _____ against people of other races.
    그녀는 다른 인종의 사람들에 대한 그녀의 편견을 제거하기 위해 재교육이 필요할 것이다.
12. Their mother _____ them for their rudeness.
    그들의 어머니는 그들이 무례한 행동에 대해 벌을 주었다.
13. When sick people become despondent about their health, it is more difficult for them to _____.
    환자들이 그들의 건강에 관해서 낙담할 때 그들은 회복하기가 더 어렵다.
14. I'm _____ there was no defect when the item left the factory.
    그 제품이 공장에서 떠날 때는 전혀 하자가 없었음이 확실하다.
15. I'll _____ plaque on my teeth in the summer vacation.
    나는 여름휴가 동안 치석을 제거할 것이다.
16. The United States has laws that _____ the numbers and kinds of immigrants allowed to enter this country.
    미국에는 이 나라에 들어올 이민의 수와 종류를 제한하는 법이 있다.
17. The soldier _____ the fleeing enemy.
    군인은 달아나는 적을 추격했다.
18. The Australian economy is experiencing a long awaited _____ after enduring several years of recession.
    호주 경제는 여러 해 동안의 경기 침체 후 오랫만에 부활되고 있다.

Hint

restrict   prejudice   overwhelm   pursue   remove   revival   positive   recover   rein
punish   overwork   premature   republic   offensive   pilgrim   obtain   produce   prior

Exercise

B. Fill in the word and meaning.

	Word	Meaning
01	overwork	
02	prior	
03	obtain	
04	remove	
05	prejudice	
06	restrict	
07	offensive	
08	pursue	
09	produce	
10	recover	
11	positive	
12	revival	
13	punish	
14	overwhelm	
15	republic	
16	premature	
17	rein	
18	pilgrim	

	Meaning	Word
01	얻다, 획득하다	
02	무례한, 불쾌한, 공격의	
03	압도하다, 질리게 하다	
04	과로하다, 과로, 초과 노동	
05	순례자, 나그네	
06	명확한, 적극적인	
07	편견, 선입관	
08	시기상조의, 조기의	
09	먼저의, ~에 우선하는	
10	생산하다, 제작하다	
11	벌주다, 응징하다	
12	추적하다, 추구하다	
13	회복하다, 되찾다	
14	고삐, 억제하다, 지배하다	
15	제거하다, 이동하다	
16	공화국	
17	제한하다, 한정하다	
18	부활, 재상영	

🎧 **C. Listen, write the word and meaning.** (Track 117)

	Word	Meaning		Word	Meaning
01			10		
02			11		
03			12		
04			13		
05			14		
06			15		
07			16		
08			17		
09			18		

Unit 39

Unit 40

🎧 **Listen and repeat.** Track 118

01 scratch [skrætʃ]
v 긁다, 할퀴다   to rub your skin with your nails
I **scratched** the place where the mosquito bit me.
모기 물린 곳을 긁었다.

02 sculpture [skʌ́lptʃər]
n 조각(품) / v 조각하다 the art of making figures or objects from stone, wood, etc
The creation of the mobile greatly extended the limits of the art of **sculpture**.
모빌의 창조는 조각이라는 예술의 한계를 대단히 확장시켰다.

03 sincerely [sinsíərli]
ad 성실히, 충심으로   honestly; faithfully
In spite of all the storms and trials of life, she has tried **sincerely** to do her duty.
인생의 모든 폭풍과 시련에도 불구하고 그녀는 자기 의무를 다하기 위해 성실히 노력했다.

04 single [síŋgəl]
a 단 하나의, 혼자의 / n 하나의 것   only one
All organisms, regardless of their complexity, begin as a **single** cell.
모든 유기체는, 그들의 복잡성에 관계없이, 단 하나의 세포로서 시작한다.

05 souvenir [sùːvəníər]
n 기념품, 선물   something that you keep to remind you of somewhere you have been
I collect **souvenirs** from various places I have visited.
나는 내가 방문하는 여러 곳에서 기념품을 수집한다.

06 specialize [spéʃəlàiz]
v 전문화하다, 전공하다   direct something to a particular object
The business is now highly **specialized**.
그 사업은 지금 매우 전문화되어 있다.

07 stethoscope [stéθəskòup]
n 청진기   the piece of equipment that a doctor uses for listening to your breathing
The doctor examined me by listening to my heart with a **stethoscope**.
의사가 청진기로 심장 소리를 들으며 검진하였다.

08 stimulate [stímjəlèit]
v 자극하다, 흥분시키다   to make something active or more active
Moderate exercise **stimulates** the blood circulation.
적절한 운동은 혈액 순환을 자극한다.

09 talent [tǽlənt]
n 재능, 재주   a natural skill or ability
His many **talents** continue to surprise and delight audiences.
그의 많은 재능은 계속 청중을 놀라게 하고 즐겁게 한다.

key words
organism n 유기체, 생물 / complexity n 복잡성 / moderate a 알맞은, 적당한

🎧 Listen and repeat. Track 119

10	**temper**	**n** 기질, 기분, 노여움 one's natural character
	[témpər]	She inherited her mother's good looks and her father's good **temper**.
		그녀는 어머니의 미모와 아버지의 좋은 기질을 물려받았다.

11	**tragedy**	**n** 비극(적인 사건) a very sad event or situation
	[trǽdʒədi]	I prayed that such a **tragedy** as this would never happen again in this sorrowful land of ours.
		나는 이와 같은 비극이 이 슬픔의 땅에서 다시 일어나지 않기를 기도했다.

12	**transfer**	**v** 이동시키다, 전송하다 to make somebody/something move from one place to another
	[trænsfə́ːr]	Have you thought about **transferring** it to another facility?
		그것을 다른 시설로 이동시키는 것에 대해 생각해 봤나요?

13	**usher**	**n** 안내인 / **v** 안내하다 a person who shows people to their seats in a theatre, church, etc
	[ʌ́ʃər]	The **usher** noticed a man stretched across three seats in the movie theater.
		안내인은 극장에서 한 남자가 대자로 누워 세 자리를 차지하고 있는 것을 알아차렸다.

14	**utensil**	**n** 용구, 기구 a type of tool that is used in the home
	[juːténsəl]	The market was overflowing with colorful clothes and a wide variety of kitchen **utensils**.
		그 시장은 화려한 색깔의 옷과 다양한 부엌 기구들로 넘쳐났다.

15	**verse**	**n** 운문, 시 a writing arranged lines which have a rhythm
	[vəːrs]	He wrote his valentine's message in **verse**.
		그는 발렌타인 데이에 보낼 편지를 시로 썼다.

16	**vice**	**n** 악덕, 결함 a moral weakness or bad habit
	[vais]	He was too upset to distinguish **vice** from virtue.
		그는 너무 화가 나서 악덕과 미덕을 구분할 수가 없었다.

17	**wound**	**n** 상처, 부상 / **v** 상처 입히다 an injury to part of your body
	[wuːnd]	It would be some time before the **wound** would heal enough for him to walk.
		그가 걸을 수 있을 만큼 상처가 낫는 데 어느 정도 시간이 걸릴 것이다.

18	**zeal**	**n** 열심, 열의 great energy or enthusiasm
	[ziːl]	His religious **zeal** borders on madness.
		그의 종교적인 열의는 광기에 가깝다.

---

key words
inherit v 물려받다 / stretch v 대자로 뻗다 / overflow v 넘치다
distinguish v 구별하다 / heal v 치료되다, 낫다

Exercise

A. Complete the sentence.

1. All organisms, regardless of their complexity, begin as a _____ cell.
   모든 유기체는, 그들의 복잡성에 관계없이, 단 하나의 세포로서 시작한다.
2. I collect _____ from various places I have visited.
   나는 내가 방문하는 여러 곳에서 기념품을 수집한다.
3. He wrote his valentine's message in _____.
   그는 발렌타인 데이에 보낼 편지를 시로 썼다.
4. She inherited her mother's good looks and her father's good _____.
   그녀는 어머니의 미모와 아버지의 좋은 기질을 물려받았다.
5. The doctor examined me by listening to my heart with a _____.
   의사가 청진기로 심장 소리를 들으며 검진하였다.
6. Moderate exercise _____ the blood circulation.
   적절한 운동은 혈액 순환을 자극한다.
7. His many _____ continue to surprise and delight audiences.
   그의 많은 재능은 계속 청중을 놀라게 하고 즐겁게 한다.
8. I _____ the place where the mosquito bit me.
   모기 물린 곳을 긁었다.
9. I prayed that such a _____ as this would never happen again in this sorrowful land of ours.
   나는 이와 같은 비극이 이 슬픔의 땅에서 다시는 일어나지 않기를 기도했다.
10. The creation of the mobile greatly extended the limits of the art of _____.
    모빌의 창조는 조각이라는 예술의 한계를 대단히 확장시켰다.
11. Have you thought about _____ it to another facility?
    그것을 다른 시설로 이동시키는 것에 대해 생각해 봤나요?
12. The _____ noticed a man stretched across three seats in the movie theater.
    안내인은 극장에서 한 남자가 대자로 누워 세 자리를 차지하고 있는 것을 알아차렸다.
13. The business is now highly _____.
    그 사업은 지금 매우 전문화되어 있다.
14. The market was overflowing with colorful clothes and a wide variety of kitchen _____.
    그 시장은 화려한 색깔의 옷과 다양한 부엌 기구들로 넘쳐났다.
15. He was too upset to distinguish _____ from virtue.
    그는 너무나 화가 나서 악덕과 미덕을 구분할 수가 없었다.
16. In spite of all the storms and trials of life, she has tried _____ to do her duty.
    인생의 모든 폭풍과 시련에도 불구하고 그녀는 자기 의무를 다하기 위해 성실히 노력했다.
17. His religious _____ borders on madness.
    그의 종교적인 열의는 광기에 가깝다.
18. It would be some time before the _____ would heal enough for him to walk.
    그가 걸을 수 있을 만큼 상처가 낫는 데 어느 정도 시간이 걸릴 것이다.

Hint

| temper | scratch | vice | stimulate | usher | sculpture | talent | stethoscope | souvenir |
| single | transfer | zeal | wound | sincerely | tragedy | verse | specialize | utensil |

Exercise

B. Fill in the word and meaning.

	Word	Meaning
01	souvenir	
02	temper	
03	scratch	
04	usher	
05	stimulate	
06	talent	
07	zeal	
08	sculpture	
09	verse	
10	wound	
11	sincerely	
12	utensil	
13	specialize	
14	vice	
15	tragedy	
16	single	
17	transfer	
18	stethoscope	

	Meaning	Word
01	긁다, 할퀴다	
02	조각(품), 조각하다	
03	성실히, 충심으로	
04	단 하나의, 혼자의, 하나의 것	
05	기념품, 선물	
06	전문화하다, 전공하다	
07	청진기	
08	자극하다, 흥분시키다	
09	재능, 재주	
10	기질, 기분, 노여움	
11	비극(적인 사건)	
12	이동시키다, 전송하다	
13	안내인, 안내하다	
14	용구, 기구	
15	운문, 시	
16	악덕, 결함	
17	상처, 부상, 상처입히다	
18	열심, 열의	

🎧 C. Listen, write the word and meaning. (Track 120)

	Word	Meaning		Word	Meaning
01			10		
02			11		
03			12		
04			13		
05			14		
06			15		
07			16		
08			17		
09			18		

Review 20

A. Read and fill in the word and meaning.

word	definition	meaning
	to grow or make something by a natural process	
	to get something	
	to take somebody/something off or away	
	coming before or earlier	
	the act of becoming strong or popular again	
	happening before the normal or expected time	
	unpleasant; insulting	
	a long thin piece of leather that is held by the rider	
	a strong unreasonable feeling of not liking somebody/something	
	follow to catch	
	to put a limit on somebody/something	
	certain; sure	
	to become well again after you have been ill	
	to be so powerful, etc that somebody cannot deal with it	
	to make somebody suffer because he/she has done wrong	
	a country that has an elected government and leader	
	a person who travels a long way to visit a religious place	
	to work too hard	

Hint

restrict prejudice overwhelm pursue remove revival positive recover rein
punish overwork premature republic offensive pilgrim obtain produce prior

B. Read and fill in the word and meaning.

word	definition	meaning
	the piece of equipment that a doctor uses for listening to your breathing	
	a writing arranged lines which have a rhythm	
	a natural skill or ability	
	the art of making figures or objects from stone, wood, etc	
	an injury to part of your body	
	to rub your skin with your nails	
	a moral weakness or bad habit	
	to make something active or more active	
	honestly; faithfully	
	a very sad event or situation	
	to make somebody/something move from one place to another	
	direct something to a particular object	
	a type of tool that is used in the home	
	one's natural character	
	only one	
	a person who shows people to their seats in a theatre, church, etc	
	great energy or enthusiasm	
	something that you keep to remind you of somewhere you have been	

Hint

temper scratch vice stimulate usher sculpture talent stethoscope souvenir
single transfer zeal wound sincerely tragedy verse specialize utensil

 MEMO

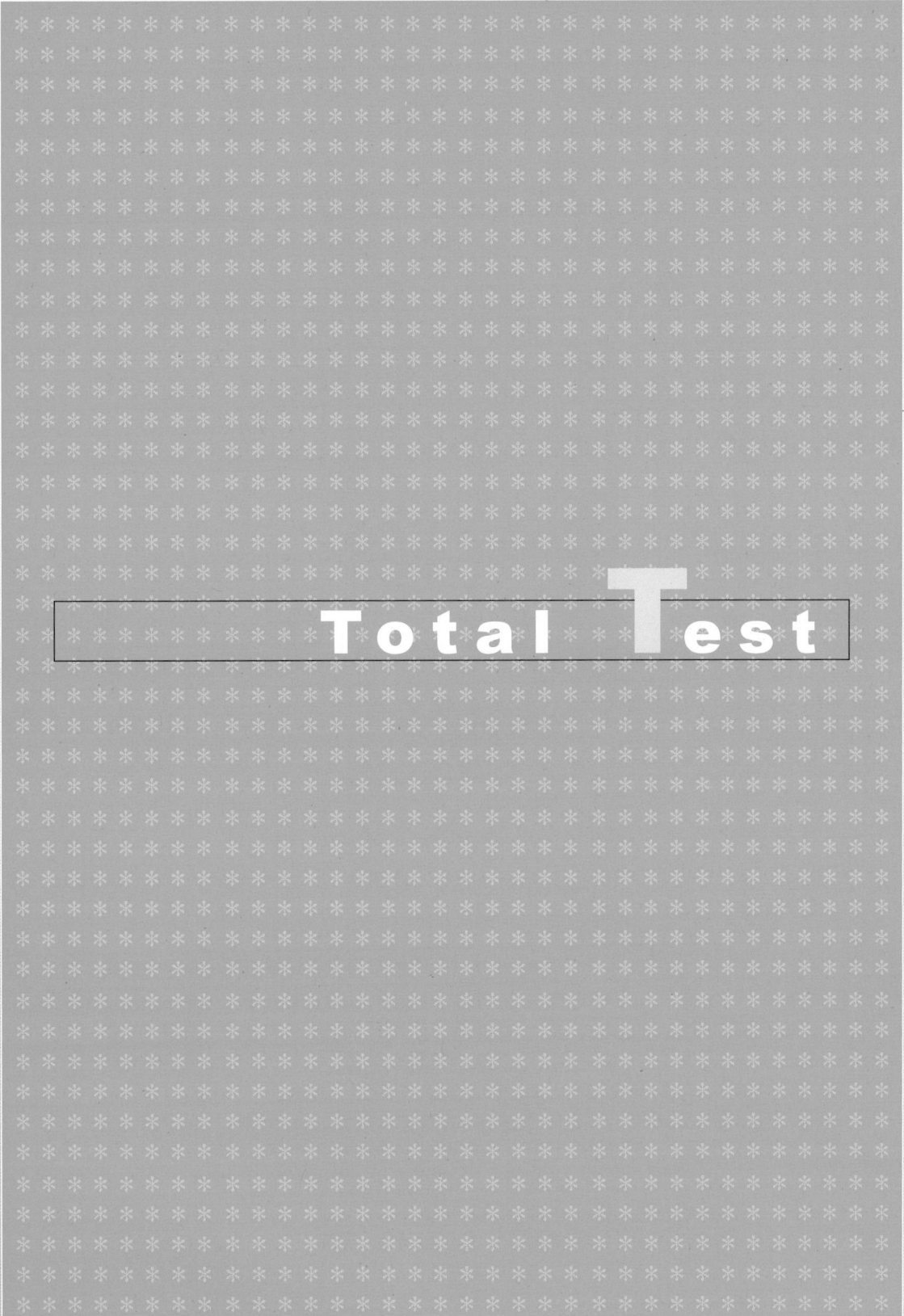

Test 1

Track 3

🎧 **Listen, write the word and meaning.**

	Word	Meaning
01		
02		
03		
04		
05		
06		
07		
08		
09		
10		
11		
12		
13		
14		
15		
16		
17		
18		

점수	점	확인	

Test 2

Track 6

🎧 **Listen, write the word and meaning.**

	Word	Meaning
01		
02		
03		
04		
05		
06		
07		
08		
09		
10		
11		
12		
13		
14		
15		
16		
17		
18		

점수	점	확인	

Test 3

Track 9

🎧 **Listen, write the word and meaning.**

	Word	Meaning
01		
02		
03		
04		
05		
06		
07		
08		
09		
10		
11		
12		
13		
14		
15		
16		
17		
18		

점수	점	확인

Test 4

Track 12

🎧 **Listen, write the word and meaning.**

	Word	Meaning
01		
02		
03		
04		
05		
06		
07		
08		
09		
10		
11		
12		
13		
14		
15		
16		
17		
18		

점수	점	확인

Test 5

Track 15

🎧 **Listen, write the word and meaning.**

	Word	Meaning
01		
02		
03		
04		
05		
06		
07		
08		
09		
10		
11		
12		
13		
14		
15		
16		
17		
18		

점수	점	확인	

Test 6

Track 18

🎧 **Listen, write the word and meaning.**

	Word	Meaning
01		
02		
03		
04		
05		
06		
07		
08		
09		
10		
11		
12		
13		
14		
15		
16		
17		
18		

점수	점	확인	

Test 7

(Track 21)

🎧 **Listen, write the word and meaning.**

	Word	Meaning
01		
02		
03		
04		
05		
06		
07		
08		
09		
10		
11		
12		
13		
14		
15		
16		
17		
18		

점수	점	확인

Test 8

(Track 24)

🎧 **Listen, write the word and meaning.**

	Word	Meaning
01		
02		
03		
04		
05		
06		
07		
08		
09		
10		
11		
12		
13		
14		
15		
16		
17		
18		

점수	점	확인

Test 9

Track 27

🎧 Listen, write the word and meaning.

	Word	Meaning
01		
02		
03		
04		
05		
06		
07		
08		
09		
10		
11		
12		
13		
14		
15		
16		
17		
18		

점수	점	확인	

Test 10

Track 30

🎧 Listen, write the word and meaning.

	Word	Meaning
01		
02		
03		
04		
05		
06		
07		
08		
09		
10		
11		
12		
13		
14		
15		
16		
17		
18		

점수	점	확인	

Test 11

Track 33

🎧 **Listen, write the word and meaning.**

	Word	Meaning
01		
02		
03		
04		
05		
06		
07		
08		
09		
10		
11		
12		
13		
14		
15		
16		
17		
18		

점수	점	확인	

Test 12

Track 36

🎧 **Listen, write the word and meaning.**

	Word	Meaning
01		
02		
03		
04		
05		
06		
07		
08		
09		
10		
11		
12		
13		
14		
15		
16		
17		
18		

점수	점	확인	

Test 13

Track 39

🎧 Listen, write the word and meaning.

	Word	Meaning
01		
02		
03		
04		
05		
06		
07		
08		
09		
10		
11		
12		
13		
14		
15		
16		
17		
18		

점수	점	확인	

Test 14

Track 42

🎧 Listen, write the word and meaning.

	Word	Meaning
01		
02		
03		
04		
05		
06		
07		
08		
09		
10		
11		
12		
13		
14		
15		
16		
17		
18		

점수	점	확인	

Test 15

Track 45

🎧 **Listen, write the word and meaning.**

	Word	Meaning
01		
02		
03		
04		
05		
06		
07		
08		
09		
10		
11		
12		
13		
14		
15		
16		
17		
18		

점수	점	확인

Test 16

Track 48

🎧 **Listen, write the word and meaning.**

	Word	Meaning
01		
02		
03		
04		
05		
06		
07		
08		
09		
10		
11		
12		
13		
14		
15		
16		
17		
18		

점수	점	확인

Test 17

Track 51

🎧 **Listen, write the word and meaning.**

	Word	Meaning
01		
02		
03		
04		
05		
06		
07		
08		
09		
10		
11		
12		
13		
14		
15		
16		
17		
18		

점수	점	확인	

Test 18

Track 54

🎧 **Listen, write the word and meaning.**

	Word	Meaning
01		
02		
03		
04		
05		
06		
07		
08		
09		
10		
11		
12		
13		
14		
15		
16		
17		
18		

점수	점	확인	

Test 19

Track 57

🎧 **Listen, write the word and meaning.**

	Word	Meaning
01		
02		
03		
04		
05		
06		
07		
08		
09		
10		
11		
12		
13		
14		
15		
16		
17		
18		

점수		점	확인	

Test 20

Track 60

🎧 **Listen, write the word and meaning.**

	Word	Meaning
01		
02		
03		
04		
05		
06		
07		
08		
09		
10		
11		
12		
13		
14		
15		
16		
17		
18		

점수		점	확인	

Test 21

Track 63

🎧 Listen, write the word and meaning.

	Word	Meaning
01		
02		
03		
04		
05		
06		
07		
08		
09		
10		
11		
12		
13		
14		
15		
16		
17		
18		

점수	점	확인	

Test 22

Track 66

🎧 Listen, write the word and meaning.

	Word	Meaning
01		
02		
03		
04		
05		
06		
07		
08		
09		
10		
11		
12		
13		
14		
15		
16		
17		
18		

점수	점	확인	

Test 23

Track 69

🎧 **Listen, write the word and meaning.**

	Word	Meaning
01		
02		
03		
04		
05		
06		
07		
08		
09		
10		
11		
12		
13		
14		
15		
16		
17		
18		

점수	점	확인	

Test 24

Track 72

🎧 **Listen, write the word and meaning.**

	Word	Meaning
01		
02		
03		
04		
05		
06		
07		
08		
09		
10		
11		
12		
13		
14		
15		
16		
17		
18		

점수	점	확인	

Test 25

Track 75

🎧 Listen, write the word and meaning.

	Word	Meaning
01		
02		
03		
04		
05		
06		
07		
08		
09		
10		
11		
12		
13		
14		
15		
16		
17		
18		

점수	점	확인	

Test 26

Track 78

🎧 Listen, write the word and meaning.

	Word	Meaning
01		
02		
03		
04		
05		
06		
07		
08		
09		
10		
11		
12		
13		
14		
15		
16		
17		
18		

점수	점	확인	

Test 27

Track 81

🎧 **Listen, write the word and meaning.**

	Word	Meaning
01		
02		
03		
04		
05		
06		
07		
08		
09		
10		
11		
12		
13		
14		
15		
16		
17		
18		

점수		점	확인	

Test 28

Track 84

🎧 **Listen, write the word and meaning.**

	Word	Meaning
01		
02		
03		
04		
05		
06		
07		
08		
09		
10		
11		
12		
13		
14		
15		
16		
17		
18		

점수		점	확인	

Test 29

Track 87

🎧 Listen, write the word and meaning.

	Word	Meaning
01		
02		
03		
04		
05		
06		
07		
08		
09		
10		
11		
12		
13		
14		
15		
16		
17		
18		

점수	점	확인	

Test 30

Track 90

🎧 Listen, write the word and meaning.

	Word	Meaning
01		
02		
03		
04		
05		
06		
07		
08		
09		
10		
11		
12		
13		
14		
15		
16		
17		
18		

점수	점	확인	

Test 31

Track 93

🎧 Listen, write the word and meaning.

	Word	Meaning
01		
02		
03		
04		
05		
06		
07		
08		
09		
10		
11		
12		
13		
14		
15		
16		
17		
18		

점수	점	확인	

Test 32

Track 96

🎧 Listen, write the word and meaning.

	Word	Meaning
01		
02		
03		
04		
05		
06		
07		
08		
09		
10		
11		
12		
13		
14		
15		
16		
17		
18		

점수	점	확인	

Test 33

Track 99

🎧 **Listen, write the word and meaning.**

	Word	Meaning
01		
02		
03		
04		
05		
06		
07		
08		
09		
10		
11		
12		
13		
14		
15		
16		
17		
18		

점수	점	확인	

Test 34

Track 102

🎧 **Listen, write the word and meaning.**

	Word	Meaning
01		
02		
03		
04		
05		
06		
07		
08		
09		
10		
11		
12		
13		
14		
15		
16		
17		
18		

점수	점	확인	

Test 35

Track 105

🎧 Listen, write the word and meaning.

	Word	Meaning
01		
02		
03		
04		
05		
06		
07		
08		
09		
10		
11		
12		
13		
14		
15		
16		
17		
18		

점수	점	확인	

Test 36

Track 108

🎧 Listen, write the word and meaning.

	Word	Meaning
01		
02		
03		
04		
05		
06		
07		
08		
09		
10		
11		
12		
13		
14		
15		
16		
17		
18		

점수	점	확인	

Test 37

Track 111

🎧 Listen, write the word and meaning.

	Word	Meaning
01		
02		
03		
04		
05		
06		
07		
08		
09		
10		
11		
12		
13		
14		
15		
16		
17		
18		

점수		점	확인	

Test 38

Track 114

🎧 Listen, write the word and meaning.

	Word	Meaning
01		
02		
03		
04		
05		
06		
07		
08		
09		
10		
11		
12		
13		
14		
15		
16		
17		
18		

점수		점	확인	

Test 39

Track 117

🎧 Listen, write the word and meaning.

	Word	Meaning
01		
02		
03		
04		
05		
06		
07		
08		
09		
10		
11		
12		
13		
14		
15		
16		
17		
18		

점수		확인	
	점		

Test 40

Track 120

🎧 Listen, write the word and meaning.

	Word	Meaning
01		
02		
03		
04		
05		
06		
07		
08		
09		
10		
11		
12		
13		
14		
15		
16		
17		
18		

점수		확인	
	점		

Answer Key

Unit 1

A
1. brand
2. access
3. dare
4. applications
5. conceal
6. arrangements
7. chaos
8. average
9. ability
10. contrary
11. aware
12. bouquet
13. ceaseless
14. amazed
15. concrete
16. arise
17. contrast
18. deaf

B
1. 지원서, 적용, 신청서
2. 꽃다발, 부케
3. 끊임없는, 부단한
4. 능력, 재능
5. 상표, 브랜드
6. 준비, 배열, 정리
7. 반대의, 적합하지 않은
8. 감히 ~하다
9. 발생하다, 일어나다
10. 대조시키다, 대조
11. 의식하고, 깨닫고
12. 유형의, 응고한
13. 깜짝 놀라게 하다
14. 감추다, 숨기다
15. 귀머거리의, 무관심한
16. 평균, 평균의
17. 무질서, 혼돈
18. 접근하다, 접근할 수 있는

1. ability
2. access
3. amaze
4. application
5. arise
6. arrangement
7. average
8. aware
9. bouquet
10. brand
11. ceaseless
12. chaos
13. conceal
14. concrete
15. contrary
16. contrast
17. dare
18. deaf

C
1. chaos — 무질서, 혼돈
2. access — 접근하다, 접근할 수 있는
3. dare — 감히 ~하다
4. conceal — 감추다, 숨기다
5. ability — 능력, 재능
6. deaf — 귀머거리의, 무관심한
7. average — 평균, 평균의
8. concrete — 유형의, 응고한
9. application — 지원서, 적용, 신청서
10. ceaseless — 끊임없는, 부단한
11. contrary — 반대의, 적합하지 않은
12. amaze — 깜짝 놀라게 하다
13. contrast — 대조시키다, 대조
14. aware — 의식하고, 깨닫고
15. bouquet — 꽃다발, 부케
16. arise — 발생하다, 일어나다
17. brand — 상표, 브랜드
18. arrangement — 준비, 배열, 정리

Unit 2

A
1. essential
2. digested
3. irregular
4. due
5. emerged
6. extension
7. gently, gently
8. differs
9. generosity
10. folks
11. foundation
12. Immigration
13. gravity
14. export
15. greeted
16. editing
17. importance
18. isolated

B
1. 온화하게, 조용히, 서서히
2. 다르다, 의견이 다르다
3. 이민, 이주
4. ~할 예정인 ~에 기인하는
5. 나타나다, 나오다
6. 기초, 설립, 기반
7. 고립된, 멀리 떨어진
8. 소화하다, 이해하다
9. 환영하다, 인사하다
10. 연장, 확대
11. 불규칙한, 고르지 못한
12. 편집하다, 교정하다
13. 중력, 진지함
14. 수출하다, 밖으로 전하다
15. 사람들, 서민의, 민속의
16. 중요성, 중대성
17. 필수의, 본질적인
18. 관대, 아량

1. differ
2. digest
3. due
4. edit
5. emerge
6. essential
7. export
8. extension
9. folk
10. foundation
11. generosity
12. gently
13. gravity
14. greet
15. immigration
16. importance
17. irregular
18. isolated

C
1. differ — 다르다, 의견이 다르다
2. digest — 소화하다, 이해하다
3. gravity — 중력, 진지함
4. foundation — 기초, 설립, 기반
5. generosity — 관대, 아량
6. greet — 환영하다, 인사하다
7. edit — 편집하다, 교정하다
8. gently — 조용히, 온화하게, 서서히
9. essential — 필수의, 본질적인
10. importance — 중요성, 중대성
11. folk — 사람들, 서민의, 민속의
12. due — ~할 예정인, ~에 기인하는
13. immigration — 이민, 이주
14. extension — 연장, 확대
15. isolated — 고립된, 멀리 떨어진
16. emerge — 나타나다, 나오다
17. irregular — 불규칙한, 고르지 못한
18. export — 수출하다, 밖으로 전하다

Review 1

A
1. chaos — 무질서, 혼돈
2. access — 접근하다, 접근할 수 있는
3. dare — 감히 ~하다
4. conceal — 감추다, 숨기다
5. ability — 능력, 재능
6. deaf — 귀머거리의, 무관심한
7. average — 평균, 평균의
8. concrete — 유형의, 응고한
9. application — 지원서, 적용, 신청서
10. ceaseless — 끊임없는, 부단한
11. contrary — 반대의, 적합하지 않은
12. amaze — 깜짝 놀라게 하다
13. contrast — 대조시키다, 대조
14. aware — 의식하고, 깨닫고
15. bouquet — 꽃다발, 부케
16. arise — 발생하다, 일어나다
17. brand — 상표, 브랜드
18. arrangement — 준비, 배열, 정리

B
1. differ — 다르다, 의견이 다르다
2. digest — 소화하다, 이해하다
3. gravity — 중력, 진지함
4. foundation — 기초, 설립, 기반
5. generosity — 관대, 아량
6. greet — 환영하다, 인사하다
7. edit — 편집하다, 교정하다
8. gently — 조용히, 온화하게, 서서히
9. essential — 필수의, 본질적인
10. importance — 중요성, 중대성
11. folk — 사람들, 서민의, 민속의
12. due — ~할 예정인, ~에 기인하는
13. immigration — 이민, 이주
14. extension — 연장, 확대
15. isolated — 고립된, 멀리 떨어진
16. emerge — 나타나다, 나오다
17. irregular — 불규칙한, 고르지 못한
18. export — 수출하다, 밖으로 전하다

Answer Key

Unit 3

A
1. logic
2. Paste
3. majestic
4. modes
5. receipt
6. location
7. numerous
8. oars
9. metropolitan
10. peninsula
11. object
12. probably
13. moderation
14. performance
15. recognize
16. process
17. reflection
18. precious

B
1. 대도시의, 주요 도시의
2. 아마, 필시
3. 노
4. 장엄한, 위엄 있는
5. 알아보다, 인정하다
6. 반도
7. 위치, 장소
8. 반영, 반사, 반성
9. 귀중한, 소중한
10. 다수의, 수많은
11. 상연, 공연, 실행
12. 영수증, 수령
13. 절제, 중용
14. 진행 과정, (가공)처리하다
15. 물체, 목적, 대상
16. 풀, 풀로 붙이다
17. 논리, 사고, 논리학
18. 방식, 방법

1. location
2. logic
3. majestic
4. metropolitan
5. mode
6. moderation
7. numerous
8. oar
9. object
10. paste
11. peninsula
12. performance
13. precious
14. probably
15. process
16. receipt
17. recognize
18. reflection

C
1. oar — 노
2. logic — 논리, 사고, 논리학
3. probably — 아마, 필시
4. receipt — 영수증, 수령
5. location — 위치, 장소
6. reflection — 반영, 반사, 반성
7. numerous — 다수의, 수많은
8. mode — 방식, 방법
9. paste — 풀, 풀로 붙이다
10. object — 물체, 목적, 대상
11. majestic — 장엄한, 위엄 있는
12. precious — 귀중한, 소중한
13. metropolitan — 대도시의, 주요 도시의
14. process — 진행, 과정, (가공)처리 하다
15. performance — 상연, 공연, 실행
16. moderation — 절제, 중용
17. peninsula — 반도
18. recognize — 알아보다, 인정하다

Unit 4

A
1. rod
2. shepherds
3. Tiny
4. shortage
5. robbed
6. spare
7. virus
8. spread
9. robbery
10. starved
11. supplies
12. violent
13. support
14. tissue
15. shore
16. torch
17. victims
18. summary

B
1. 막대, 낚싯대
2. 해안, 호숫가
3. 희생자, 피해자
4. 요약, 개요
5. 빼앗다, 훔치다
6. 펴다, 늘이다
7. 바이러스, 병균
8. 조직, 티슈
9. 나누어주다, 절약하다, 여분의
10. 강도(짓), 약탈
11. 공급하다, 보충하다
12. 굶주리다, 굶어 죽다
13. 격렬한, 맹렬한
14. 횃불, 태우다
15. 부족, 결핍
16. 매우 작은, 작은 것
17. 지지하다, 후원하다
18. 양치는 사람, 이끌다

1. rob
2. robbery
3. rod
4. shepherd
5. shore
6. shortage
7. spare
8. spread
9. starve
10. summary
11. supply
12. support
13. tiny
14. tissue
15. torch
16. victim
17. violent
18. virus

C
1. rob — 빼앗다, 훔치다
2. shortage — 부족, 결핍
3. virus — 바이러스, 병균
4. spare — 나누어주다, 절약하다, 여분의
5. robbery — 강도(짓), 약탈
6. shore — 해안, 호숫가
7. support — 지지하다, 후원하다
8. rod — 막대, 낚싯대
9. tiny — 매우 작은, 작은 것
10. shepherd — 양치는 사람, 이끌다
11. torch — 횃불, 태우다
12. summary — 요약, 개요
13. tissue — 조직, 티슈
14. starve — 굶주리다, 굶어 죽다
15. supply — 공급하다, 보충하다
16. victim — 희생자, 피해자
17. spread — 펴다, 늘이다
18. violent — 격렬한, 맹렬한

Review 2

A
1. oar — 노
2. logic — 논리, 사고, 논리학
3. probably — 아마, 필시
4. receipt — 영수증, 수령
5. location — 위치, 장소
6. reflection — 반영, 반사, 반성
7. numerous — 다수의, 수많은
8. mode — 방식, 방법
9. paste — 풀, 풀로 붙이다
10. object — 물체, 목적, 대상
11. majestic — 장엄한, 위엄 있는
12. precious — 귀중한, 소중한
13. metropolitan — 대도시의, 주요 도시의
14. process — 진행, 과정, (가공)처리하다
15. performance — 상연, 공연, 실행
16. moderation — 절제, 중용
17. peninsula — 반도
18. recognize — 알아보다, 인정하다

B
1. rob — 빼앗다, 훔치다
2. shortage — 부족, 결핍
3. virus — 바이러스, 병균
4. spare — 나누어주다, 절약하다, 여분의
5. robbery — 강도(짓), 약탈
6. shore — 해안, 호숫가
7. support — 지지하다, 후원하다
8. rod — 막대, 낚싯대
9. tiny — 매우 작은, 작은 것
10. shepherd — 양치는 사람, 이끌다
11. torch — 횃불, 태우다
12. summary — 요약, 개요
13. tissue — 조직, 티슈
14. starve — 굶주리다, 굶어 죽다
15. supply — 공급하다, 보충하다
16. victim — 희생자, 피해자
17. spread — 펴다, 늘이다
18. violent — 격렬한, 맹렬한

Unit 5

A
1. confess
2. accomplishes
3. deck
4. accounting
5. colonial
6. animated
7. bald
8. beams
9. awful
10. bumped
11. conveniences
12. ancient
13. bunch
14. arrested
15. civilized
16. aside
17. courteous
18. decade

B
1. 무서운, 대단한
2. 벗어진, 대머리의
3. 이룩하다, 성취하다, 완성하다
4. 문명화하다, 세련되게 하다
5. 설명, 이유, 은행구좌
6. 충돌하다, 부딪히다
7. 편리, 편의
8. 체포하다, 저지하다, 체포
9. 식민(지)의, 식민지풍의
10. 10년간
11. 옆에(으로), 떨어져서
12. 예의 바른, 친절한
13. 다발, 묶음
14. 고대의, 옛날의, 구식의
15. 갑판
16. 광선, 기둥, 빛나다
17. 자백하다, 인정하다, 고백하다
18. 만화영화의

1. accomplish
2. account
3. ancient
4. animated
5. arrest
6. aside
7. awful
8. bald
9. beam
10. bump
11. bunch
12. civilize
13. colonial
14. confess
15. convenience
16. courteous
17. decade
18. deck

C
1. confess — 자백하다, 인정하다, 고백하다
2. bald — 벗어진, 대머리의
3. accomplish — 이룩하다, 성취하다, 완성하다
4. convenience — 편리, 편의
5. awful — 무서운, 대단한
6. deck — 갑판
7. account — 설명, 이유, 은행구좌
8. courteous — 예의 바른, 친절한
9. beam — 광선, 기둥, 빛나다
10. ancient — 고대의, 옛날의, 구식의
11. decade — 10년간
12. animated — 만화영화의
13. colonial — 식민(지)의, 식민지풍의
14. aside — 옆에(으로), 떨어져서
15. bunch — 다발, 묶음
16. arrest — 체포하다, 저지하다, 체포
17. civilize — 문명화하다, 세련되게 하다
18. bump — 충돌하다, 부딪히다

Unit 6

A
1. gestures
2. disappointment
3. industrious
4. efficiency
5. elected
6. establish
7. facilities
8. declared
9. fancies
10. Financial
11. estates
12. geography
13. growth
14. fossil
15. jail
16. homesick
17. influence
18. issue

B
1. 실망, 실망거리
2. 화석, 화석의, 구식의
3. 광대한 토지, 재산
4. 성장, 발육
5. 선언하다, 단언하다
6. 재정(상)의, 재무의
7. 몸짓, 제스처
8. 영향, 세력, 영향을 미치다
9. 뽑다, 선거하다
10. 문제, 논쟁, 발행
11. 근면한, 부지런한
12. 설립하다, 확립하다
13. 감옥, 교도소
14. 공상, 상상, 공상하다
15. 향수병에 걸린
16. 지리학, 지리
17. 시설, 특징, 장소
18. 능률, 효율

1. declare
2. disappointment
3. efficiency
4. elect
5. establish
6. estate
7. facility
8. fancy
9. financial
10. fossil
11. geography
12. gesture
13. growth
14. homesick
15. industrious
16. influence
17. issue
18. jail

C
1. gesture — 몸짓, 제스처
2. disappointment — 실망, 실망거리
3. elect — 뽑다, 선거하다
4. geography — 지리학, 지리
5. declare — 선언하다, 단언하다
6. growth — 성장, 발육
7. efficiency — 능률, 효율
8. industrious — 근면한, 부지런한
9. fossil — 화석, 화석의, 구식의
10. estate — 광대한 토지, 재산
11. homesick — 향수병에 걸린
12. financial — 재정(상)의, 재무의
13. influence — 영향, 세력, 영향을 미치다
14. establish — 설립하다, 확립하다
15. facility — 시설, 특징, 장소
16. issue — 문제, 논쟁, 발행
17. fancy — 공상, 상상, 공상하다
18. jail — 감옥, 교도소

Review 3

A
1. confess — 자백하다, 인정하다, 고백하다
2. bald — 벗어진, 대머리의
3. accomplish — 이룩하다, 성취하다, 완성하다
4. convenience — 편리, 편의
5. awful — 무서운, 대단한
6. deck — 갑판
7. account — 설명, 이유, 은행구좌
8. courteous — 예의 바른, 친절한
9. beam — 광선, 기둥, 빛나다
10. ancient — 고대의, 옛날의, 구식의
11. decade — 10년간
12. animated — 만화영화의
13. colonial — 식민(지)의, 식민지풍의
14. aside — 옆에(으로), 떨어져서
15. bunch — 다발, 묶음
16. arrest — 체포하다, 저지하다, 체포
17. civilize — 문명화하다, 세련되게 하다
18. bump — 충돌하다, 부딪히다

B
1. gesture — 몸짓, 제스처
2. disappointment — 실망, 실망거리
3. elect — 뽑다, 선거하다
4. geography — 지리학, 지리
5. declare — 선언하다, 단언하다
6. growth — 성장, 발육
7. efficiency — 능률, 효율
8. industrious — 근면한, 부지런한
9. fossil — 화석, 화석의, 구식의
10. estate — 광대한 토지, 재산
11. homesick — 향수병에 걸린
12. financial — 재정(상)의, 재무의
13. influence — 영향, 세력, 영향을 미치다
14. establish — 설립하다, 확립하다
15. facility — 시설, 특징, 장소
16. issue — 문제, 논쟁, 발행
17. fancy — 공상, 상상, 공상하다
18. jail — 감옥, 교도소

Answer Key

Unit 7

A
1. Permit
2. minimum
3. mostly
4. religion
5. murder
6. perplexes
7. maintenance
8. occupy
9. occur
10. offended
11. plentiful
12. mine
13. progress
14. manner
15. properly
16. reaction
17. products
18. relatives

B
1. 최소의, 최소
2. 차지하다, 점령하다
3. 풍부한, 넉넉한
4. 유지, 정비, 주장
5. 산물, 생산품
6. 성나게하다, 위반하다
7. 살인사건, 살해하다
8. 당혹하다, 복잡케하다
9. 반작용, 반동, 반응
10. 태도, 방법
11. 종교, 신앙
12. 허락하다, 용인하다
13. 적당히, 정확히
14. 광산, 채광하다
15. 친척, 상대적인
16. 전진, 진보
17. 일어나다, 생기다
18. 주로, 대개

1. maintenance
2. manner
3. mine
4. minimum
5. mostly
6. murder
7. occupy
8. occur
9. offend
10. permit
11. perplex
12. plentiful
13. product
14. progress
15. properly
16. reaction
17. relative
18. religion

C
1. occupy — 차지하다, 점령하다
2. reaction — 반작용, 반동, 반응
3. minimum — 최소의, 최소
4. relative — 친척, 상대적인
5. properly — 적당히, 정확히
6. maintenance — 유지, 정비, 주장
7. progress — 전진, 진보
8. mine — 광산, 채광하다
9. religion — 종교, 신앙
10. product — 산물, 생산품
11. manner — 태도, 방법
12. plentiful — 풍부한, 넉넉한
13. mostly — 주로, 대개
14. perplex — 당혹케하다, 복잡케하다
15. offend — 성나게 하다, 위반하다
16. permit — 허락하다, 용인하다
17. murder — 살인사건, 살해하다
18. occur — 일어나다, 생기다

Unit 8

A
1. similar
2. Rubbing
3. shuttle
4. vogue
5. silly
6. rotate
7. statistics
8. stock, stocks
9. track
10. swallowing
11. rumor
12. symbolizes
13. toward
14. status
15. traditional
16. visible
17. sympathy
18. vomiting

B
1. 왕복운행, 왕복하다
2. ~쪽으로, ~편으로
3. 동정, 공감
4. 회전하다, 교대하다
5. 어리석은, 시시한
6. 전통적인, 전통의
7. 삼키다, 들이켜다
8. 문지르다, 비비다
9. 유사한, 닮은
10. 유행, 인기, 유행 하는
11. 지위, 신분
12. 토하다, 게우다
13. 통계, 통계학
14. 눈에 보이는, 명백한
15. 주식, 재고
16. 통로, 흔적
17. 상징하다, 부호로 나타내다
18. 소문, 풍문

1. rotate
2. rub
3. rumor
4. shuttle
5. silly
6. similar
7. statistics
8. status
9. stock
10. swallow
11. symbolize
12. sympathy
13. toward
14. track
15. traditional
16. visible
17. vogue
18. vomit

C
1. swallow — 삼키다, 들이켜다
2. rotate — 회전하다, 교대하다
3. vomit — 토하다, 게우다
4. stock — 주식, 재고
5. rub — 문지르다, 비비다
6. symbolize — 상징하다, 부호로 나타내다
7. shuttle — 왕복 운행, 왕복하다
8. toward — ~쪽으로, ~편으로
9. sympathy — 동정, 공감
10. rumor — 소문, 풍문
11. status — 지위, 신분
12. track — 통로, 흔적
13. silly — 어리석은, 시시한
14. traditional — 전통적인, 전통의
15. statistics — 통계, 통계학
16. visible — 눈에 보이는, 명백한
17. similar — 유사한, 닮은
18. vogue — 유행, 인기, 유행하는

Review 4

A
1. occupy — 차지하다, 점령하다
2. reaction — 반작용, 반동, 반응
3. minimum — 최소의, 최소
4. relative — 친척, 상대적인
5. properly — 적당히, 정확히
6. maintenance — 유지, 정비, 주장
7. progress — 전진, 진보
8. mine — 광산, 채광하다
9. religion — 종교, 신앙
10. product — 산물, 생산품
11. manner — 태도, 방법
12. plentiful — 풍부한, 넉넉한
13. mostly — 주로, 대개
14. perplex — 당혹케하다, 복잡케하다
15. offend — 성나게 하다, 위반하다
16. permit — 허락하다, 용인하다
17. murder — 살인사건, 살해하다
18. occur — 일어나다, 생기다

B
1. swallow — 삼키다, 들이켜다
2. rotate — 회전하다, 교대하다
3. vomit — 토하다, 게우다
4. stock — 주식, 재고
5. rub — 문지르다, 비비다
6. symbolize — 상징하다, 부호로 나타내다
7. shuttle — 왕복 운행, 왕복하다
8. toward — ~쪽으로, ~편으로
9. sympathy — 동정, 공감
10. rumor — 소문, 풍문
11. status — 지위, 신분
12. track — 통로, 흔적
13. silly — 어리석은, 시시한
14. traditional — 전통적인, 전통의
15. statistics — 통계, 통계학
16. visible — 눈에 보이는, 명백한
17. similar — 유사한, 닮은
18. vogue — 유행, 인기, 유행하는

Unit 9

A
1. clockwise
2. admired
3. annoying
4. cancer
5. defeated
6. bankrupt
7. coward
8. announcer
9. deducted
10. associate
11. classified
12. defects
13. astronomical
14. blended
15. confidence
16. Congress
17. actually
18. bushes

B
1. 섞다, 섞이다
2. 현실로, 실제로
3. 빼다, 공제하다
4. 암
5. 감탄하다, 칭찬하다
6. 의회, 국회
7. 천문학(상)의
8. 결함, 장애
9. 괴롭히다, 귀찮다
10. 분류하다, 등급으로 나누다
11. 쳐부수다, 패배시키다
12. 연상하다 연합하다 교체하다
13. 신뢰, 신용, 자신감
14. 파산한, 파산자
15. 겁쟁이, 소심한 사람
16. 관목, 덤불, 수풀
17. 아나운서, 발표자
18. 시계 방향의

1. actually
2. admire
3. announcer
4. annoy
5. associate
6. astronomical
7. bankrupt
8. blend
9. bush
10. cancer
11. classify
12. clockwise
13. confidence
14. congress
15. coward
16. deduct
17. defeat
18. defect

C
1. astronomical — 천문학(상)의
2. bankrupt — 파산한, 파산자
3. classify — 분류하다, 등급으로 나누다
4. actually — 현실로, 실제로
5. associate — 연상하다,연합하다, 교체하다
6. confidence — 신뢰, 신용, 자신감
7. clockwise — 시계 방향의
8. blend — 섞다, 섞이다
9. announcer — 아나운서, 발표자
10. coward — 겁쟁이, 소심한 사람
11. admire — 감탄하다, 칭찬하다
12. cancer — 암
13. annoy — 괴롭히다, 귀찮다
14. congress — 의회, 국회
15. deduct — 빼다, 공제하다
16. bush — 관목, 덤불, 수풀
17. defect — 결함, 장애
18. defeat — 쳐부수다, 패배시키다

Unit 10

A
1. embarrassed
2. fertile
3. discomfort
4. insulted
5. gliding
6. Evaluation
7. journey
8. horizon
9. dispute
10. eternal
11. fantastic
12. genuine
13. definite
14. global
15. hunchback
16. insured
17. frail
18. justifies

B
1. 비옥한, 풍부한
2. 진짜의, 순수한
3. 명확한, 확실한
4. 곱사등(이)
5. 곤란케 하다, 당황케 하다
6. 미끄러지다, 미끄러지듯 나가다
7. 모욕하다, 무례한 짓을 하다
8. 논쟁, 논쟁하다
9. 지구의, 전 세계의
10. 영원한, 불후의
11. 여행, 여정
12. 평가, 값을 구함
13. 보험 계약하다, 보증하다
14. 수평선, 지평선
15. 불편, 불쾌
16. 약한, 덧없는
17. 정당화 하다, 옳다고 하다
18. 환상적인, 멋진

1. definite
2. discomfort
3. dispute
4. embarrass
5. eternal
6. evaluation
7. fantastic
8. fertile
9. frail
10. genuine
11. glide
12. global
13. horizon
14. hunchback
15. insult
16. insure
17. journey
18. justify

C
1. fertile — 비옥한, 풍부한
2. evaluation — 평가, 값을 구함
3. journey — 여행, 여정
4. fantastic — 환상적인, 멋진
5. glide — 미끄러지다,미끄러지듯 나가다
6. embarrass — 곤란케 하다, 당황케 하다
7. genuine — 진짜의, 순수한
8. insure — 보험 계약하다, 보증하다
9. frail — 약한, 덧없는
10. dispute — 논쟁, 논쟁하다
11. eternal — 영원한, 불후의
12. hunchback — 곱사등(이)
13. global — 지구의, 전 세계의
14. discomfort — 불편, 불쾌
15. insult — 모욕하다, 무례한 짓을 하다
16. horizon — 수평선, 지평선
17. justify — 정당화하다, 옳다고 하다
18. definite — 명확한, 확실한

Review 5

A
1. astronomical — 천문학(상)의
2. bankrupt — 파산한, 파산자
3. classify — 분류하다, 등급으로 나누다
4. actually — 현실로, 실제로
5. associate — 연상하다, 연합하다, 교체하다
6. confidence — 신뢰, 신용, 자신감
7. clockwise — 시계 방향의
8. blend — 섞다, 섞이다
9. announcer — 아나운서, 발표자
10. coward — 겁쟁이, 소심한 사람
11. admire — 감탄하다, 칭찬하다
12. cancer — 암
13. annoy — 괴롭히다, 귀찮다
14. congress — 의회, 국회
15. deduct — 빼다, 공제하다
16. bush — 관목, 덤불, 수풀
17. defect — 결함, 장애
18. defeat — 쳐부수다, 패배시키다

B
1. fertile — 비옥한, 풍부한
2. evaluation — 평가, 값을 구함
3. journey — 여행, 여정
4. fantastic — 환상적인, 멋진
5. glide — 미끄러지다, 미끄러지듯 나가다
6. embarrass — 곤란케 하다, 당황케 하다
7. genuine — 진짜의, 순수한
8. insure — 보험 계약하다, 보증하다
9. frail — 약한, 덧없는
10. dispute — 논쟁, 논쟁하다
11. eternal — 영원한, 불후의
12. hunchback — 곱사등(이)
13. global — 지구의, 전 세계의
14. discomfort — 불편, 불쾌
15. insult — 모욕하다, 무례한 짓을 하다
16. horizon — 수평선, 지평선
17. justify — 정당화하다, 옳다고 하다
18. definite — 명확한, 확실한

Unit 11

A
1. organize
2. marble
3. remodeling
4. minstrels
5. narrator
6. odd
7. manufactures
8. opponent
9. plow
10. offence
11. political
12. property
13. minor
14. punched
15. remedy
16. mystery
17. protect
18. remote

B
1. 기묘한, 홀수의
2. 쟁기, 쟁기로 갈다
3. 제조하다, 제조
4. 상대, 반대자
5. 재산, 소유물
6. 대리석, 대리석의, 단단한
7. 주먹으로 치다
8. 위반, 화냄
9. 치료, 치료약, 고치다
10. 주요하지 않은, 미성년
11. 조직하다, 계획하다
12. 개조하다, 개작하다
13. 보호하다, 막다
14. 신비, 불가사의
15. 먼, 외딴
16. 해설자, 내레이터
17. 정치상의, 정치적인
18. 음유시인

C
1. manufacture
2. marble
3. minor
4. minstrel
5. mystery
6. narrator
7. odd
8. offence
9. opponent
10. organize
11. plow
12. political
13. property
14. protect
15. punch
16. remedy
17. remodel
18. remote

1. remedy — 치료, 치료약, 고치다
2. protect — 보호하다, 막다
3. minor — 주요하지 않은, 미성년자
4. odd — 기묘한, 홀수의
5. remodel — 개조하다, 개작하다
6. offence — 위반, 화냄
7. punch — 주먹으로 치다
8. remote — 먼, 외딴
9. opponent — 상대, 반대자
10. political — 정치상의, 정치적인
11. mystery — 신비, 불가사의
12. organize — 조직하다, 계획하다
13. narrator — 해설자, 내레이터
14. property — 재산, 소유물
15. minstrel — 음유시인
16. manufacture — 제조하다, 제조
17. plow — 쟁기, 쟁기로 갈다
18. marble — 대리석, 대리석의, 단단한

Unit 12

A
1. scanned
2. unified
3. strict
4. tame
5. satisfied
6. tapped
7. stomachache
8. translate
9. skyscraper
10. transport
11. straighten
12. voted
13. slippery
14. weeds
15. scary
16. symptom
17. western
18. skills

B
1. 똑바르게 하다, 정리하다
2. 번역하다 통역하다 바꾸다
3. 만족시키다, 충족시키다
4. 징후, 증상
5. 길든, 유순한
6. 훑어보다 자세히 조사하다
7. 엄격한, 엄밀한
8. 통합하다, 통일하다
9. 무서운, 두려운
10. 잡초, 쓸모없는 것
11. 복통, 위통
12. 서쪽의, 서부 지방의
13. 기술, 실력
14. 수송하다, 수송, 운송
15. 고층건물
16. 투표하다, 투표
17. 가볍게 두드리다
18. 미끄러운, 잘 빠져나가는

1. satisfy
2. scan
3. scary
4. skill
5. skyscraper
6. slippery
7. stomachache
8. straighten
9. strict
10. symptom
11. tame
12. tap
13. translate
14. transport
15. unify
16. vote
17. weed
18. western

C
1. strict — 엄격한, 엄밀한
2. tame — 길든, 유순한
3. western — 서쪽의, 서부 지방의
4. satisfy — 만족시키다, 충족시키다
5. tap — 가볍게 두드리다
6. straighten — 똑바르게 하다, 정리하다
7. weed — 잡초, 쓸모없는 것
8. symptom — 징후, 증상
9. scan — 훑어 보다, 자세히 조사하다
10. translate — 번역하다, 통역하다, 바꾸다
11. slippery — 미끄러운, 잘 빠져나가는
12. transport — 수송하다, 수송, 운송
13. stomachache — 복통, 위통
14. scary — scary
15. unify — 통합하다, 통일하다
16. vote — 투표하다, 투표
17. skill — 기술, 실력
18. skyscraper — 고층건물

Review 6

A
1. remedy — 치료, 치료약, 고치다
2. protect — 보호하다, 막다
3. minor — 주요하지 않은, 미성년자
4. odd — 기묘한, 홀수의
5. remodel — 개조하다, 개작하다
6. offence — 위반, 화냄
7. punch — 주먹으로 치다
8. remote — 먼, 외딴
9. opponent — 상대, 반대자
10. political — 정치상의, 정치적인
11. mystery — 신비, 불가사의
12. organize — 조직하다, 계획하다
13. narrator — 해설자, 내레이터
14. property — 재산, 소유물
15. minstrel — 음유시인
16. manufacture — 제조하다, 제조
17. plow — 쟁기, 쟁기로 갈다
18. marble — 대리석, 대리석의, 단단한

B
1. strict — 엄격한, 엄밀한
2. tame — 길든, 유순한
3. western — 서쪽의, 서부 지방의
4. satisfy — 만족시키다, 충족시키다
5. tap — 가볍게 두드리다
6. straighten — 똑바르게 하다, 정리하다
7. weed — 잡초, 쓸모없는 것
8. symptom — 징후, 증상
9. scan — 훑어보다, 자세히 조사하다
10. translate — 번역하다, 통역하다, 바꾸다
11. slippery — 미끄러운, 잘 빠져나가는
12. transport — 수송하다, 수송, 운송
13. stomachache — 복통, 위통
14. scary — scary
15. unify — 통합하다, 통일하다
16. vote — 투표하다, 투표
17. skill — 기술, 실력
18. skyscraper — 고층건물

Unit 13

A

1. bless
2. admitted
3. constantly
4. adolescence
5. cloning
6. appetite
7. deposited
8. attractive
9. bet
10. capacity
11. captured
12. athletes
13. compare
14. conscious
15. defending
16. crisis
17. apologized
18. crowded

B

1. 은총을 내리다, 축복하다	1. admit
2. 붙잡다, 생포하다	2. adolescence
3. 인정하다, 허가하다	3. apologize
4. 의식이 있는, 의식적인	4. appetite
5. 매력적인, 흥미를 돋우는	5. athlete
6. 복제하다	6. attractive
7. 붐비는, 혼잡한	7. bet
8. 사춘기, 청년기	8. bless
9. 위기, 어려운 상황	9. capacity
10. 걸다, 내기를 하다	10. capture
11. 항상, 끊임 없이, 자주	11. clone
12. 식욕, 욕구	12. compare
13. 비교하다, 비유하다	13. conscious
14. 예금하다, 두다, 쌓이다	14. constantly
15. 사과하다, 변명하다	15. crisis
16. 수용력, 능력	16. crowded
17. 막다, 지키다	17. defend
18. 운동선수	18. deposit

C

1. capture	붙잡다, 생포하다
2. crowded	붐비는, 혼잡한
3. admit	인정하다, 허가하다
4. clone	복제하다
5. capacity	수용력, 능력
6. deposit	예금하다, 두다, 쌓이다
7. adolescence	사춘기, 청년기
8. bless	은총을 내리다, 축복하다
9. defend	막다, 지키다
10. compare	비교하다, 비유하다
11. apologize	사과하다, 변명하다
12. bet	걸다, 내기를 하다
13. attractive	매력적인, 흥미를 돋우는
14. crisis	위기, 어려운 상황
15. appetite	식욕, 욕구
16. conscious	의식이 있는, 의식적인
17. constantly	항상, 끊임없이, 자주
18. athlete	운동선수

Unit 14

A

1. disposed
2. governor
3. emotion
4. firm
5. evidence
6. landscape
7. disease
8. independent
9. eventual
10. finance
11. employed
12. frustrated
13. invaded
14. glorious
15. frightened
16. immoral
17. intend
18. lack

B

1. 최종적인, 최후의	1. disease
2. 병, 질병	2. dispose
3. 주지사, 총독	3. emotion
4. 재정, 자금, 융자하다	4. employ
5. 의도하다, 작정이다	5. eventual
6. 배치하다, 배열하다	6. evidence
7. 침입하다, 침해하다	7. finance
8. 단단한, 굳은	8. firm
9. 영광스러운, 장려한, 유쾌한	9. frighten
10. 풍경, 경치	10. frustrate
11. 감정, 감동, 감격	11. glorious
12. 독립한, 독립심이 강한	12. governor
13. 두려워하게 하다, 놀라게 하다	13. immoral
14. 부족, 결핍	14. independent
15. 고용하다, 사용하다	15. intend
16. 부도덕한, 품행이 나쁜	16. invade
17. 실패하게 하다, 헛되게 하다	17. lack
18. 증거, 흔적	18. landscape

C

1. glorious	영광스러운, 장려한, 유쾌한
2. immoral	부도덕한, 품행이 나쁜
3. lack	부족, 결핍
4. employ	고용하다, 사용하다
5. governor	주지사, 총독
6. dispose	배치하다, 배열하다
7. frustrate	실패하게 하다, 헛되게 하다
8. independent	독립한, 독립심이 강한
9. emotion	감정, 감동, 감격
10. frighten	두려워하게 하다, 놀라게 하다
11. intend	의도하다, 작정이다
12. firm	단단한, 굳은
13. disease	병, 질병
14. landscape	풍경, 경치
15. invade	침입하다, 침해하다
16. eventual	최종적인, 최후의
17. finance	재정, 자금, 융자하다
18. evidence	증거, 흔적

Review 7

A

1. capture	붙잡다, 생포하다
2. crowded	붐비는, 혼잡한
3. admit	인정하다, 허가하다
4. clone	복제하다
5. capacity	수용력, 능력
6. deposit	예금하다, 두다, 쌓이다
7. adolescence	사춘기, 청년기
8. bless	은총을 내리다, 축복하다
9. defend	막다, 지키다
10. compare	비교하다, 비유하다
11. apologize	사과하다, 변명하다
12. bet	걸다, 내기를 하다
13. attractive	매력적인, 흥미를 돋우는
14. crisis	위기, 어려운 상황
15. appetite	식욕, 욕구
16. conscious	의식이 있는, 의식적인
17. constantly	항상, 끊임없이, 자주
18. athlete	운동선수

B

1. glorious	영광스러운, 장려한, 유쾌한
2. immoral	부도덕한, 품행이 나쁜
3. lack	부족, 결핍
4. employ	고용하다, 사용하다
5. governor	주지사, 총독
6. dispose	배치하다, 배열하다
7. frustrate	실패하게 하다, 헛되게 하다
8. independent	독립한, 독립심이 강한
9. emotion	감정, 감동, 감격
10. frighten	두려워하게 하다, 놀라게 하다
11. intend	의도하다, 작정이다
12. firm	단단한, 굳은
13. disease	병, 질병
14. landscape	풍경, 경치
15. invade	침입하다, 침해하다
16. eventual	최종적인, 최후의
17. finance	재정, 자금, 융자하다
18. evidence	증거, 흔적

Unit 15

A
1. Oriental
2. match
3. Politicians
4. reservation
5. quarreling
6. miserable
7. neglected
8. opportunity
9. polite
10. marine
11. pollutes
12. purpose
13. quoting
14. resembles
15. original
16. necessary
17. misleading
18. result

B
1. 필요한, 필연적인
2. 독창적인, 원본
3. 공손한, 예의 바른
4. 바다의, 해양의
5. 목적, 의도, 요점
6. 무시하다, 방치하다
7. 오염시키다, 불결하게 하다
8. 어울리다, 시합
9. 인용하다, 예시하다, 인용구
10. 기회, 호기
11. 예약, 보류
12. 싸우다, 싸움
13. 불쌍한, 비참한, 궁핍한
14. 결과, 성과
15. 정치가, 출세주의자
16. 오해하게 하는, 현혹시키는
17. 닮다, 공통점이 있다
18. 동양의, 동양적인

1. marine
2. match
3. miserable
4. misleading
5. necessary
6. neglect
7. opportunity
8. oriental
9. original
10. polite
11. politician
12. pollute
13. purpose
14. quarrel
15. quote
16. resemble
17. reservation
18. result

C
1. polite — 공손한, 예의 바른
2. result — 결과, 성과
3. original — 독창적인, 원본
4. pollute — 오염시키다, 불결하게 하다
5. marine — 바다의, 해양의
6. politician — 정치가, 출세주의자
7. oriental — 동양의, 동양적인
8. purpose — 목적, 의도, 요점
9. quarrel — 싸우다, 싸움
10. match — 어울리다, 시합
11. neglect — 무시하다, 방치하다
12. resemble — 닮다, 공통점이 있다
13. opportunity — 기회, 호기
14. miserable — 불쌍한, 비참한, 궁핍한
15. quote — 인용하다, 예시하다, 인용구
16. necessary — 필요한, 필연적인
17. reservation — 예약, 보류
18. misleading — 오해하게 하는, 현혹시키는

Unit 16

A
1. Suddenly
2. witty
3. scattered
4. Wetlands
5. utility
6. semester
7. urban
8. snatched
9. Solid
10. strumbles
11. tender
12. separate
13. term
14. soaking
15. terrific
16. unconscious
17. while
18. submit

B
1. 와락 붙잡다, 잡아채다
2. 갑자기, 별안간
3. 부드러운, 다정한, 예민한
4. 흩뿌리다, 흩어지다
5. 실용성, 공공사업
6. 고체의, 단결된
7. 기간, 임기
8. 한 학기, 반 년간
9. 도시의, 도회풍의
10. 주춤하다, 비틀거리다
11. 잠시, ~하는 동안
12. 아주 좋은, 멋진
13. 분리된, 분산된
14. 재치 있는, 기지 있는
15. 복종하다, 제출하다
16. 습지대
17. 젖다, 적시다
18. ~을 모르는, 무의식의

1. scatter
2. semester
3. separate
4. snatch
5. soak
6. solid
7. stumble
8. submit
9. suddenly
10. tender
11. term
12. terrific
13. unconscious
14. urban
15. utility
16. wetland
17. while
18. witty

C
1. soak — 젖다, 적시다
2. witty — 재치 있는, 기지 있는
3. snatch — 와락 붙잡다, 잡아채다
4. wetland — 습지대
5. solid — 고체의, 단결된
6. while — 잠시, ~하는 동안
7. separate — 분리된, 분산된
8. unconscious — ~을 모르는, 무의식의
9. stumble — 주춤하다, 비틀거리다
10. scatter — 흩뿌리다, 흩어지다
11. terrific — 아주 좋은, 멋진
12. semester — 한 학기, 반 년간
13. utility — 실용성, 공공사업
14. suddenly — 갑자기, 별안간
15. tender — 부드러운, 다정한, 예민한
16. urban — 도시의, 도회풍의
17. submit — 제출하다, 복종하다
18. term — 기간, 임기

Review 8

A
1. polite — 공손한, 예의 바른
2. result — 결과, 성과
3. original — 독창적인, 원본
4. pollute — 오염시키다, 불결하게 하다
5. marine — 바다의, 해양의
6. politician — 정치가, 출세주의자
7. oriental — 동양의, 동양적인
8. purpose — 목적, 의도, 요점
9. quarrel — 싸우다, 싸움
10. match — 어울리다, 시합
11. neglect — 무시하다, 방치하다
12. resemble — 닮다, 공통점이 있다
13. opportunity — 기회, 호기
14. miserable — 불쌍한, 비참한, 궁핍한
15. quote — 인용하다, 예시하다, 인용구
16. necessary — 필요한, 필연적인
17. reservation — 예약, 보류
18. misleading — 오해하게 하는, 현혹시키는

B
1. soak — 젖다, 적시다
2. witty — 재치 있는, 기지 있는
3. snatch — 와락 붙잡다, 잡아채다
4. wetland — 습지대
5. solid — 고체의, 단결된
6. while — 잠시, ~하는 동안
7. separate — 분리된, 분산된
8. unconscious — ~을 모르는, 무의식의
9. stumble — 주춤하다, 비틀거리다
10. scatter — 흩뿌리다, 흩어지다
11. terrific — 아주 좋은, 멋진
12. semester — 한 학기, 반 년간
13. utility — 실용성, 공공사업
14. suddenly — 갑자기, 별안간
15. tender — 부드러운, 다정한, 예민한
16. urban — 도시의, 도회풍의
17. submit — 제출하다, 복종하다
18. term — 기간, 임기

Unit 17

A
1. approve
2. Despite
3. blossoms
4. curious
5. advertising
6. contract
7. appreciated
8. continents
9. bold
10. available
11. bonds
12. abolished
13. boundary
14. cultural
15. approach
16. complex
17. diameter
18. competitive

B
1. 찬성하다, 승인하다
2. 경계, 경계선
3. 폐지하다, 없애다
4. 대륙, 육지
5. 꽃, 꽃이 피다
6. 문화의, 교양의
7. 광고하다, 알리다
8. ~에도 불구하고
9. 대담한, 뻔뻔스러운
10. 인정하다 감상하다 인식하다
11. 호기심 있는, 기묘한
12. 경쟁력 있는, 경쟁에 의한
13. ~에 접근하다, 가까이 가다
14. 지름, 직경
15. 유대, 결속, 끈
16. 계약, 계약서
17. 이용할 수 있는, 입수 가능한
18. 복잡한, 복합시설, 열등감

C
1. contract — 계약, 계약서
2. cultural — 문화의, 교양의
3. despite — ~에도 불구하고
4. available — 이용할 수 있는, 입수 가능한
5. continent — 대륙, 육지
6. curious — 호기심 있는, 기묘한
7. abolish — 폐지하다, 없애다
8. complex — 복잡한, 복합시설, 열등감
9. blossom — 꽃, 꽃이 피다
10. diameter — 지름, 직경
11. advertise — 광고하다, 알리다
12. bond — 유대, 결속, 끈
13. approach — ~에 접근하다, 가까이 가다
14. bold — 대담한, 뻔뻔스러운
15. competitive — 경쟁력 있는, 경쟁에 의한
16. appreciate — 인정하다, 감상하다, 인식하다
17. boundary — 경계, 경계선
18. approve — 찬성하다, 승인하다

Unit 18

A
1. flexible
2. diminish
3. invasion
4. grabbed
5. employees
6. gallons
7. equality
8. existence
9. immediate
10. explorers
11. dictations
12. generally
13. graduating
14. invest
15. leaked
16. flushed
17. illustrates
18. loaf

B
1. 구부리기 쉬운, 유연성이 있는
2. 구술, 받아쓰기
3. 대개, 일반적으로
4. 즉석의, 가장 가까운
5. 줄어들다, 감소하다
6. 졸업하다, 학위를 수여하다
7. 얼굴이 붉어지다, 분출하다
8. 새다, 새는 곳
9. 평등, 같음
10. 덩어리
11. 침입, 침략
12. 탐험가, 조사자
13. 붙잡다, 가로채다
14. 피고용자, 종업원
15. 투자하다, 돈을 쓰다
16. 갤런, 대량
17. 설명하다, 삽화를 넣다
18. 존재, 생존

C
1. employee — 피고용자, 종업원
2. grab — 붙잡다, 가로채다
3. invest — 투자하다, 돈을 쓰다
4. diminish — 줄어들다, 감소하다
5. graduate — 졸업하다, 학위를 수여하다
6. equality — 평등, 같음
7. leak — 새다, 새는 곳
8. illustrate — 설명하다, 삽화를 넣다
9. flush — 얼굴이 붉어지다, 분출하다
10. existence — 존재, 생존
11. immediate — 즉석의, 가장 가까운
12. explorer — 탐험가, 조사자
13. dictation — 구술, 받아쓰기
14. loaf — 덩어리
15. gallon — 갤런, 대량
16. invasion — 침입, 침략
17. generally — 대개, 일반적으로
18. flexible — 구부리기 쉬운, 유연성이 있는

Review 9

A
1. contract — 계약, 계약서
2. cultural — 문화의, 교양의
3. despite — ~에도 불구하고
4. available — 이용할 수 있는, 입수 가능한
5. continent — 대륙, 육지
6. curious — 호기심 있는, 기묘한
7. abolish — 폐지하다, 없애다
8. complex — 복잡한, 복합시설, 열등감
9. blossom — 꽃, 꽃이 피다
10. diameter — 지름, 직경
11. advertise — 광고하다, 알리다
12. bond — 유대, 결속, 끈
13. approach — ~에 접근하다, 가까이 가다
14. bold — 대담한, 뻔뻔스러운
15. competitive — 경쟁력 있는, 경쟁에 의한
16. appreciate — 인정하다, 감상하다, 인식하다
17. boundary — 경계, 경계선
18. approve — 찬성하다, 승인하다

B
1. employee — 피고용자, 종업원
2. grab — 붙잡다, 가로채다
3. invest — 투자하다, 돈을 쓰다
4. diminish — 줄어들다, 감소하다
5. graduate — 졸업하다, 학위를 수여하다
6. equality — 평등, 같음
7. leak — 새다, 새는 곳
8. illustrate — 설명하다, 삽화를 넣다
9. flush — 얼굴이 붉어지다, 분출하다
10. existence — 존재, 생존
11. immediate — 즉석의, 가장 가까운
12. explorer — 탐험가, 조사자
13. dictation — 구술, 받아쓰기
14. loaf — 덩어리
15. gallon — 갤런, 대량
16. invasion — 침입, 침략
17. generally — 대개, 일반적으로
18. flexible — 구부리기 쉬운, 유연성이 있는

Answer Key

Unit 19

A

1. parliament
2. riddle
3. Mixtures
4. rarely
5. march
6. roasted
7. misunderstand
8. raps
9. particular
10. meadow
11. passive
12. melted
13. posed
14. possess
15. portrait
16. realize
17. mass
18. revolution

B

1. 특별한, 특정한
2. 행진, 행진하다
3. 톡톡 두드림, 두드리다
4. 소극적인, 수동의
5. 대중, 집단
6. 깨닫다, 실현하다
7. 의회, 국회
8. 수수께끼, 난문
9. 오해하다, 진가를 못 알아보다
10. 굽다, 볶다
11. 소유하다, 지니다
12. 풀밭, 목초지
13. 혁명, 회전
14. 초상화
15. 좀처럼 ~하지 않다
16. 녹다, 녹이다
17. 자세를 취하다, 제기하다
18. 혼합물, 혼합

1. march
2. mass
3. meadow
4. melt
5. misunderstand
6. mixture
7. parliament
8. particular
9. passive
10. portrait
11. pose
12. possess
13. rap
14. rarely
15. realize
16. revolution
17. riddle
18. roast

C

1. rarely	좀처럼 ~하지 않다
2. roast	굽다, 볶다
3. realize	깨닫다, 실현하다
4. mass	대중, 집단
5. particular	특별한, 특정한
6. rap	톡톡 두드림, 두드리다
7. march	행진, 행진하다
8. possess	소유하다, 지니다
9. parliament	의회, 국회
10. meadow	풀밭, 목초지
11. passive	소극적인, 수동의
12. revolution	혁명, 회전
13. melt	녹다, 녹이다
14. pose	자세를 취하다, 제기하다
15. mixture	혼합물, 혼합
16. portrait	초상화
17. misunderstand	오해하다, 진가를 못 알아보다
18. riddle	수수께끼, 난문

Unit 20

A

1. worsened
2. shed
3. tremendous
4. various
5. youth
6. somewhat
7. thrilled
8. suffer
9. sufficient
10. suicide
11. tighten
12. wreck
13. share
14. utilized
15. somewhere
16. shaved
17. vary
18. sorrow

B

1. 얼마간, 다소
2. 스릴, 전율
3. 자살
4. 공유하다, 분배하다
5. 죄다, 단단하게 하다
6. 경험하다 ,앓다, 괴로워하다
7. 다양한, 다방면의
8. 깎다, 면도하다
9. 난파, 난파시키다
10. 충분한, 흡족한
11. 악화되다, 악화시키다
12. 떨어뜨리다, 뿌리다
13. 거대한, 무서운
14. 젊음, 청년
15. 어딘가에
16. 변화하다, 다양하게 하다
17. 활용하다, 이용하다
18. 슬픔, 비애

1. share
2. shave
3. shed
4. somewhat
5. somewhere
6. sorrow
7. suffer
8. sufficient
9. suicide
10. thrill
11. tighten
12. tremendous
13. utilize
14. various
15. vary
16. worsen
17. wreck
18. youth

C

1. utilize	활용하다, 이용하다
2. suicide	자살
3. thrill	스릴, 전율
4. various	다양한, 다방면의
5. share	공유하다, 분배하다
6. tighten	죄다, 단단하게 하다
7. shed	떨어뜨리다, 뿌리다
8. worsen	악화되다, 악화시키다
9. vary	변화하다, 다양하게 하다
10. shave	깎다, 면도하다
11. tremendous	거대한, 무서운
12. somewhere	어딘가에
13. wreck	난파, 난파시키다
14. suffer	경험하다, 앓다, 괴로워하다
15. somewhat	얼마간, 다소
16. sufficient	충분한, 흡족한
17. youth	젊음, 청년
18. sorrow	슬픔, 비애

Review 10

A

1. rarely	좀처럼 ~하지 않다
2. roast	굽다, 볶다
3. realize	깨닫다, 실현하다
4. mass	대중, 집단
5. particular	특별한, 특정한
6. rap	톡톡 두드림, 두드리다
7. march	행진, 행진하다
8. possess	소유하다, 지니다
9. parliament	의회, 국회
10. meadow	풀밭, 목초지
11. passive	소극적인, 수동의
12. revolution	혁명, 회전
13. melt	녹다, 녹이다
14. pose	자세를 취하다, 제기하다
15. mixture	혼합물, 혼합
16. portrait	초상화
17. misunderstand	오해하다, 진가를 못 알아보다
18. riddle	수수께끼, 난문

B

1. utilize	활용하다, 이용하다
2. suicide	자살
3. thrill	스릴, 전율
4. various	다양한, 다방면의
5. share	공유하다, 분배하다
6. tighten	죄다, 단단하게 하다
7. shed	떨어뜨리다, 뿌리다
8. worsen	악화되다, 악화시키다
9. vary	변화하다, 다양하게 하다
10. shave	깎다, 면도하다
11. tremendous	거대한, 무서운
12. somewhere	어딘가에
13. wreck	난파, 난파시키다
14. suffer	경험하다, 앓다, 괴로워하다
15. somewhat	얼마간, 다소
16. sufficient	충분한, 흡족한
17. youth	젊음, 청년
18. sorrow	슬픔, 비애

Unit 21

A
1. confided
2. barrier
3. abandon
4. drowned
5. declared
6. afflicted
7. cooperate
8. applauded
9. banquet
10. abruptly
11. beguiled
12. comfort
13. apparent
14. contributed
15. accurate
16. burden
17. debt
18. disappointed

B
1. 부담, 짐, 짐을 지우다
2. 협력하다, 협동하다
3. 버리다, 포기하다
4. 은혜, 빚
5. 정확한, 신중한
6. 물에 빠지다, 익사시키다
7. 현혹하다, 속이다
8. 갑자기, 퉁명스럽게
9. 선언하다, 단언하다
10. 위로, 위안, 위로 하다
11. 괴롭히다
12. 털어놓다, 맡기다
13. 박수 갈채하다
14. 실망시키다, 좌절시키다
15. 장벽, 장애
16. 명백한, 겉보기의
17. 기부하다, 기여하다
18. 연회, 진수성찬

C
1. cooperate — 협력하다, 협동하다
2. declare — 선언하다, 단언하다
3. abandon — 버리다, 포기하다
4. debt — 은혜, 빚
5. abruptly — 갑자기, 퉁명스럽게
6. disappoint — 실망시키다, 좌절시키다
7. afflict — 괴롭히다
8. beguile — 현혹하다, 속이다
9. contribute — 기부하다, 기여하다
10. drown — 물에 빠지다, 익사시키다
11. accurate — 정확한, 신중한
12. burden — 부담, 짐, 짐을 지우다
13. applaud — 박수 갈채하다
14. confide — 털어놓다, 맡기다
15. apparent — 명백한, 겉보기의
16. banquet — 연회, 진수성찬
17. comfort — 위로, 위안, 위로하다
18. barrier — 장벽, 장애

Unit 22

A
1. Hydrogen
2. grace
3. examined
4. minister
5. fierce
6. magnitude
7. guaranteed
8. howling
9. hygiene
10. equipment
11. meager
12. insert
13. legacy
14. Freeze
15. legend
16. majority
17. insight
18. mend

B
1. 짖다, 울부짖다
2. 삽입하다, 게재하다
3. 장비, 설비
4. 전설, 일화집
5. 보증하다, 보증
6. 크기, 중대함
7. 조사하다, 시험하다
8. 고치다, 수선하다
9. 유산, 물려받은 것
10. 사나운, 격렬한
11. 통찰, 통찰력
12. 적은, 빈약한
13. 얼다, 얼게 하다
14. 장관, 목사
15. 수소
16. 대다수, 과반수, 다수파
17. 우아, 은혜
18. 위생, 위생법

C
1. fierce — 사나운, 격렬한
2. insight — 통찰, 통찰력
3. legend — 전설, 일화집
4. equipment — 장비, 설비
5. legacy — 유산, 물려받은 것
6. mend — 고치다, 수선하다
7. examine — 조사하다, 시험하다
8. minister — 장관, 목사
9. freeze — 얼다, 얼게 하다
10. magnitude — 크기, 중대함
11. grace — 우아, 은혜
12. majority — 대다수, 과반수, 다수파
13. howl — 짖다, 울부짖다
14. meager — 적은, 빈약한
15. guarantee — 보증하다, 보증
16. hydrogen — 수소
17. insert — 삽입하다, 게재하다
18. hygiene — 위생, 위생법

Review 11

A
1. cooperate — 협력하다, 협동하다
2. declare — 선언하다, 단언하다
3. abandon — 버리다, 포기하다
4. debt — 은혜, 빚
5. abruptly — 갑자기, 퉁명스럽게
6. disappoint — 실망시키다, 좌절시키다
7. afflict — 괴롭히다
8. beguile — 현혹하다, 속이다
9. contribute — 기부하다, 기여하다
10. drown — 물에 빠지다, 익사시키다
11. accurate — 정확한, 신중한
12. burden — 부담, 짐, 짐을 지우다
13. applaud — 박수 갈채하다
14. confide — 털어놓다, 맡기다
15. apparent — 명백한, 겉보기의
16. banquet — 연회, 진수성찬
17. comfort — 위로, 위안, 위로하다
18. barrier — 장벽, 장애

B
1. fierce — 사나운, 격렬한
2. insight — 통찰, 통찰력
3. legend — 전설, 일화집
4. equipment — 장비, 설비
5. legacy — 유산, 물려받은 것
6. mend — 고치다, 수선하다
7. examine — 조사하다, 시험하다
8. minister — 장관, 목사
9. freeze — 얼다, 얼게 하다
10. magnitude — 크기, 중대함
11. grace — 우아, 은혜
12. majority — 대다수, 과반수, 다수파
13. howl — 짖다, 울부짖다
14. meager — 적은, 빈약한
15. guarantee — 보증하다, 보증
16. hydrogen — 수소
17. insert — 삽입하다, 게재하다
18. hygiene — 위생, 위생법

Unit 23

A
1. prevail
2. nourish
3. resentful
4. novelty
5. profound
6. reproduce
7. optimistic
8. paralyzed
9. persist
10. owed
11. postponed
12. operator
13. recruited
14. pretending
15. racial
16. posture
17. related
18. puzzled

B
1. 빚지고 있다, 은혜를 입고 있다
2. ~인 체하다
3. (영양분을)주다, 기르다
4. 당황하게 하다, 이리저리 생각하다
5. 고집하다, 지속하다
6. 인종의, 종족의
7. 진기함, 새로운 것
8. 우세하다, 보급되다
9. 번식하다, 재생하다
10. 마비시키다, 무력케하다
11. 분개한, 골을 잘 내는
12. 교환수, 조작자
13. 깊이가 있는, 심오한
14. 이야기하다, 관계 짓다
15. 연기하다, 차위에 두다
16. 채용하다, 모집하다
17. 자세, 태도
18. 낙천적인, 낙관적인

1. nourish
2. novelty
3. operator
4. optimistic
5. owe
6. paralyze
7. persist
8. postpone
9. posture
10. pretend
11. prevail
12. profound
13. puzzle
14. racial
15. recruit
16. relate
17. reproduce
18. resentful

C
1. persist 고집하다, 지속하다
2. racial 인종의, 종족의
3. relate 이야기하다, 관계 짓다
4. paralyze 마비시키다, 무력케하다
5. prevail 우세하다, 보급되다
6. resentful 분개한, 골을 잘 내는
7. postpone 연기하다, 차위에 두다
8. recruit 채용하다, 모집하다
9. optimistic 낙천적인, 낙관적인
10. posture 자세, 태도
11. novelty 진기함, 새로운 것
12. pretend ~인 체하다
13. reproduce 번식하다, 재생하다
14. nourish (영양분을)주다, 기르다
15. puzzle 당황하게 하다, 이리 저리 생각하다
16. operator 교환수, 조작자
17. profound 깊이가 있는, 심오한
18. owe 빚지고 있다, 은혜를 입고 있다

Unit 24

A
1. slope
2. transplant
3. strength
4. ridiculous
5. sequence
6. slip
7. voluntary
8. spectacular
9. rigid
10. spectators
11. Temperate
12. seized
13. transform
14. utmost
15. Virtue
16. sting
17. temporary
18. utter

B
1. 찌르다, 괴롭히다, 찌름
2. 임시의, 일시적인
3. 우스꽝스러운, 어리석은
4. 옮겨 심다, 이식하다 이식
5. 경사지, 비탈
6. 변형시키다, 변모시키다
7. 단단한, 엄격한
8. 최고의, 최대의
9. 장관의, 구경거리의
10. 덕, 장점
11. (붙)잡다, 파악하다
12. 자발적인, 임의의
13. 구경꾼, 관객
14. 말하다, 완전한
15. 연속, 순서
16. 절제하는, 온화한
17. 힘, 세기, 강점
18. 미끄러지다, 몰래 나오다

1. ridiculous
2. rigid
3. seize
4. sequence
5. slip
6. slope
7. spectacular
8. spectator
9. sting
10. strength
11. temperate
12. temporary
13. transform
14. transplant
15. utmost
16. utter
17. virtue
18. voluntary

C
1. transplant 옮겨 심다, 이식하다, 이식
2. seize (붙)잡다, 파악하다
3. spectacular 장관의, 구경거리의
4. utter 말하다, 완전한
5. spectator 구경꾼, 관객
6. transform 변형시키다, 변모시키다
7. strength 힘, 세기, 강점
8. ridiculous 우스꽝스러운, 어리석은
9. temporary 임시의, 일시적인
10. sting 찌르다, 괴롭히다, 찌름
11. virtue 덕, 장점
12. temperate 절제하는, 온화한
13. slope 경사지, 비탈
14. utmost 최고의, 최대의
15. slip 미끄러지다, 몰래 나오다
16. voluntary 자발적인, 임의의
17. rigid 단단한, 엄격한
18. sequence 연속, 순서

Review 12

A
1. persist 고집하다, 지속하다
2. racial 인종의, 종족의
3. relate 이야기하다, 관계 짓다
4. paralyze 마비시키다, 무력케하다
5. prevail 우세하다, 보급되다
6. resentful 분개한, 골을 잘 내는
7. postpone 연기하다, 차위에 두다
8. recruit 채용하다, 모집하다
9. optimistic 낙천적인, 낙관적인
10. posture 자세, 태도
11. novelty 진기함, 새로운 것
12. pretend ~인 체하다
13. reproduce 번식하다, 재생하다
14. nourish (영양분을)주다, 기르다
15. puzzle 당황하게 하다, 이리 저리 생각하다
16. operator 교환수, 조작자
17. profound 깊이가 있는, 심오한
18. owe 빚지고 있다, 은혜를 입고 있다

B
1. transplant 옮겨 심다, 이식하다, 이식
2. seize (붙)잡다, 파악하다
3. spectacular 장관의, 구경거리의
4. utter 말하다, 완전한
5. spectator 구경꾼, 관객
6. transform 변형시키다, 변모시키다
7. strength 힘, 세기, 강점
8. ridiculous 우스꽝스러운, 어리석은
9. temporary 임시의, 일시적인
10. sting 찌르다, 괴롭히다, 찌름
11. virtue 덕, 장점
12. temperate 절제하는, 온화한
13. slope 경사지, 비탈
14. utmost 최고의, 최대의
15. slip 미끄러지다, 몰래 나오다
16. voluntary 자발적인, 임의의
17. rigid 단단한, 엄격한
18. sequence 연속, 순서

Unit 25

A
1. correctly
2. absolutely
3. delight
4. allies
5. dumped
6. colony
7. appliances
8. Beneath
9. besides
10. canal
11. astonished
12. comfortably
13. aim
14. coordinate
15. delegate
16. absurd
17. dumb
18. column

B
1. 편안하게, 기분 좋게
2. 절대적으로, 완전히
3. ~의 밑(아래)에
4. 위임하다, 대표자
5. 부조리한, 불합리한
6. 운하, 수로
7. 기쁨, 기쁨을 주는 것
8. 목표, 목적, 겨누다
9. 조정하다, 조화시키다
10. 놀라게 하다
11. 식민지, 집단
12. 벙어리의, 말을 하지 않는
13. 동맹국, 협력자
14. (쓰레기를)내버리다, 내려뜨리다
15. 게다가, 그 밖에, ~외에도
16. 정확히, 바르게
17. 기구, 장치, 설비
18. (신문의)란, 기둥

C
1. absolutely
2. absurd
3. aim
4. ally
5. appliance
6. astonish
7. beneath
8. besides
9. canal
10. colony
11. column
12. comfortably
13. coordinate
14. correctly
15. delegate
16. delight
17. dumb
18. dump

C
1. dumb — 벙어리의, 말을 하지 않는
2. absolutely — 절대적으로, 완전히
3. dump — (쓰레기를)내버리다, 내려뜨리다
4. coordinate — 조정하다, 조화시키다
5. absurd — 부조리한, 불합리한
6. correctly — 정확히, 바르게
7. colony — 식민지, 집단
8. delegate — 위임하다, 대표자
9. aim — 목표, 목적, 겨누다
10. besides — 게다가, 그 밖에, ~외에도
11. delight — 기쁨, 기쁨을 주는 것
12. canal — 운하, 수로
13. ally — 동맹국, 협력자
14. beneath — ~의 밑(아래)에
15. astonish — 놀라게 하다
16. column — (신문의)란, 기둥
17. appliance — 기구, 장치, 설비
18. comfortably — 편안하게, 기분 좋게

Unit 26

A
1. fled
2. explored
3. manipulate
4. firm
5. exploded
6. further
7. guardians
8. monument
9. halt
10. iceberg
11. Frost
12. indigenous
13. insisted
14. instruments
15. liberal
16. immediately
17. mutual
18. legislate

B
1. 더욱이, 더 먼
2. 빙산
3. 폭발시키다, 격발하다
4. 주장하다, 강력히 요구하다
5. 정지, 정지하다
6. 법률을 제정하다
7. 탐험하다, 탐구하다
8. 조작하다, (기계) 잘 다루다
9. 곧, 즉시
10. 굳은, 확고한
11. 서로의, 공동의
12. 기계, 기구, 도구
13. 서리, 서리로 덮다
14. 기념비, 기념물
15. 토착의, 원산의
16. 달아나다, 도망치다
17. 너그러운, 자유주의의
18. 보호자, 후견인

C
1. explode
2. explore
3. firm
4. flee
5. frost
6. further
7. guardian
8. halt
9. iceberg
10. immediately
11. indigenous
12. insist
13. instrument
14. legislate
15. liberal
16. manipulate
17. monument
18. mutual

C
1. frost — 서리, 서리로 덮다
2. guardian — 보호자, 후견인
3. further — 더욱이, 더 먼
4. legislate — 법률을 제정하다
5. flee — 달아나다, 도망치다
6. mutual — 서로의, 공동의
7. instrument — 기계, 기구, 도구
8. halt — 정지, 정지하다
9. firm — 굳은, 확고한
10. liberal — 너그러운, 자유주의의
11. insist — 주장하다, 강력히 요구하다
12. explore — 탐험하다, 탐구하다
13. iceberg — 빙산
14. manipulate — 조작하다, (기계) 잘 다루다
15. immediately — 곧, 즉시
16. explode — 폭발시키다, 격발하다
17. monument — 기념비, 기념물
18. indigenous — 토착의, 원산의

Review 13

A
1. dumb — 벙어리의, 말을 하지 않는
2. absolutely — 절대적으로, 완전히
3. dump — (쓰레기를)내버리다, 내려뜨리다
4. coordinate — 조정하다, 조화시키다
5. absurd — 부조리한, 불합리한
6. correctly — 정확히, 바르게
7. colony — 식민지, 집단
8. delegate — 위임하다, 대표자
9. aim — 목표, 목적, 겨누다
10. besides — 게다가, 그 밖에, ~외에도
11. delight — 기쁨, 기쁨을 주는 것
12. canal — 운하, 수로
13. ally — 동맹국, 협력자
14. beneath — ~의 밑(아래)에
15. astonish — 놀라게 하다
16. column — (신문의)란, 기둥
17. appliance — 기구, 장치, 설비
18. comfortably — 편안하게, 기분 좋게

B
1. frost — 서리, 서리로 덮다
2. guardian — 보호자, 후견인
3. further — 더욱이, 더 먼
4. legislate — 법률을 제정하다
5. flee — 달아나다, 도망치다
6. mutual — 서로의, 공동의
7. instrument — 기계, 기구, 도구
8. halt — 정지, 정지하다
9. firm — 굳은, 확고한
10. liberal — 너그러운, 자유주의의
11. insist — 주장하다, 강력히 요구하다
12. explore — 탐험하다, 탐구하다
13. iceberg — 빙산
14. manipulate — 조작하다, (기계) 잘 다루다
15. immediately — 곧, 즉시
16. explode — 폭발시키다, 격발하다
17. monument — 기념비, 기념물
18. indigenous — 토착의, 원산의

Answer Key

Unit 27

A
1. resist
2. nursery
3. primary
4. outlet
5. parcel
6. relay
7. prairies
8. patriotism
9. nurtured
10. preview
11. prohibit
12. pronunciation
13. radical
14. outstanding
15. random
16. poverty
17. residence
18. pliable

B
1. 애국심
2. 금지하다, 방해하다
3. 육아실, 탁아소
4. 가난, 결핍
5. 근본적인, 근본의
6. 양육하다, 교육하다
7. 대초원, 목초지
8. 전달하다, 중계하다
9. 배출구, 판매 대리점, 콘센트
10. 주요한, 본래의, 첫째의
11. 미리 보기, 시사회
12. 거주, 주거
13. 눈에 띄는, 현저한
14. 발음, 발음표기
15. 유연한, 융통성이 있는
16. 견디다, 저항하다
17. 소포, 꾸러미로 하다
18. 임의의, 되는 대로

1. nursery
2. nurture
3. outlet
4. outstanding
5. parcel
6. patriotism
7. pliable
8. poverty
9. prairie
10. preview
11. primary
12. prohibit
13. pronunciation
14. radical
15. random
16. relay
17. residence
18. resist

C
1. poverty 가난, 결핍
2. nurture 양육하다, 교육하다
3. residence 거주, 주거
4. prairie 대초원, 목초지
5. nursery 육아실, 탁아소
6. resist 견디다, 저항하다
7. preview 미리 보기, 시사회
8. relay 전달하다, 중계하다
9. outlet 배출구, 판매 대리점, 콘센트
10. radical 근본적인, 근본의
11. pronunciation 발음, 발음표기
12. primary 주요한, 본래의, 첫째의
13. patriotism 애국심
14. outstanding 눈에 띄는, 현저한
15. pliable 유연한, 융통성이 있는
16. random 임의의, 되는 대로
17. parcel 소포, 꾸러미로 하다
18. prohibit 금지하다, 방해하다

Unit 28

A
1. triumph
2. sniffed
3. voyage
4. servants
5. splashed
6. ultimate
7. spots
8. roaring
9. struggling
10. tempt
11. tense
12. sacrifice
13. vague
14. sobbing
15. vain
16. settled
17. superb
18. whiskers

B
1. 희생, 희생하다
2. 승리, 승리하다
3. 투쟁하다, 애쓰다
4. 으르렁거리다, 울부짖다
5. 장소, 반점, 더럽히다
6. 헛된, 허영심이 강한
7. 하인, 봉사자
8. 막연한, 모호한, 희미한
9. 긴장한, 시제
10. 흐느껴 울다, 흐느낌
11. 여행, 항해, 여행 하다
12. 이주하다, 결정하다
13. 구레나룻
14. 최후의, 궁극적인
15. 튀기다, 첨벙거리다
16. 유혹하다, 꾀다
17. 냄새 맡다
18. 뛰어난, 멋진

1. roar
2. sacrifice
3. servant
4. settle
5. sniff
6. sob
7. splash
8. spot
9. struggle
10. superb
11. tempt
12. tense
13. triumph
14. ultimate
15. vague
16. vain
17. voyage
18. whisker

C
1. struggle 투쟁하다, 애쓰다
2. sob 흐느껴 울다, 흐느낌
3. sacrifice 희생, 희생하다
4. whisker 구레나룻
5. superb 뛰어난, 멋진
6. roar 으르렁거리다, 울부짖다
7. spot 장소, 반점, 더럽히다
8. voyage 여행, 항해, 여행하다
9. sniff 냄새 맡다
10. ultimate 최후의, 궁극적인
11. splash 튀기다, 첨벙거리다
12. vague 막연한, 모호한, 희미한
13. tense 긴장한, 시제
14. tempt 유혹하다, 꾀다
15. vain 헛된, 허영심이 강한
16. settle 이주하다, 결정하다
17. triumph 승리, 승리하다
18. servant 하인, 봉사자

Review 14

A
1. poverty 가난, 결핍
2. nurture 양육하다, 교육하다
3. residence 거주, 주거
4. prairie 대초원, 목초지
5. nursery 육아실, 탁아소
6. resist 견디다, 저항하다
7. preview 미리 보기, 시사회
8. relay 전달하다, 중계하다
9. outlet 배출구, 판매 대리점, 콘센트
10. radical 근본적인, 근본의
11. pronunciation 발음, 발음표기
12. primary 주요한, 본래의, 첫째의
13. patriotism 애국심
14. outstanding 눈에 띄는, 현저한
15. pliable 유연한, 융통성이 있는
16. random 임의의, 되는 대로
17. parcel 소포, 꾸러미로 하다
18. prohibit 금지하다, 방해하다

B
1. struggle 투쟁하다, 애쓰다
2. sob 흐느껴 울다, 흐느낌
3. sacrifice 희생, 희생하다
4. whisker 구레나룻
5. superb 뛰어난, 멋진
6. roar 으르렁거리다, 울부짖다
7. spot 장소, 반점, 더럽히다
8. voyage 여행, 항해, 여행하다
9. sniff 냄새 맡다
10. ultimate 최후의, 궁극적인
11. splash 튀기다, 첨벙거리다
12. vague 막연한, 모호한, 희미한
13. tense 긴장한, 시제
14. tempt 유혹하다, 꾀다
15. vain 헛된, 허영심이 강한
16. settle 이주하다, 결정하다
17. triumph 승리, 승리하다
18. servant 하인, 봉사자

Unit 29

A
1. elaborate
2. beyond
3. amazing
4. biography
5. analyzes
6. attendant
7. carved
8. abused
9. Cemetery
10. attempting
11. accent
12. comparison
13. costume
14. crew
15. deserve
16. communicate
17. desire
18. election

B
1. 받을 가치가 있다, ~할 만하다
2. 새기다, 조각하다
3. 학대하다, 남용하다
4. 승무원
5. 시중드는 사람, 참석자
6. 비교, 유사
7. 강세, 강조
8. 묘지
9. 정교한, 공들여 만들다
10. 시도하다, 시도
11. 선거, 투표
12. 놀랄 만한, 굉장한
13. 바램, 소망
14. 전기, 일대기
15. 복장, 의상
16. 분석하다, 분해하다
17. ~의 저편에, ~을 넘어서
18. 의사소통하다, 전달하다

1. abuse
2. accent
3. amazing
4. analyze
5. attempt
6. attendant
7. beyond
8. biography
9. carve
10. cemetery
11. communicate
12. comparison
13. costume
14. crew
15. desire
16. elaborate
17. election

C
1. carve — 새기다, 조각하다
2. elaborate — 정교한, 공들여 만들다
3. abuse — 학대하다, 남용하다
4. biography — 전기, 일대기
5. cemetery — 묘지
6. desire — 바램, 소망
7. accent — 강세, 강조
8. election — 선거, 투표
9. communicate — 의사소통하다, 전달하다
10. amazing — 놀랄 만한, 굉장한
11. beyond — ~의 저편에, ~을 넘어서
12. deserve — 받을 가치가 있다, ~할 만하다
13. attempt — 시도하다, 시도
14. comparison — 비교, 유사
15. analyze — 분석하다, 분해하다
16. costume — 복장, 의상
17. attendant — 시중드는 사람, 참석자
18. crew — 승무원

Unit 30

A
1. extract
2. interferes
3. gay
4. fluent
5. intimate
6. extracurricular
7. foremost
8. immigrant
9. garments
10. hardship
11. imported
12. minorities
13. literature
14. myth
15. intelligent
16. Likewise
17. needy
18. mandatory

B
1. 수입하다, ~의 뜻을 내포하다
2. 마찬가지로, 똑같이
3. 추출하다, 뽑다
4. 유창한, 능변의
5. 간섭하다, 방해하다
6. 과외의, 정식 과목이외
7. 신화, 전설
8. 고난, 역경
9. 매우 가난한
10. 이해력 있는, 지적인, 총명한
11. 의류, 옷가지
12. 문학, 문헌
13. 친밀한, 깊은
14. 최고의, 맨 처음의
15. 명령의, 강제의
16. 이민자, 이주하는
17. 소수, 소수파
18. 명랑한, 화려한

1. extract
2. extracurricular
3. fluent
4. foremost
5. garment
6. gay
7. hardship
8. immigrant
9. import
10. intelligent
11. interfere
12. intimate
13. likewise
14. literature
15. mandatory
16. minority
17. myth
18. needy

C
1. interfere — 간섭하다, 방해하다
2. extract — 추출하다, 뽑다
3. needy — 매우 가난한
4. intimate — 친밀한, 깊은
5. hardship — 고난, 역경
6. intelligent — 이해력 있는, 지적인, 총명한
7. likewise — 마찬가지로, 똑같이
8. extracurricular — 과외의, 정식 과목이외
9. minority — 소수, 소수파
10. gay — 명랑한, 화려한
11. myth — 신화, 전설
12. immigrant — 이민자, 이주하는
13. literature — 문학, 문헌
14. fluent — 유창한, 능변의
15. garment — 의류, 옷가지
16. import — 수입하다, ~의 뜻을 내포하다
17. mandatory — 명령의, 강제의
18. foremost — 최고의, 맨 처음의

Review 15

A
1. carve — 새기다, 조각하다
2. elaborate — 정교한, 공들여 만들다
3. abuse — 학대하다, 남용하다
4. biography — 전기, 일대기
5. cemetery — 묘지
6. desire — 바램, 소망
7. accent — 강세, 강조
8. election — 선거, 투표
9. communicate — 의사소통하다, 전달하다
10. amazing — 놀랄 만한, 굉장한
11. beyond — ~의 저편에, ~을 넘어서
12. deserve — 받을 가치가 있다, ~할 만하다
13. attempt — 시도하다, 시도
14. comparison — 비교, 유사
15. analyze — 분석하다, 분해하다
16. costume — 복장, 의상
17. attendant — 시중드는 사람, 참석자
18. crew — 승무원

B
1. interfere — 간섭하다, 방해하다
2. extract — 추출하다, 뽑다
3. needy — 매우 가난한
4. intimate — 친밀한, 깊은
5. hardship — 고난, 역경
6. intelligent — 이해력 있는, 지적인, 총명한
7. likewise — 마찬가지로, 똑같이
8. extracurricular — 과외의, 정식 과목이외
9. minority — 소수, 소수파
10. gay — 명랑한, 화려한
11. myth — 신화, 전설
12. immigrant — 이민자, 이주하는
13. literature — 문학, 문헌
14. fluent — 유창한, 능변의
15. garment — 의류, 옷가지
16. import — 수입하다, ~의 뜻을 내포하다
17. mandatory — 명령의, 강제의
18. foremost — 최고의, 맨 처음의

Unit 31

A
1. petals
2. proceed
3. nutrition
4. Overall
5. rare
6. responsible
7. pessimistic
8. principal
9. Oath
10. prosperity
11. protested
12. rear
13. released
14. prime
15. precautions
16. overheard
17. relieve
18. resources

B
1. 맹세, 선서
2. 번영, 부유
3. 교장, 장, 주요한
4. 뒤쪽, 후방의
5. 영양(분), 영양 공급
6. 계속하다, 나아가다
7. 자원, 재료
8. 전체적으로, 전체의
9. 구원하다, 덜다
10. 꽃잎
11. 책임이 있는, 신뢰할 수 있는
12. 엿듣다, 우연히 듣다
13. 항의하다, 주장하다
14. 첫째의, 주요한
15. 드문, 희귀한
16. 조심, 예방책
17. 놓아주다, 공개하다, 개봉하다
18. 비관적인, 염세적인

C
1. precaution — 조심, 예방책
2. responsible — 책임이 있는, 신뢰할 수 있는
3. oath — 맹세, 선서
4. petal — 꽃잎
5. resource — 자원, 재료
6. overhear — 엿듣다, 우연히 듣다
7. prime — 첫째의, 주요한
8. nutrition — 영양(분), 영양 공급
9. release — 놓아주다, 공개하다, 개봉하다
10. pessimistic — 비관적인, 염세적인
11. prosperity — 번영, 부유
12. principal — 교장, 장, 주요한
13. relieve — 구원하다, 덜다
14. overall — 전체적으로, 전체의
15. rare — 드문, 희귀한
16. proceed — 계속하다, 나아가다
17. rear — 뒤쪽, 후방의
18. protest — 항의하다, 주장하다

Unit 32

A
1. scars
2. transmit
3. suspended
4. shift
5. valid
6. stared
7. transition
8. unity
9. satellite
10. unlettered
11. solemn
12. unwind
13. solitary
14. vain
15. whistles
16. startled
17. Shrug
18. wilderness

B
1. 옮기다, 이동시키다
2. 통일, 일치
3. 보류하다 매달다, 중지하다
4. (인공)위성, (인공)위성의
5. 변천(기), 변이
6. 헛된, 무익한
7. 상처, 흔적
8. 전송하다, 전도하다
9. 휘파람, 휘파람을 불다
10. 엄숙한, 근엄한, 중대한
11. 황야, 미개지
12. 깜짝 놀라게 하다
13. 타당한, 유효한
14. 으쓱하다 어깨를 으쓱하기
15. 풀리다, 풀다
16. 혼자의, 외로운
17. 문맹의, 무학의
18. 응시하다, 빤히 보다

C
1. stare — 응시하다, 빤히 보다
2. unlettered — 문맹의, 무학의
3. shift — 옮기다, 이동시키다
4. transmit — 전송하다, 전도하다
5. unity — 통일, 일치
6. satellite — (인공)위성, (인공)위성의
7. solemn — 엄숙한, 근엄한, 중대한
8. transition — 변천(기), 변이
9. shrug — 으쓱하다, 어깨를 으쓱하기
10. wilderness — 황야, 미개지
11. unwind — 풀리다, 풀다
12. scar — 상처, 흔적
13. whistle — 휘파람, 휘파람을 불다
14. suspend — 보류하다, 매달다, 중지하다
15. solitary — 혼자의, 외로운
16. vain — 헛된, 무익한
17. startle — 깜짝 놀라게 하다
18. valid — 타당한, 유효한

Review 16

A
1. precaution — 조심, 예방책
2. responsible — 책임이 있는, 신뢰할 수 있는
3. oath — 맹세, 선서
4. petal — 꽃잎
5. resource — 자원, 재료
6. overhear — 엿듣다, 우연히 듣다
7. prime — 첫째의, 주요한
8. nutrition — 영양(분), 영양 공급
9. release — 놓아주다, 공개하다, 개봉하다
10. pessimistic — 비관적인, 염세적인
11. prosperity — 번영, 부유
12. principal — 교장, 장, 주요한
13. relieve — 구원하다, 덜다
14. overall — 전체적으로, 전체의
15. rare — 드문, 희귀한
16. proceed — 계속하다, 나아가다
17. rear — 뒤쪽, 후방의
18. protest — 항의하다, 주장하다

B
1. stare — 응시하다, 빤히 보다
2. unlettered — 문맹의, 무학의
3. shift — 옮기다, 이동시키다
4. transmit — 전송하다, 전도하다
5. unity — 통일, 일치
6. satellite — (인공)위성, (인공)위성의
7. solemn — 엄숙한, 근엄한, 중대한
8. transition — 변천(기), 변이
9. shrug — 으쓱하다, 어깨를 으쓱하기
10. wilderness — 황야, 미개지
11. unwind — 풀리다, 풀다
12. scar — 상처, 흔적
13. whistle — 휘파람, 휘파람을 불다
14. suspend — 보류하다, 매달다, 중지하다
15. solitary — 혼자의, 외로운
16. vain — 헛된, 무익한
17. startle — 깜짝 놀라게 하다
18. valid — 타당한, 유효한

Unit 33

A
1. awfully
2. charming
3. accused
4. biology
5. damage
6. encourages
7. announcement
8. cruel
9. anthem
10. bother
11. acquire
12. clamor
13. compliments
14. attracting
15. despise
16. competent
17. elementary
18. detective

B
1. 괴롭히다, 귀찮게 하다
2. 칭찬, 찬사
3. 고발하다, 비난하다
4. 손해, 피해 손해(피해)를 입다
5. 유능한, 능력이 있는
6. 얻다, 취득하다
7. 경멸하다, 싫어하다
8. 아주, 몹시
9. 초보의, 기본의
10. 공고, 발표
11. 격려하다, 촉진하다
12. 매력적인, 매우 재미있는
13. 성가, 찬송가
14. 생물학, 생물학 책
15. 탐정, 탐정의
16. 잔인한, 참혹한
17. (주의 흥미 등을)끌다, 매혹하다
18. 아우성, 시끄럽게 요구하다

C
1. charming 매력적인, 매우 재미있는
2. damage 손해,피해,손해(피해)를 입다
3. elementary 초보의, 기본의
4. bother 괴롭히다, 귀찮게 하다
5. accuse 고발하다, 비난하다
6. clamor 아우성,시끄럽게 요구하다
7. detective 탐정, 탐정의
8. despise 경멸하다, 싫어하다
9. acquire 얻다, 취득하다
10. compliment 칭찬, 찬사
11. awfully 아주, 몹시
12. competent 유능한, 능력이 있는
13. announcement 공고, 발표
14. encourage 격려하다, 촉진하다
15. attract (주의, 흥미 등을) 끌다, 매혹하다
16. biology 생물학, 생물학 책
17. anthem 성가, 찬송가
18. cruel 잔인한, 참혹한

Unit 34

A
1. generates
2. extraordinary
3. master
4. formal
5. figure
6. gazing
7. hardworking
8. foresaw
9. heritages
10. extrovert
11. independent
12. haste
13. invader
14. located
15. mediate
16. norms
17. industrial
18. luxurious

B
1. 특별한, 범상치 않은
2. 산업의, 공업의
3. 전통문화, 유산
4. 외향적인 사람
5. 독립의, 자주의
6. 응시하다, 바라보다
7. 숙달하다, 주인, 대가
8. 예견하다, 예지하다
9. 위치하다, 위치를 정하다
10. 조정하다, 화해시키다
11. 형식적인, 정규의
12. 사치스러운, 호화로운
13. 급함, 서두름
14. 표준, 평균
15. 생산하다, 발생하다
16. 주목할 만한, 유명한
17. 침입자, 침략자
18. 부지런한, 열심히 일하는

C
1. locate 위치하다, 위치를 정하다
2. notable 주목할 만한, 유명한
3. extraordinary 특별한, 범상치 않은
4. industrial 산업의, 공업의
5. foresee 예견하다, 예지하다
6. master 숙달하다, 주인, 대가
7. hardworking 부지런한, 열심히 일하는
8. extrovert 외향적인 사람
9. invader 침입자, 침략자
10. luxurious 사치스러운, 호화로운
11. formal 형식적인, 정규의
12. independent 독립의, 자주의
13. heritage 전통문화, 유산
14. gaze 응시하다, 바라보다
15. mediate 조정하다, 화해시키다
16. generate 생산하다, 발생하다
17. haste 급함, 서두름
18. norm 표준, 평균

Review 17

A
1. charming 매력적인, 매우 재미있는
2. damage 손해, 피해, 손해(피해)를 입다
3. elementary 초보의, 기본의
4. bother 괴롭히다, 귀찮게 하다
5. accuse 고발하다, 비난하다
6. clamor 아우성, 시끄럽게 요구하다
7. detective 탐정, 탐정의
8. despise 경멸하다, 싫어하다
9. acquire 얻다, 취득하다
10. compliment 칭찬, 찬사
11. awfully 아주, 몹시
12. competent 유능한, 능력이 있는
13. announcement 공고, 발표
14. encourage 격려하다, 촉진하다
15. attract (주의, 흥미 등을) 끌다, 매혹하다
16. biology 생물학, 생물학 책
17. anthem 성가, 찬송가
18. cruel 잔인한, 참혹한

B
1. locate 위치하다, 위치를 정하다
2. notable 주목할 만한, 유명한
3. extraordinary 특별한, 범상치 않은
4. industrial 산업의, 공업의
5. foresee 예견하다, 예지하다
6. master 숙달하다, 주인, 대가
7. hardworking 부지런한, 열심히 일하는
8. extrovert 외향적인 사람
9. invader 침입자, 침략자
10. luxurious 사치스러운, 호화로운
11. formal 형식적인, 정규의
12. independent 독립의, 자주의
13. heritage 전통문화, 유산
14. gaze 응시하다, 바라보다
15. mediate 조정하다, 화해시키다
16. generate 생산하다, 발생하다
17. haste 급함, 서두름
18. norm 표준, 평균

Unit 35

A
1. revive
2. observing
3. revealing
4. precise
5. recite
6. physical
7. obliged
8. preference
9. overtake
10. pervaded
11. privileges
12. rely
13. proudly
14. overlooked
15. private
16. remain
17. physicist
18. recently

B
1. 자랑스럽게, 거만하게
2. 강요하다, 고맙게 여기다
3. 신체의, 물질의
4. 낭송하다, 말하다
5. 널리 퍼지다, 충만하다
6. 관찰하다(규칙 등을)준수하다
7. 의지하다, 믿다
8. 선호, 좋아하는 물건
9. 간과하다, 내려다보다
10. 소생하다, 부활하다
11. 개인적인, 사적인
12. 남다, ~인 상태로 있다, 유적
13. 따라 잡다, 덮치다
14. 특권, 특권을 주다
15. 드러내다, 폭로하다
16. 정확한, 정밀한
17. 최근에, 요즈음
18. 물리학자

1. oblige
2. observe
3. overlook
4. overtake
5. physical
6. physicist
7. precise
8. preference
9. pervade
10. private
11. privilege
12. proudly
13. recently
14. recite
15. rely
16. remain
17. reveal
18. revive

C
1. private — 개인적인, 사적인
2. oblige — 강요하다, 고맙게 여기다
3. revive — 소생하다, 부활하다
4. privilege — 특권, 특권을 주다
5. observe — 관찰하다, 준수하다
6. recently — 최근에, 요즈음
7. reveal — 드러내다, 폭로하다
8. preference — 선호, 좋아하는 물건
9. overlook — 간과하다, 내려다보다
10. physical — 신체의, 물질의
11. rely — 의지하다, 믿다
12. pervade — 널리 퍼지다, 충만하다
13. overtake — 따라 잡다, 덮치다
14. remain — 남다, ~인 상태로 있다, 유적
15. physicist — 물리학자
16. recite — 낭송하다, 말하다
17. precise — 정확한, 정밀한
18. proudly — 자랑스럽게, 거만하게

Unit 36

A
1. similarities
2. tough
3. scarcely
4. sophomores
5. wireless
6. suspicion
7. tradition
8. significant
9. urgent
10. steady
11. useless
12. scholar
13. swear
14. vapor
15. solution
16. witness
17. vanished
18. steep

B
1. 중요한 의미 있는, 상당한
2. 맹세하다, 선서하다
3. 강인한, 질긴, 힘든
4. 거의 ~않다, 간신히
5. 의심, 혐의
6. 쓸모 없는, 무익한
7. 학자, 고전학자
8. 긴급한, 절박한
9. 사라지다, 희미해지다
10. 해결, 용해
11. 증거, 목격자
12. 2학년생, 2학년생
13. 무선의, 무선전신
14. 가파른, 적시다
15. 증기, 증발하다
16. 비슷함, 유사점
17. 전통, 전설
18. 확고한, 착실한, 한결같은

1. scarcely
2. scholar
3. significant
4. similarity
5. solution
6. sophomore
7. steady
8. steep
9. suspicion
10. swear
11. tough
12. tradition
13. urgent
14. useless
15. vanish
16. vapor
17. wireless
18. witness

C
1. vapor — 증기, 증발하다
2. useless — 쓸모 없는, 무익한
3. steep — 가파른, 적시다
4. scholar — 학자, 고전학자
5. wireless — 무선의, 무선전신
6. suspicion — 의심, 혐의
7. tradition — 전통, 전설
8. vanish — 사라지다, 희미해지다
9. significant — 중요한, 의미 있는, 상당한
10. steady — 확고한, 착실한, 한결같은
11. scarcely — 거의 ~않다, 간신히
12. solution — 해결, 용해
13. tough — 강인한, 질긴, 힘든
14. urgent — 긴급한, 절박한
15. sophomore — 2학년생, 2학년생의
16. witness — 증거, 목격자
17. similarity — 비슷함, 유사점
18. swear — 맹세하다, 선서하다

Review 18

A
1. private — 개인적인, 사적인
2. oblige — 강요하다, 고맙게 여기다
3. revive — 소생하다, 부활하다
4. privilege — 특권, 특권을 주다
5. observe — 관찰하다, 준수하다
6. recently — 최근에, 요즈음
7. reveal — 드러내다, 폭로하다
8. preference — 선호, 좋아하는 물건
9. overlook — 간과하다, 내려다보다
10. physical — 신체의, 물질의
11. rely — 의지하다, 믿다
12. pervade — 널리 퍼지다, 충만하다
13. overtake — 따라 잡다, 덮치다
14. remain — 남다, ~인 상태로 있다, 유적
15. physicist — 물리학자
16. recite — 낭송하다, 말하다
17. precise — 정확한, 정밀한
18. proudly — 자랑스럽게, 거만하게

B
1. vapor — 증기, 증발하다
2. useless — 쓸모 없는, 무익한
3. steep — 가파른, 적시다
4. scholar — 학자, 고전학자
5. wireless — 무선의, 무선전신
6. suspicion — 의심, 혐의
7. tradition — 전통, 전설
8. vanish — 사라지다, 희미해지다
9. significant — 중요한, 의미 있는, 상당한
10. steady — 확고한, 착실한, 한결같은
11. scarcely — 거의 ~않다, 간신히
12. solution — 해결, 용해
13. tough — 강인한, 질긴, 힘든
14. urgent — 긴급한, 절박한
15. sophomore — 2학년생, 2학년생의
16. witness — 증거, 목격자
17. similarity — 비슷함, 유사점
18. swear — 맹세하다, 선서하다

Unit 37

A
1. compulsory
2. barks
3. affections
4. directly
5. apologies
6. engaged
7. banished
8. breakthrough
9. cleave
10. coeducation
11. donations
12. additional
13. consists
14. anxiety
15. breakdown
16. deal
17. endurance
18. discharge

B
1. 짖다, 소리치며 말하다
2. 이루어지다, ~에 있다
3. 부가된, 추가의
4. 기부, 기증
5. 중요한 성과, 획기적 발전
6. 애정, 감동
7. 인내, 지구력, 내구성
8. 거래, 다루다, 거래하다
9. 추방하다, 내쫓다
10. 이행하다, 해임하다, 방출하다
11. 쇠약, 고장
12. 고용하다, 약속하다
13. 걱정, 불안
14. 의무적인, 강제적인
15. 곧장, 직접, 즉시
16. 쪼개다, 찢다
17. 사과, 변명
18. 남녀 공학

C
1. breakdown — 쇠약, 고장
2. directly — 곧장, 직접, 즉시
3. engage — 고용하다, 약속하다
4. breakthrough — 중요한 성과, 획기적 발전
5. additional — 부가된, 추가의
6. discharge — 이행하다, 해임하다, 방출하다
7. coeducation — 남녀 공학
8. banish — 추방하다, 내쫓다
9. cleave — 쪼개다, 찢다
10. donation — 기부, 기증
11. affection — 애정, 감동
12. bark — 짖다, 소리치며 말하다
13. endurance — 인내, 지구력, 내구성
14. compulsory — 의무적인, 강제적인
15. deal — 거래, 다루다, 거래하다
16. anxiety — 걱정, 불안
17. consist — 이루어지다, ~에 있다
18. apology — 사과, 변명

Unit 38

A
1. laboratory
2. fainted
3. notion
4. fortunately
5. magnifies
6. genetic
7. hesitate
8. infant
9. fate
10. infected
11. lectures
12. flagrant
13. magnificent
14. guild
15. medieval
16. hollows
17. Mediterranean
18. notify

B
1. 동업 조합, 연맹
2. 전염시키다, 영향을 미치다
3. 기절하다, 희미한, 어질어질한
4. 주저하다, 망설이다
5. 웅대한, 장엄한
6. 운명, 숙명
7. 강의, 훈계
8. 실험실, 실습실
9. 악명 높은, 극악한
10. 중세의, 중고의
11. 유아, 유아의
12. 지중해
13. 운 좋게, 다행히
14. 알리다, 신고하다
15. 확대하다, 과장하다
16. 유전의, 유전학의
17. 개념, 생각, 의견
18. 구멍, 우묵한 곳

C
1. infant — 유아, 유아의
2. fortunately — 운 좋게, 다행히
3. hollow — 구멍, 우묵한 곳
4. notify — 알리다, 신고하다
5. genetic — 유전의, 유전학의
6. hesitate — 주저하다, 망설이다
7. Mediterranean — 지중해
8. infect — 전염시키다, 영향을 미치다
9. notion — 개념, 생각, 의견
10. guild — 동업 조합, 연맹
11. lecture — 강의, 훈계
12. flagrant — 악명 높은, 극악한
13. magnificent — 웅대한, 장엄한
14. laboratory — 실험실, 실습실
15. faint — 기절하다, 희미한, 어질어질한
16. medieval — 중세의, 중고의
17. fate — 운명, 숙명
18. magnify — 확대하다, 과장하다

Review 19

A
1. breakdown — 쇠약, 고장
2. directly — 곧장, 직접, 즉시
3. engage — 고용하다, 약속하다
4. breakthrough — 중요한 성과, 획기적 발전
5. additional — 부가된, 추가의
6. discharge — 이행하다, 해임하다, 방출하다
7. coeducation — 남녀 공학
8. banish — 추방하다, 내쫓다
9. cleave — 쪼개다, 찢다
10. donation — 기부, 기증
11. affection — 애정, 감동
12. bark — 짖다, 소리치며 말하다
13. endurance — 인내, 지구력, 내구성
14. compulsory — 의무적인, 강제적인
15. deal — 거래, 다루다, 거래하다
16. anxiety — 걱정, 불안
17. consist — 이루어지다, ~에 있다
18. apology — 사과, 변명

B
1. infant — 유아, 유아의
2. fortunately — 운 좋게, 다행히
3. hollow — 구멍, 우묵한 곳
4. notify — 알리다, 신고하다
5. genetic — 유전의, 유전학의
6. hesitate — 주저하다, 망설이다
7. Mediterranean — 지중해
8. infect — 전염시키다, 영향을 미치다
9. notion — 개념, 생각, 의견
10. guild — 동업 조합, 연맹
11. lecture — 강의, 훈계
12. flagrant — 악명 높은, 극악한
13. magnificent — 웅대한, 장엄한
14. laboratory — 실험실, 실습실
15. faint — 기절하다, 희미한, 어질어질한
16. medieval — 중세의, 중고의
17. fate — 운명, 숙명
18. magnify — 확대하다, 과장하다

Answer Key

Unit 39

A
1. prior
2. obtain
3. republic
4. reins
5. overwhelme
6. pilgrims
7. overworked
8. premature
9. offensive
10. produce
11. prejudices
12. punished
13. recover
14. positive
15. remove
16. restrict
17. pursued
18. revival

B
1. 과로하다, 과로, 초과 노동
2. 먼저의, ~에 우선하는
3. 얻다, 획득하다
4. 제거하다, 이동하다
5. 편견, 선입관
6. 제한하다, 한정하다
7. 무례한, 불쾌한, 공격의
8. 추적하다, 추구하다
9. 생산하다, 제작하다
10. 회복하다, 되찾다
11. 명확한, 적극적인
12. 부활, 재상영
13. 벌주다, 응징하다
14. 압도하다, 질리게 하다
15. 공화국
16. 시기상조의, 조기의
17. 고삐, 억제하다, 지배하다
18. 순례자, 나그네

1. obtain
2. offensive
3. overwhelm
4. overwork
5. pilgrim
6. positive
7. prejudice
8. premature
9. prior
10. produce
11. punish
12. pursue
13. recover
14. rein
15. remove
16. republic
17. restrict
18. revival

C
1. produce — 생산하다, 제작하다
2. obtain — 얻다, 획득하다
3. remove — 제거하다, 이동하다
4. prior — 먼저의, ~에 우선하는
5. revival — 부활, 재상영
6. premature — 시기상조의, 조기의
7. offensive — 무례한, 불쾌한, 공격의
8. rein — 고삐, 억제하다, 지배하다
9. prejudice — 편견, 선입관
10. pursue — 추적하다, 추구하다
11. restrict — 제한하다, 한정하다
12. positive — 명확한, 적극적인
13. recover — 회복하다, 되찾다
14. overwhelm — 압도하다, 질리게 하다
15. punish — 벌주다, 응징하다
16. republic — 공화국
17. pilgrim — 순례자, 나그네
18. overwork — 과로하다, 과로, 초과 노동

Unit 40

A
1. single
2. souvenirs
3. verse
4. temper
5. stethoscope
6. stimulates
7. talents
8. scratched
9. tragedy
10. sculpture
11. transferring
12. usher
13. specialized
14. utensils
15. vice
16. sincerely
17. zeal
18. wound

B
1. 기념품, 선물
2. 기질, 기분, 노여움
3. 긁다, 할퀴다
4. 안내인, 안내하다
5. 자극하다, 흥분시키다
6. 재능, 재주
7. 열심, 열의
8. 조각(품), 조각하다
9. 운문, 시
10. 상처, 부상, 상처 입히다
11. 성실히, 충심으로
12. 용구, 기구
13. 전문화하다, 전공하다
14. 악덕, 결함
15. 비극(적인 사건)
16. 단 하나의, 혼자의, 하나의 것
17. 이동시키다, 전송하다
18. 청진기

1. scratch
2. sculpture
3. sincerely
4. single
5. souvenir
6. specialize
7. stethoscope
8. stimulate
9. talent
10. temper
11. tragedy
12. transfer
13. usher
14. utensil
15. verse
16. vice
17. wound
18. zeal

C
1. stethoscope — 청진기
2. verse — 운문, 시
3. talent — 재능, 재주
4. sculpture — 조각(품), 조각하다
5. wound — 상처, 부상, 상처 입히다
6. scratch — 긁다, 할퀴다
7. vice — 악덕, 결함
8. stimulate — 자극하다, 흥분시키다
9. sincerely — 성실히, 충심으로
10. tragedy — 비극(적인 사건)
11. transfer — 이동시키다, 전송하다
12. specialize — 전문화하다, 전공하다
13. utensil — 용구, 기구
14. temper — 기질, 기분, 노여움
15. single — 단 하나의, 혼자의, 하나의 것
16. usher — 안내인, 안내하다
17. zeal — 열심, 열의
18. souvenir — 기념품, 선물

Review 20

A
1. produce — 생산하다, 제작하다
2. obtain — 얻다, 획득하다
3. remove — 제거하다, 이동하다
4. prior — 먼저의, ~에 우선하는
5. revival — 부활, 재상영
6. premature — 시기상조의, 조기의
7. offensive — 무례한, 불쾌한, 공격의
8. rein — 고삐, 억제하다, 지배하다
9. prejudice — 편견, 선입관
10. pursue — 추적하다, 추구하다
11. restrict — 제한하다, 한정하다
12. positive — 명확한, 적극적인
13. recover — 회복하다, 되찾다
14. overwhelm — 압도하다, 질리게 하다
15. punish — 벌주다, 응징하다
16. republic — 공화국
17. pilgrim — 순례자, 나그네
18. overwork — 과로하다, 과로, 초과 노동

B
1. stethoscope — 청진기
2. verse — 운문, 시
3. talent — 재능, 재주
4. sculpture — 조각(품), 조각하다
5. wound — 상처, 부상, 상처 입히다
6. scratch — 긁다, 할퀴다
7. vice — 악덕, 결함
8. stimulate — 자극하다, 흥분시키다
9. sincerely — 성실히, 충심으로
10. tragedy — 비극(적인 사건)
11. transfer — 이동시키다, 전송하다
12. specialize — 전문화하다, 전공하다
13. utensil — 용구, 기구
14. temper — 기질, 기분, 노여움
15. single — 단 하나의, 혼자의, 하나의 것
16. usher — 안내인, 안내하다
17. zeal — 열심, 열의
18. souvenir — 기념품, 선물

Total Test — 해당 Unit별 Exercise 3번 문제의 정답과 일치

MEMO

 MEMO